James Joyce's Dubliners
A Critical Handbook

edited by

James R. Baker
San Diego State College

and

Thomas F. Staley
University of Tulsa

Wadsworth Publishing Company, Inc.
Belmont, California

L. C. Cat. Card No.: 69–14780

Printed in the United States of America
By American Book–Stratford Press, Inc.

PREFACE

James Joyce's *Dubliners* (1914) is one of the classics in the literature of modern urban life. It is an especially remarkable achievement when we consider that the fifteen stories in the volume were written by the time Joyce was twenty-five and were based on theories about culture and art he had formulated even earlier. Nevertheless, *Dubliners* is widely read and admired not merely for its literary qualities but for its contemporary relevance. It also serves as a vital introduction to the famous works of Joyce's later years: *A Portrait of the Artist as a Young Man* (1916), *Ulysses* (1922), and *Finnegans Wake* (1939). All of these books are about Dublin and Dubliners. Joyce's subject is the city and her people, and his great ingenuity as an artist is dedicated to the task of making that scene reflect timeless and universal motifs in human experience.

This collection of materials on *Dubliners* is designed as a companion volume to the stories. We have kept in mind the needs of the student approaching serious study of Joyce for the first time as well as the advanced student or scholar who wishes to undertake a thorough analysis. With this audience in mind, we have tried to make selections which most clearly reveal Joyce's intentions and the consensus of judgment reached by the best scholarship.

The contents are arranged in what seems a natural order: (1) remarks on theory, sources, and influences; (2) scholarly assessments of the structure and unity of the volume as a whole; (3) critical analyses of the individual stories; (4) a chronology outlining Joyce's life and career; (5) suggestions for study and research; (6) a bibliography of criticism for guidance in further research by student or professor.

Part One contains excerpts from Joyce's own aesthetic theories. He was a precocious and erudite student of literary history and aesthetics. We have selected passages from these writings close in spirit and conception to the stories and those most frequently cited in scholarly writing. The youthful essay "Drama and Life" (1900), in spite of some obscurities, provides a useful introduction to the art of *Dubliners*. It is not simply a discussion of the history of drama. Actually, the essay is important primarily as Joyce's first effort to formalize his ideas on what he called "dramatic art," and *Dubliners* represents the first successful application of these theories and ideals.

In 1904 Joyce began writing short stories in which he hoped to dramatize as objectively as possible the true spiritual condition of the people of Dublin. By the end of the year he had written "The Sisters," "Eveline," "After the Race," and a first version of "Clay." In 1905 he wrote eight more stories and worked out a first plan for arranging the whole group in a book. "Two Gallants" and "A Little Cloud" were completed in 1906, and "The Dead" (the final story) was finished early in 1907. Within four years the fifteen stories were written, but they were not to be published as a collection until 1914.

The many letters to Grant Richards, Joyce's British publisher, reveal some of the frustrations the young author experienced with moralistic printers. This long struggle in the Victorian twilight seems to the modern reader a quaint episode in literary censorship, but the three letters included here also contain many important statements on the theory and intention behind *Dubliners*. For those who wish to trace the arguments over the manuscript and the complex publishing history of the various stories, we recommend the collections of Joyce's letters edited by Stuart Gilbert and Richard Ellmann, and, of course, Ellmann's invaluable biography.

A group of stories written over a brief period of time reflects a common purpose, and the essays in Part Two examine the structure and basic unity of *Dubliners* as a whole. We wish to point out, however, that these commentaries contain some analysis of particular stories and passages. The student is urged to consult the Index to Critical Discussions (p. vii) as the quickest means of locating and comparing all of the scholarly perspectives on a given story.

Part Three presented the most difficult editorial choices. We have included at least one selection on each story; but, as one notes immediately on glancing at the bibliography, some of the stories have attracted a great deal of critical attention while others have been virtually ignored. Where only a little professional work has been done, we have chosen articles or excerpts offering a sound general statement or suggestions worth pursuing and developing further.

Students may document their research according to page numbers in the original sources by utilizing the exact bibliographical data furnished in the notes and by reference to the original page numbers enclosed in brackets in each section. Although materials are generally reprinted as they first appeared, we have added descriptive titles for a few of the excerpts taken from longer works, and we have renumbered the original footnotes as required for consistency and clarity. Only those footnotes designated [Eds.] are by the editors of this guide-book.

We have not included page references for quotations from the stories. Since most of the stories are quite short, quotations of some length or those of crucial importance to the scholar's analysis may be found easily in any one of the three available editions of *Dubliners*: the Compass Books edition originally issued by The Viking Press in 1958 and recently reissued with Joyce's original punctuation; the *Portable James Joyce,* edited by Harry Levin and first published by The Viking Press in 1947; and the Modern Library edition originally published by Random House in 1926 with a preface by Padraic Colum.

James R. Baker
Thomas F. Staley

CONTENTS

INDEX TO CRITICAL DISCUSSIONS

PART ONE. THE AUTHOR'S THEORIES AND THE SHORT-STORY GENRE

Drama and Life

JAMES JOYCE

ALTHOUGH THE RELATIONS BETWEEN DRAMA AND LIFE ARE, AND MUST be, of the most vital character, in the history of drama itself these do not seem to have been at all times, consistently in view. The earliest and best known drama, this side of the Caucasus, is that of Greece. I do not propose to attempt anything in the nature of a historical survey but cannot pass it by. Greek drama arose out of the cult of Dionysos, who, god of fruitage, joyfulness and earliest art, offered in his life-story a practical groundplan for the erection of a tragic and a comic theatre. In speaking of Greek drama it must be borne in mind that its rise dominated its form. The conditions of the Attic stage suggested a syllabus of greenroom proprieties and cautions to authors, which in after ages were foolishly set up as the canons of dramatic art, in all lands. Thus the Greeks handed down a code of laws which their descendants with purblind wisdom forthwith advanced to the dignity of inspired pronouncements. Beyond this, I say nothing. It may be a vulgarism, but it is literal truth to say that Greek drama is played out.[1] For good or for bad it has done its work, which, if wrought in gold, was not upon lasting pillars. Its revival is not of dramatic but of pedagogic significance. Even in its own camp it has been superseded. When it had thriven over long in hieratic custody and in ceremonial form, it began to pall on the Aryan genius. A reaction ensued, as was inevitable; and as the classical drama had been born of religion, its follower arose out of a movement in literature. In this reaction Eng-

---

[1] In *Stephen Hero*, p. 101 (88), a student objects "that Mr. Daedalus did not understand the beauty of the Attic theatre. He pointed out that Eschylus was an imperishable name and he predicted that the drama of the Greeks would outlive many civilizations."

1

land played an important part, for it was the power of the Shake-
spearean clique that dealt the deathblow to the already dying drama.
Shakespeare was before all else a literary artist; humour, eloquence,
a gift of seraphic music, theatrical instincts—he had a rich dower of
these. The work, to which he gave such splendid impulse, was of a
higher nature than that which it followed. It was far from mere
drama, it was literature in dialogue. Here I must draw a line of demarcation between literature and drama.[2] [39]

Human society is the embodiment of changeless laws which the
whimsicalities and circumstances of men and women involve and
overwrap. The realm of literature is the realm of these accidental
manners and humours—a spacious realm; and the true literary artist
concerns himself mainly with them. Drama has to do with the under-
lying laws first, in all their nakedness and divine severity, and only
secondarily with the motley agents who bear them out. When so
much is recognized an advance has been made to a more rational and
true appreciation of dramatic art. Unless some such distinction be
made the result is chaos. Lyricism parades as poetic drama, psychological conversation as literary drama, and traditional farce moves
over the boards with the label of comedy affixed to it.

Both of these dramas having done their work as prologues to the
swelling act, they may be relegated to the department of literary
curios. It is futile to say that there is no new drama or to contend that
its proclamation is a huge boom. Space is valuable and I cannot combat
these assertions. However, it is to me day-clear that dramatic drama
must outlive its elders, whose life is only eked by the most dexterous
management and the carefullest husbanding. Over this New School
some hard hits have been given and taken. The public is slow to
seize truth, and its leaders quick to miscall it. Many, whose palates
have grown accustomed to the old food, cry out peevishly against
a change of diet. To these use and want is the seventh heaven. Loud
are their praises of the bland blatancy of Corneille, the starchglaze of
Trapassi's[3] godliness, the Pumblechookian[4] woodenness of Calderon.
Their infantile plot juggling sets them agape, so superfine it is. Such
critics are not to be taken seriously but they are droll figures! It is
of course patently true that the 'new' school masters them on their
own ground. Compare the skill of Haddon Chambers and Douglas
Jerrold, of Sudermann and Lessing. The 'new' school in this branch of

---

[2] Joyce was impressed by Verlaine's line in "Art Poetique," "Et tout le reste
est litterature." His dismissal of "literature" here as an inferior form of verbal expression is repeated in "James Clarence Mangan" (*Critical Writings*, p. 75), and in
the review of Rooney's *Poems and Ballads* (*Critical Writings*, p. 86), then in
Stephen Hero, p. 78 (65); in the *Portrait*, however, he gives up this distinction,
and has Stephen refer to literature as "the highest and most spiritual art."

[3] Pietro Metastasio (1698–1782), born Trapassi.

[4] From Pumblechook, a servile character in Dickens' *Great Expectations*.

its art is superior. This superiority is only natural, as it accompanies work of immeasurably higher calibre. Even the least part of Wagner—his music—is beyond Bellini. Spite of the outcry of these lovers of the past, the masons are building for Drama an [40] ampler and loftier home, where there shall be light for gloom, and wide porches for drawbridge and keep.

Let me explain a little as to this great visitant. By drama I understand the interplay of passions to portray truth; drama is strife, evolution, movement in whatever way unfolded; it exists, before it takes form, independently; it is conditioned but not controlled by its scene. It might be said fantastically that as soon as men and women began life in the world there was above them and about them, a spirit, of which they were dimly conscious, which they would have had sojourn in their midst in deeper intimacy and for whose truth they became seekers in after times, longing to lay hands upon it. For this spirit is as the roaming air, little susceptible of change, and never left their vision, shall never leave it, till the firmament is as a scroll rolled away. At times it would seem that the spirit had taken up his abode in this or that form—but on a sudden he is misused, he is gone and the abode is left idle. He is, one might guess, somewhat of an elfish nature, a nixie, a very Ariel. So we must distinguish him and his house. An idyllic portrait, or an environment of haystacks does not constitute a pastoral play, no more than rhodomontade and sermonizing build up a tragedy.[5] Neither quiescence nor vulgarity shadow forth drama. However subdued the tone of passions may be, however ordered the action or commonplace the diction, if a play or a work of music or a picture presents the everlasting hopes, desires and hates of us, or deals with a symbolic presentment of our widely related nature, albeit a phase of that nature, then it is drama. I shall not speak here of its many forms. In every form that was not fit for it, it made an outburst, as when the first sculptor separated the feet. Morality, mystery, ballet, pantomime, opera, all these it speedily ran through and discarded. Its proper form 'the drama' is yet intact. 'There are many candles on the high altar, though one fall.'

Whatever form it takes must not be superimposed or conventional. In literature we allow conventions, for literature is a comparatively low form of art. Literature is kept alive by tonics, it flourishes through conventions in all human relations, in all actuality. Drama will be for the future at war with convention, if it is to realize itself truly. If you have a clear thought of the body [41] of drama, it will be manifest what raiment befits it. Drama of so wholehearted and admirable a nature cannot but draw all hearts from the spectacular and the theatrical, its note being truth and freedom in every aspect of it. It may be asked

---

[5] From here to the end of this paragraph, Joyce paraphrases a passage in "Royal Hibernian Academy 'Ecce Homo'" (*Critical Writings*, p. 32).

what are we to do, in the words of Tolstoi.[6] First, clear our minds of cant and alter the falsehoods to which we have lent our support. Let us criticize in the manner of free people, as a free race, recking little of ferula and formula. The Folk is, I believe, able to do so much. *Securus judicat orbis terrarum,*[7] is not too high a motto for all human artwork. Let us not overbear the weak, let us treat with a tolerant smile the stale pronouncements of those matchless serio-comics—the 'litterateurs.' If a sanity rules the mind of the dramatic world there will be accepted what is now the faith of the few, there will be past dispute written up the respective grades of *Macbeth* and *The Master Builder.*[8] The sententious critic of the thirtieth century may well say of them— Between him and these there is a great gulf fixed.

There are some weighty truths which we cannot overpass, in the relations between drama and the artist. Drama is essentially a communal art and of widespread domain. The drama—its fittest vehicle almost presupposes an audience, drawn from all classes. In an artloving and art-producing society the drama would naturally take up its position at the head of all artistic institutions. Drama is moreover of so unswayed, so unchallengeable a nature that in its highest forms it all but transcends criticism. It is hardly possible to criticize *The Wild Duck,* for instance; one can only brood upon it as upon a personal woe. Indeed in the case of all Ibsen's later work dramatic criticism, properly so called, verges on impertinence. In every other art personality, mannerisms of touch, local sense, are held as adornments, as additional charms. But here the artist forgoes his very self and stands a mediator in awful truth before the veiled face of God.

If you ask me what occasions drama or what is the necessity for it at all, I answer Necessity. It is mere animal instinct applied to [42] the mind. Apart from his world-old desire to get beyond the flaming ramparts, man has a further longing to become a maker and a moulder. That is the necessity of all art. Drama is again the least dependent of all arts on its material. If the supply of mouldable earth or stone gives out, sculpture becomes a memory, if the yield of vegetable pigments ceases, the pictorial art ceases. But whether there be marble or paints, there is always the artstuff for drama. I believe further that drama arises spontaneously out of life and is coeval with it. Every race has made its own myths and it is in these that early drama often finds an outlet. The author of Parsifal has recognized this and hence his work is solid as a rock. When the mythus passes over the borderline and invades the temple of worship, the possibilities of its drama have

---

[6] *What Are We to Do?* is the title of a book by Tolstoy.

[7] "Untroubled, the world judges," St. Augustine, *Contra Epistolam Parmeniani,* III, 24.

[8] A speaker objects, in *Stephen Hero,* p. 78 (65), "Everyone knew that *Macbeth* would be famous when the unknown authors of whom Mr. Dedalus was so fond were dead and forgotten."

lessened considerably. Even then it struggles back to its rightful place, much to the discomfort of the stodgy congregation.

As men differ as to the rise, so do they as to the aims of drama. It is in most cases claimed by the votaries of the antique school that the drama should have special ethical claims, to use their stock phrase, that it should instruct, elevate, and amuse. Here is yet another gyve that the jailers have bestowed. I do not say that drama may not fulfil any or all of these functions, but I deny that it is essential that it should fulfil them. Art, elevated into the overhigh sphere of religion, generally loses its true soul in stagnant quietism. As to the lower form of this dogma it is surely funny. This polite request to the dramatist to please point a moral, to rival Cyrano, in iterating through each act "A la fin de l'envoi je touche" is amazing. Bred as it is of an amiable-parochial disposition we can but waive it. Mr. Beoerly sacked with strychnine, or M. Coupeau in the horrors are nothing short of piteous in a surplice and dalmatic apiece. However this absurdity is eating itself fast, like the tiger of story, tail first.

A yet more insidious claim is the claim for beauty. As conceived by the claimants beauty is as often anaemic spirituality as hardy animalism. Then, chiefly because beauty is to men an arbitrary quality and often lies no deeper than form, to pin drama to dealing with it, would be hazardous. Beauty is the swerga[9] of the aesthete; but truth has a more ascertainable and more real dominion.[10] Art [43] is true to itself when it deals with truth. Should such an untoward event as a universal reformation take place on earth, truth would be the very threshold of the house beautiful.

I have just one other claim to discuss, even at the risk of exhausting your patience. I quote from Mr. Beerbohm Tree. "In these days when faith is tinged with philosophic doubt, I believe it is the function of art to give us light rather than darkness. It should not point to our relationship with monkeys but rather remind us of our affinity with the angels." In this statement there is a fair element of truth which however requires qualification. Mr. Tree contends that men and women will always look to art as the glass wherein they may see themselves idealized. Rather I should think that men and women seldom think gravely on their own impulses towards art. The fetters of convention bind them too strongly. But after all art cannot be governed by the insincerity of the compact majority but rather by those eternal conditions, says Mr. Tree, which have governed it from the first. I admit this as irrefutable truth. But it were well we had in mind that those eternal conditions are not the conditions of modern communities. Art is marred by such mistaken insistence on its religious, its moral, its

[9] The heaven of the Gods in Hindu literature.
[10] Compare the treatment of truth and beauty in the Pola Notebook (*Critical Writings*, pp. 146–148).

beautiful, its idealizing tendencies. A single Rembrandt is worth a gallery full of Van Dycks. And it is this doctrine of idealism in art which has in notable instances disfigured manful endeavour, and has also fostered a babyish instinct to dive under blankets at the mention of the bogey of realism. Hence the public disowns Tragedy, unless she rattles her dagger and goblet, abhors Romance which is not amenable to the laws of prosody, and deems it a sad effect in art, if, from the outpoured blood of hapless heroism, there does not at once spring up a growth of sorrowful blossoms. As in the very madness and frenzy of this attitude, people want the drama to befool them, Purveyor supplies plutocrat with a parody of life which the latter digests medicinally in a darkened theatre, the stage literally battening on the mental offal of its patrons.

Now if these views are effete what will serve the purpose? Shall we put life—real life—on the stage? No, says the Philistine chorus, for it will not draw. What a blend of thwarted sight and smug commercialism. Parnassus and the city Bank divide the souls of the pedlars. Life indeed nowadays is often a sad bore. Many feel like the Frenchman that they have been born too late in a [44] world too old, and their wanhope and nerveless unheroism point on ever sternly to a last nothing, a vast futility and meanwhile—a bearing of fardels. Epic savagery is rendered impossible by vigilant policing, chivalry has been killed by the fashion oracles of the boulevards. There is no clank of mail, no halo about gallantry, no hat-sweeping, no roystering! The traditions of romance are upheld only in Bohemia. Still I think out of the dreary sameness of existence, a measure of dramatic life may be drawn. Even the most commonplace, the deadest among the living, may play a part in a great drama. It is a sinful foolishness to sigh back for the good old times, to feed the hunger of us with the cold stones they afford. Life we must accept as we see it before our eyes, men and women as we meet them in the real world, not as we apprehend them in the world of faery. The great human comedy in which each has share, gives limitless scope to the true artist, to-day as yesterday and as in years gone. The forms of things, as the earth's crust, are changed. The timbers of the ships of Tarshish[11] are falling asunder or eaten by the wanton sea; time has broken into the fastness of the mighty; the gardens of Armida[12] are become as treeless wilds. But the deathless passions, the human verities which so found expression then, are indeed deathless, in the heroic cycle, or in the scientific age. Lohengrin, the drama of which unfolds itself in a scene of seclusion, amid half-lights, is not an Antwerp legend but a world drama. Ghosts, the action of which passes in a common parlour, is of universal import—a deepset branch on the tree, Igdrasil,

[11] "Jehoshaphat made ships of Tarshish to go to Ophir for gold." I Kings 22:48.
[12] Gardens of sweet indolence in Tasso's Gersualemme Liberata.

whose roots are struck in earth, but through whose higher leafage the stars of heaven are glowing and astir. It may be that many have nothing to do with such fable, or think that their wonted fare is all that is of need to them. But as we stand on the mountains today, looking before and after, pining for what is not, scarcely discerning afar the patches of open sky; when the spurs threaten, and the track is grown with briers, what does it avail that into our hands we have given us a clouded cane for an alpenstock, or that we have dainty silks to shield us against the eager, upland wind? The sooner we understand our true position, the better; and the sooner then will we be up and doing on our way. In the meantime, art, and chiefly drama, may help us to make our resting places with a greater insight and [45] a greater foresight, that the stones of them may be bravely builded, and the windows goodly and fair. ". . . what will you do in our Society, Miss Hessel?" asked Rörlund—"I will let in fresh air, Pastor."—answered Lona.[13]

JAS A. JOYCE
January 10, 1900 [46]

[13] The curtain speech of Act I, Ibsen's *Pillars of Society*.

The Dramatic Form

JAMES JOYCE

. . . ART NECESSARILY DIVIDES ITSELF INTO THREE FORMS PROGRESSING from one to the next. These forms are: the lyrical form, the form wherein the artist presents his image in immediate relation to himself; the epical form, the form wherein he presents his image in mediate relation to himself and to others; the dramatic form, the form wherein he presents his image in immediate relation to others.

. . . .

—Lessing, said Stephen, should not have taken a group of statues to write of. The art, being inferior, does not present the forms I spoke of distinguished clearly one from another. Even in literature, the highest and most spiritual art, the forms are often confused. The lyrical form is in fact the simplest verbal gesture of an instant of emotion, a rhythmical cry such as ages ago cheered on the man who pulled at the oar or dragged stones up a slope. He who utters it is more conscious of the instant of emotion than of himself as feeling emotion. The simplest epical form is seen emerging out of lyrical literature when the artist prolongs and broods upon himself as the centre of an epical event and this form progresses till the centre of emotional gravity is equidistant from the artist [214] himself and from others. The narrative is no longer purely personal. The personality of the artist passes into the narration itself, flowing round and round the persons and the action like a vital sea. This progress you will see easily in that old English ballad *Turpin Hero* which begins in the first person and ends in the third person. The dramatic form is reached when the vitality which has flowed and eddied round each person fills every person with such vital force that he or she assumes a proper and intangible esthetic life. The personality of the artist, at first a cry or a cadence or a mood and then a fluid and lambent narrative, finally refines itself out of existence, impersonalises itself, so to speak. The esthetic image in the dramatic form is life purified in and reprojected from the human imagination. The mystery of esthetic like that of material creation is accomplished. The artist, like the God of the creation, remains within or behind or beyond or above his handiwork, invisible, refined out of existence, indifferent, paring his fingernails. [215]

Epiphany

JAMES JOYCE

HE WAS PASSING THROUGH ECCLES' ST ONE EVENING, ONE MISTY EVENING, with [210] all these thoughts dancing the dance of unrest in his brain when a trivial incident set him composing some ardent verses which he entitled a "Vilanelle of the Temptress."[1] A young lady was standing on the steps of one of those brown brick houses which seem the very incarnation of Irish paralysis.[2] A young gentleman was leaning on the rusty railings of the area. Stephen as he passed on his quest heard the following fragment of colloquy out of which he received an impression keen enough to afflict his sensitiveness very severely.

[1] In *A Portrait of the Artist as a Young Man* (New York, 1964, pp. 223–224) the temptress is E. C. (Emma Clery) and the vilanelle which appears there is addressed to her. [Eds.]
[2] Cf. Mangan's sister in "Araby" and the description of the houses in the opening lines of the story. [Eds.]

From James Joyce, *Stephen Hero*, edited by Theodore Spencer. New York: New Directions, 1944. Pp. 210–213. Reprinted by permission of The Society of Authors as the literary representative of the Estate of the late James Joyce.

The Young Lady—(drawling discreetly) . . . O, yes . . . I was . . . at the . . . cha . . . pel . . .

The Young Gentleman—(inaudibly) . . . I . . . (again inaudibly) . . . I . . .

The Young Lady—(softly) . . . O . . . but you're . . . ve . . . ry . . . wick . . . ed . . .

This triviality made him think of collecting many such moments together in a book of epiphanies. By an epiphany he meant a sudden spiritual manifestation, whether in the vulgarity of speech or of gesture or in a memorable phase of the mind itself. He believed that it was for the man of letters to record these epiphanies with extreme care, seeing that they themselves are the most delicate and evanescent of moments. He told Cranly that the clock of the Ballast Office was capable of an epiphany. Cranly questioned the inscrutable dial of the Ballast Office with his no less inscrutable countenance:

—Yes, said Stephen. I will pass it time after time, allude to it, refer to it, catch a glimpse of it. It is only an item in the catalogue of Dublin's street furniture. Then all at once I see it and I know at once what it is: epiphany.

—What?

—Imagine my glimpses at that clock as the gropings of a spiritual eye which seeks to adjust its vision to an exact focus. The moment the focus is reached the object is epiphanised. It is just in this epiphany that I find the third, the supreme quality of beauty.

—Yes? said Cranly absently. [211]

—No esthetic theory, pursued Stephen relentlessly, is of any value which investigates with the aid of the lantern of tradition. What we symbolise in black the Chinaman may symbolise in yellow: each has his own tradition. Greek beauty laughs at Coptic beauty and the American Indian derides them both. It is almost impossible to reconcile all tradition whereas it is by no means impossible to find the justification of every form of beauty which has ever been adored on the earth by an examination into the mechanism of esthetic apprehension whether it be dressed in red, white, yellow or black. We have no reason for thinking that the Chinaman has a different system of digestion from that which we have though our diets are quite dissimilar. The apprehensive faculty must be scrutinised in action.

—Yes . . .

—You know what Aquinas says: The three things requisite for beauty are, integrity, a wholeness, symmetry and radiance. Some day I will expand that sentence into a treatise. Consider the performance of your own mind when confronted with any object, hypothetically beautiful. Your mind to apprehend that object divides the entire universe into two parts, the object, and the void which is not the object. To apprehend it you must lift it away from everything else: and then you perceive that it is one integral thing, that is a thing. You recognise its integrity. Isn't that so?

—And then?

—That is the first quality of beauty: it is declared in a simple sudden synthesis of the faculty which apprehends. What then? Analysis then. The mind considers the object in whole and in part, in relation to itself and to other objects, examines the balance of its parts, contemplates the form of the object, traverses every cranny of the structure. So the mind receives the impression of the symmetry of the object. The mind recognises that the object is in the strict sense of the word, a *thing*, a definitely constituted entity. You see?

—Let us turn back, said Cranly.

They had reached the corner of Grafton St and as the foot-path [212] was overcrowded they turned back northwards. Cranly had an inclination to watch the antics of a drunkard who had been ejected from a bar in Suffolk St but Stephen took his arm summarily and led him away.

—Now for the third quality. For a long time I couldn't make out what Aquinas meant. He uses a figurative word (a very unusual thing for him) but I have solved it. *Claritas* is *quidditas*. After the analysis which discovers the second quality the mind makes the only logically possible synthesis and discovers the third quality. This is the moment which I call epiphany. First we recognise that the object is *one* integral thing, then we recognise that it is an organised composite structure, a *thing* in fact: finally, when the relation of the parts is exquisite, when the parts are adjusted to the special point, we recognise that it is *that* thing which it is. Its soul, its whatness, leaps to us from the vestment of its appearance. The soul of the commonest object, the structure of which is so adjusted, seems to us radiant. The object achieves its epiphany.

Having finished his argument Stephen walked on in silence. He felt Cranly's hostility and he accused himself of having cheapened the eternal images of beauty. For the first time, too, he felt slightly awkward in his friend's company and to restore a mood of flippant familiarity he glanced up at the clock of the Ballast Office and smiled:

—It has not epiphanised yet, he said. [213]

A Succession of Epiphanies

THEODORE SPENCER

THIS THEORY SEEMS TO ME CENTRAL TO AN UNDERSTANDING OF JOYCE AS an artist, and we might describe his successive works as illustrations, intensifications and enlargements of it. *Dubliners*, we [16] may say, is a series of epiphanies describing apparently trivial but actually crucial and revealing moments in the lives of different characters. The *Portrait*

From Theodore Spencer's Introduction to James Joyce, *Stephen Hero*. New York: New Directions, 1944. Pp. 16–17. Copyright 1944 by New Directions. Reprinted by permission of New Directions Publishing Corporation.

may be seen as a kind of epiphany—a showing forth—of Joyce himself as a young man; *Ulysses,* by taking one day in the life of the average man, describes that man, according to Joyce's intention, more fully than any human being had ever been described before; it is the epiphany of Leopold Bloom, just as, years earlier, the trivial conversation overheard on a misty evening in Eccles Street (where, incidentally, Mr. Bloom lived) was the epiphany of those two people's lives, shown forth in a moment. And *Finnegans Wake* may be seen as a vast enlargement, of course unconceived by Joyce as a young man, of the same view. Here it is not any one individual that is "epiphanized"; it is all of human history, symbolized in certain types the representatives of which combine with one another as the words describing them combine various meanings, so that H. C. Earwicker and his family, his acquaintances, the city of Dublin where he lives, his morality and religion, become symbols of an epiphanic view of human life as a whole, and the final end of the artist is achieved. [17]

Three Letters to Grant Richards

JAMES JOYCE

TO GRANT RICHARDS
MS. HARVARD
15 October 1905
Via S. Nicolo 30, II°,
Trieste, Austria

Dear Mr. Grant Richards Mr. Symons wrote to me saying that Messrs Constable & Co, to whom he had spoken of me, had invited me to send them the MSS of my two books. Accordingly I made a copy of *Chamber Music* and sent it to them today. I am not sure whether you will think this act of mine discourteous but I hardly know what to do. I think you had better keep my verses as it is most probable that Messrs Constable & Co will refuse the book.

The second book which I have ready is called *Dubliners.* It is a collection of twelve short stories. It is possible that you would consider it to be of a commercial nature. I would gladly submit it to you before sending it to Messrs Constable and, if you could promise to publish it soon, I would gladly agree. Unfortunately I am in such circumstances that it is necessary for me to have either of the books published as soon as possible.

I do not think that any writer has yet presented Dublin to the world. It has been a capital of Europe for thousands of years, it is supposed to be the second city of the British Empire and it is nearly three times as big as Venice. Moreover, on account of many circumstances which I cannot detail here, the expression "Dubliner" seems to me to have some meaning and I doubt whether the same can be said for such words as "Londoner" and "Parisian" both of which have been used by writers as titles. From time to time I see in publishers' lists announcements of [122] books on Irish subjects, so that I think people might be willing to pay for the special odour of corruption which, I hope, floats over my stories. Faithfully yours

JAS A JOYCE¹ [123]

TO GRANT RICHARDS   MS. HARVARD
5 May 1906   Via Giovanni Boccaccio 1, II,
                                  Trieste, Austria

Dear Mr. Grant Richards, I am sorry you do not tell me why the printer, who seems to be the barometer of English opinion, refuses to print *Two Gallants* and makes marks in the margin of *Counterparts*.² Is it the small gold coin in the former story or the code of honour which the two [132] gallants live by which shocks him? I see nothing which should shock him in either of these things. His idea of gallantry

---

¹ Grant Richards replied on 18 October 1905, "Of course I cannot for a moment complain of your having sent your manuscript to Messrs. Constable, and I hope for your sake that that firm will decide to publish the poems. . . . If they do not, then I shall still hope that we may be able to do something with them here. It will give me great pleasure to have the opportunity of reading 'Dubliners.' "

² Richards had written Joyce on 23 April, "I am sorry, but I am afraid we cannot publish 'The Two Gallants' as it stands; indeed, the printers, to whom it was sent before I read it myself, say that they won't print it. You see that there are still limitations imposed on the English publisher! I am therefore sending it back to you to ask you either to suppress it, or better, to modify it in such a way as to enable it to pass. Perhaps you can see your way to do this at once.

"The same thing has to be done with two passages marked in blue pencil on page 15 of 'Counterparts.'

"Also—you will think I am very troublesome, but I don't want the critics to come down on your book like a cart load of bricks—I want you to give me a word that we can use instead of 'bloody' in the story 'Grace.' "

Joyce replied on 26 April (*Letters*, ed. Gilbert, pp. 60–61) that he would change nothing, regardless of the printer's point of view. On 1 May Richards answered that the printer's opinion might be valueless in itself, but was indicative of the probable opinion of an "inconveniently large section of the general public."

has grown up in him (probably) during the reading of the novels of the elder Dumas and during the performance of romantic plays which presented to him cavaliers and ladies in full dress. But I am sure he is willing to modify his fantastic views. I would strongly recommend to him the chapters wherein Ferrero[3] examines the moral code of the soldier and (incidentally) of the gallant. But it would be useless for I am sure that in his heart of hearts he is a militarist.

He has marked three passages in *Counterparts:*

"a man with two establishments to keep up, of course he couldn't . . ."

"Farrington said he wouldn't mind having the far one and began to smile at her. . . ."

"She continued to cast bold glances at him and changed the position of her legs often; and when she was going out she brushed against his chair and said 'Pardon!' in a Cockney accent."[4]

His marking of the first passage makes me think that there is priestly blood in him: the scent for immoral allusions is certainly very keen here. To me this passage seems as childlike as the reports of divorce cases in *The Standard.* Or is it possible that this same printer (or maybe some near relative of his) will read (nay more, actually collaborate in) that solemn journal which tells its readers not merely that Mrs So and So misconducted herself with Captain So and So but even how often she misconducted herself with him! The word "establishment" is surely as inoffensive as the word "misconducted."

It is easier to understand why he has marked the second passage, and evident why he has marked the third. But I would refer him again to that respectable organ the reporters of which are allowed to speak of such intimate things as even I, a poor artist, have but dared to suggest. O one-eyed printer! Why has he descended with his blue pencil, full of the Holy Ghost, upon these passages and allowed his companions to set up in type reports of divorce cases, and ragging cases and cases of criminal assault—reports, moreover, which are to be read by an "inconveniently large section of the general public." [133]

There remains his final objection to the word "bloody." I cannot know, of course, from what he derives the word or whether, in his plain blunt way, he accepts it as it stands. In the latter case his objection is absurd and in the former case (if he follows the only derivation I have heard for it) it is strange that he should object more strongly to a profane use of the Virgin than to a profane use of the name of

---

[3] Guglielmo Ferrero (1871–1942), Italian historian and antifascist social critic. In *L'Europa giovane* (Milan, 1898), pp. 163–170, Ferrero finds a secret alliance between Puritanism, sexual aberration, and military destructiveness, using Bismarck as his example.

[4] When *Dubliners* was finally published by Grant Richards in 1914, Joyce omitted the first two passages and modified the third to read, "She glanced at him once or twice and, when the party was leaving the rooms, she brushed against his chair and said 'O, pardon!' in a London accent."

scrupulous meanness (handwritten annotation)

God. Where is his English Protestantism? I myself can bear witness that I have seen in modern English print such expressions as "by God" and "damn." Some cunning Jesuit must have tempted our stout Protestant from the path of righteousness that he defends the honour of the Virgin with such virgin ardour.

As for my part and share in the book I have already told all I have to tell. My intention was to write a chapter of the moral history of my country and I chose Dublin for the scene because that city seemed to me the centre of paralysis. I have tried to present it to the indifferent public under four of its aspects: childhood, adolescence, maturity and public life. The stories are arranged in this order. I have written it for the most part in a style of scrupulous meanness and with the conviction that he is a very bold man who dares to alter in the presentment, still more to deform, whatever he has seen and heard. I cannot do any more than this. I cannot alter what I have written. All these objections of which the printer is now the mouthpiece arose in my mind when I was writing the book, both as to the themes of the stories and their manner of treatment. Had I listened to them I would not have written the book. I have come to the conclusion that I cannot write without offending people. The printer denounces *Two Gallants* and *Counterparts*. A Dubliner would denounce *Ivy Day in the Committee-Room*. The more subtle inquisitor will denounce *An Encounter*, the enormity of which the printer cannot see because he is, as I said, a plain blunt man. The Irish priest will denounce *The Sisters*. The Irish boarding-house keeper will denounce *The Boarding-House*. Do not let the printer imagine, for goodness' sake, that he is going to have all the barking to himself.

I can see plainly that there are two sides to the matter but unfortunately I can occupy only one of them. I will not fall into the error of suggesting to you which side you should occupy but it seems to me that you credit the printer with too infallible a knowledge of the future. I know very little of the state of English literature at present nor do I know whether it deserves or not the eminence which it occupies as the laughing-stock of Europe. But I suspect that it will follow the other countries of Europe as it did in Chaucer's time. You have opportunities to observe the phenomenon at close range. Do you think that *The* [134] *Second Mrs. Tanqueray*[5] would not have been denounced by a manager of the middle Victorian period, or that a publisher of that period would not have rejected a book by George Moore or Thomas Hardy? And if a change is to take place I do not see why it should not begin now.

You tell me in conclusion that I am endangering my future and your reputation. I have shown you earlier in the letter the frivolity of

---

[5] A play (1893) about a man who marries a "notorious" woman, by Sir Arthur Wing Pinero.

the printer's objections and I do not see how the publication of *Dubliners* as it now stands in manuscript could possibly be considered an outrage on public morality. I am willing to believe that when you advise me not to persist in the publication of stories such as those you have returned to me you do so with a kind intention towards me: and I am sure you will think me wrong-headed in persisting. But if the art were any other, if I were a painter and my book were a picture you would be less ready to condemn me for wrong-headedness if I refused to alter certain details. These details may now seem to you unimportant but if I took them away *Dubliners* would seem to me like an egg without salt. In fact, I am somewhat curious to know what, if these and similar points have been condemned, has been admired in the book at all.

I see now that my letter is becoming nearly as long as my book. I have touched on every point you raise in order to give you reason for the faith that is in me. I have not, however, said what a disappointment it would be to me if you were unable to share my views. I do not speak so much of a material as of a moral disappointment. But I think I could more easily reconcile myself to such a disappointment than to the thousand little regrets and self-reproaches which would certainly make me their prey afterwards. Believe me, dear Mr Grant Richards, Faithfully yours

JAS A JOYCE. [135]

TO GRANT RICHARDS

23 June 1906   *Via Giovanni Boccaccio 1, Trieste*

Dear Mr Grant Richards: I have received the manuscript safely. For the next few days I shall be engaged on a translation but during next week I shall read over the whole book and try to do what I can with it. I shall delete the word "bloody" wherever it occurs except in one passage in *The Boarding-House.* I shall modify the passage in *Counterparts* as best I can. Since you object to it so strongly. These are operations which I dislike from the bottom of my heart and I am only conceding so much to your objections in order that *Two Gallants* may be included. If you cannot see your way to publish it I will have only wasted my time for nothing. As for the fourteenth story *A Little Cloud* I do not expect you will find anything in it to object to. In any case I will send it back with the others, as you direct me.

Some of my suggestions may have seemed to you rather farcical: and I suppose it would be useless for me to suggest that you should find another printer. I would prefer a person who was dumb from his birth, or, if none such can be found, a person who will not "argue the point." But let that pass.

Your suggestion that those concerned in the publishing of *Dubliners* may be prosecuted for indecency is in my opinion an extraordinary contribution to the discussion. I know that some amazing imbecilities have been perpetrated in England but I really cannot see how any civilised tribunal could listen for two minutes to such an accusation against my book. I care little or nothing whether what I write is indecent or not but, if I understand the meaning of words, I have written nothing whatever indecent in *Dubliners*.

I send you a Dublin paper by this post. It is the leading satirical paper of the Celtic nations, corresponding to *Punch* or *Pasquino*. I send it to you that you may see how witty the Irish are as all the world knows. The style of the caricaturist will show you how artistic they are: and you will see for yourself that the Irish are the most spiritual race on the face of the earth. Perhaps this may reconcile you to *Dubliners*. It is not my [63] fault that the odour of ashpits and old weeds and offal hangs round my stories. I seriously believe that you will retard the course of civilisation in Ireland by preventing the Irish people from having one good look at themselves in my nicely polished looking-glass. [64]

Dubliners and the Short Story

MARVIN MAGALANER AND RICHARD M. KAIN

THE SHORT STORY FORM AS WE KNOW IT, IS VERY YOUNG, DATING BACK to the middle years of the nineteenth century. Before that time, a short story was simply a story that was not long. The developments which were to change the short story from the status of truncated novel to that of a highly specialized artistic form came not from England or Ireland but from Russia, France, Germany, and America. England, where tastes in the nineteenth century ran to bulk, and standard novels to three heavy volumes, was hardly in a position to effect a revolution in reading tastes. Circulating libraries encouraged the triteness and artificiality of the ordinary novel. They helped to prevent literary reform. Finally, as H. E. Bates points out in his excellent discussion of the problem, explicit moralizing and preaching and the taboo on honest discussion of sex in literature robbed the English novel of the elements

From Marvin Magalaner and Richard M. Kain, *Joyce: The Man, the Work, the Reputation*. New York: New York University Press, 1956. Pp. 68–82. Reprinted by permission of the authors and the publisher.

that might have produced a new view of the short story. Such writing
impelled a large audience to reject the very qualities on which modern
short stories depend for their effect.[1]

The conventions of this heavy English novel had, for instance,
ruled out impressionist narration, with its accompanying gaps in temporal and spatial arrangement of episodes, it had discouraged any but
the most obvious symbolic representations, and it had by its example
relegated the quality of poetic concentration to disuse. It is impossible
to imagine a story like Joyce's "The Sisters" lacking these attributes and
yet retaining much of the power that resides in it.[2]

Joyce's kind of short story begins, perhaps, with Gogol, whose
quiet, intense characters have become the norm in modern tales. The
profusion of detail, the ugliness yet warmth of the subject, the handling
of ordinary lives of ordinary civil servants are common to both writers.
(Notice the resemblance [69] of Gogol's copyist, Akaky Akakyevitch,
to Farrington of Joyce's "Counterparts.") Both Gogol and Joyce looked
at commonplace people and found within them such powerful internal
conflicts that there was no reason to seek material elsewhere.

Critics of *Dubliners* most frequently cite Chekhov and Maupassant
as Joyce's models. Louis Cazamian finds the stories in the tradition of
the latter.[3] In his book on Joyce, Louis Golding agrees.[4] Allen Tate and
Mary Colum see at work the influence of Maupassant's teacher, Flaubert.[5] The frequency of such claims merits examination.

Joyce and Maupassant are really quite different in their approach
to the short story. In that genre, the Frenchman is usually the cele-
brator of violent emotion, passion, love, undying hate; of flamboyant,
startling action: dueling, rape, brutal murder, assassination. Joyce, on
the other hand, seldom raises his voice as he examines the less overt
manifestations of human behavior: the inhibitions, the frustrations, and
the disappointments of the ordinary person. The conclusion of a story
by the French writer finds the lives of his characters sharply altered
in a very obvious way: in "The Vendetta," the widow Saverini returns
peacefully to her home after seeing to it that her enemy has died a
bloody death; the vicious Prussian officer in "Mademoiselle Fifi" lies
stabbed to death while his murderess flees to safety; the noisy athlete
in "The Duel" destroys himself rather than risk the disgrace of failure.

---

[1] H. E. Bates, *The Modern Short Story: A Critical Survey* (London: Thomas
Nelson and Sons, Ltd., 1941), pp. 36–41.

[2] Elizabeth Bowen, *The Faber Book of Modern Stories* (London: Faber and
Faber, Ltd., 1937), p. 8.

[3] Louis Cazamian, *Essais en deux langues* (Paris: Henri Didier, Editeur,
1938), p. 48.

[4] Louis Golding, *James Joyce* (London: Thornton Butterworth, Ltd., 1933),
p. 28.

[5] Allen Tate, "Three Commentaries: Poe, James, and Joyce," *The Sewanee
Review*, LVIII (Winter 1950), 10; Mary Colum, *From These Roots* (New York:
Charles Scribner's Sons, 1938), p. 350.

In just the opposite way, Joyce gains his effects. It is the shock of having nothing happen, overtly at least, that brings home sharply the emptiness of the lives that he reveals. In "Two Gallants," a gigolo tries to wheedle a coin from his servant girl companion and is successful. Chandler, of "A Little Cloud," dreams of escape from narrow family problems and a debilitating suburban life, but realizes that such escape is impossible. Joyce's stories are keyed to the tempo of routine middle-class life, while Maupassant usually selects the extraordinary moment in an ordinary existence.

To maintain the interest of his readers in story after story whose center is sensuous animal passion, Maupassant must supply an artificial device, the trick ending. This he does with great skill; yet artful con-trivance does not entirely make up for the profusion of artificial jolts that he uses to give point and climax to his tales. Joyce would never ask his readers to accept, as the Frenchman does, a series of extremely unlikely actions leading up to a melodramatic denouement. [70] Joyce's brother Stanislaus, while agreeing that his brother admired Maupas-sant, remembers that Joyce criticized him for being too concise, for his "insistent wish to define things in a phrase," and for his brutality in judging the fictional characters he had created. His "characters seem to rise to a momentary interest only to fall back again into banality." In Joyce's writing, on the other hand, Stanislaus finds everyday life foremost, "and the incident, in itself so slight . . . serves only to il-luminate a certain moment of the everyday life. Judgment is always suspended. . . ."[6]

Other points of difference in technique may easily be adduced. Maupassant is not especially interested in symbolic presentation. He usually tells his story in a flat, clean, clear, brittle, and totally admirable way, presenting his account on the realistic level only. Joyce was not content to stop at this point. Edmund Wilson puts emphasis on an-other difference—the difference between poetry and prose.[7] It is unfair, of course, to speak of the sound and rhythm of Maupassant's writing in translation, but even in its French original, his prose is only prose, simple and lucid. Joyce's short stories carry a rhythm and cadence, however, rarely found in short stories. It is unnecessary to quote the melodious final paragraph of "The Dead" to indicate Joyce's superiority in writing musical prose. In short, Joyce may have learned a great deal about fictional technique from reading Maupassant, but there is little evidence in *Dubliners* to show that he made use of it in his own work. We know from Gorman that Joyce devoured "several volumes" of Maupassant,[8] but differences in temperament, habits of life, and ap-

    [6] Stanislaus Joyce, *Recollections of James Joyce by His Brother* (New York: The James Joyce Society, 1950), p. 18.
    [7] Edmund Wilson, *Axel's Castle: A Study in the Imaginative Literature of 1870–1930* (New York: Charles Scribner's Sons, 1931), p. 191.
    [8] Herman Gorman, *James Joyce* (New York: Rinehart and Company, 1939).

proach to art would not have been conducive to Joyce's finding the influence he needed in this pupil of Flaubert.

It is quite a different matter with Chekhov—and a much more difficult one. Perhaps Joyce did not know of the existence of the Russian while *Dubliners* was in preparation, for Chekhov's reputation was scarcely international in the early years of the twentieth century. Very occasionally, in the 1890's, an English translation of one of his stories would appear in *Temple Bar* or elsewhere.[9] And *The Fortnightly Review*, which ran Joyce's review of Ibsen, did publish two of Chekhov's stories (1903 and 1906), but there is no certainty that Joyce ever saw them.[10] It is very likely, however, that he did see a collection of Chekhov's stories called *The Black Monk*, published in London in 1903, with an introduction by an Irishman, Robert Long.[11] It contained, among [71] others, "The Black Monk," "In Exile," "Rothschild's Fiddle," "Sleepyhead," and "Ward No. 6." That a man interested in significant Continental literature, and especially in the short story, would have been unaware of this revolutionary publication is hard to believe.

Both writers tried in their stories to represent the flat surface and the twisted core of life. The visible portion of the iceberg was to be reproduced faithfully and with acute sensitivity to realistic detail. The smell of the peasantry, their wretched cottages, their brutality to servants or to horses—the daily affairs of life—were to be sketched with stark and unremittant fidelity. Joyce demanded that his pictures of middle-class politicians at work, or Irish priests, or tea salesmen, be accurate and immediately recognizable. But both artists recognized, in addition, the key role in life played by less material, less tangible elements in the human personality. At a time when it was not popular to plumb beneath the surface, they acquiesced in the artistic necessity of considering in their stories the great mass of iceberg under water— the hopes, the dreams, the self-deceiving illusions, the unconscious motivations, and the contradictions of the emotional life. Because both Joyce and Chekhov understood that the delineation of life required consideration of the whole iceberg, their stories have distinctive similarities. The discovery by both artists that the tension set up between

[9] Avrahm Yarmolinsky, Foreword to "Chekhov in English: A List of Works by and about Him," by Anna Heifetz, in *Bulletin of The New York Public Library*, LIII (January 1949), 27–28; see also Vivienne C. Koch, "Anton Chekhov," unpublished Master's thesis, Columbia University, 1933; and Anton Chekhov, "Two Tales from the Russian of Anton Tschechow" [*sic*], *Temple Bar*, CXI (May 1897), 104–113. [328]The stories in *Temple Bar* are "The Biter Bit" and "Sorrow."

[10] Anton Chekhov, "Darling: A Story by A. Tchekhof" [*sic*], trans. A. B. and E. A., with an Afterword by Leo Tolstoy, *The Fortnightly Review*, CCCCLXXVII (September 1, 1906), 560–571. This periodical had also published Chekhov's "In Exile" in September 1903.

[11] Chekhov's *The Black Monk*, ed. R. Long (London: Duckworth and Company, 1903).

life-as-it-is and life-as-it-should-be constitutes "the story" provides them with a common theme.[12]

Chekhov uses this motif most notably in "Ward No. 6." The creeping paralysis of small-town officialdom wears down the ambitions and distorts the mind of the local doctor until he finds stimulation only in conversation with a village madman and is himself adjudged insane. Joyce employs the slip between illusion and reality throughout *Dubliners*, recognizing no explicit demarcation between them.

It is most certainly present in "Araby," where the exotic Oriental motif is deliberately employed so that it may be contrasted with the banal reality of the salesgirl's flirtatious interlude and the bareness of the darkened suburban bazaar. When Maria, the laundress, sings in the quavering voice of an elderly spinster of how "I dreamt that I dwelt in marble halls," the theme is reiterated. It is equally apparent in Gabriel Conroy, in "The Dead," who, in spite of constant self-examination, fails to see himself as others see him. The revelation of all the shifting undercurrents to such a personality [72] would have been impossible for most writers in the short story, which demands brevity and yet completeness. Joyce and Chekhov were probably best fitted, fifty years ago, to show the way.

All novelists, of course, deal in some way with the struggle of the individual against the world and against his inner self. But Joyce and his Russian counterpart are alike in more specific ways. They are concerned with the same kinds of characters and situations. Avoiding Maupassant's overt action, they deal, as Matthew Josephson has pointed out, with "people who find themselves in a trap, or a 'box' . . . who plan to escape. . . . But nothing happens, or at least nothing happens as they planned. . . ."[13] To mention Joyce's main characters is to establish a gallery of thwarted escapees: Farrington, Eveline, Gabriel, Little Chandler, the boy in "An Encounter," and Polly Mooney's husband.

When a writer depicts life in realistic detail, he must be careful not to suggest artificiality by arranging his plot so that the details are too pat, too obvious and artful, for that is not how events seem to happen in life. Maupassant, with his structural hardness, his fixed opening and trick closing, disregarded that modern dictum. Chekhov made it his trademark. He felt that "a story should have neither beginning nor end." Like Joyce, he preferred to seem "inconclusive." That is one of the reasons why the reader does not have to stretch his imagination too far in going from *Dubliners* to *A Portrait*. Joyce's characters and situations extend themselves far beyond the pages on which they actually appear and take on an independent life of their own. What

---

[12] See William Gerhardi, *Anton Chekhov: A Critical Study* (New York: Duffield and Company, 1923).

[13] Matthew Josephson, *The Personal Papers of Anton Chekhov* (New York: Lear Publishers, 1948), p. 10.

happened to them before they walked across the stage and what will happen after the curtain descends are important to the reader. "Ivy Day in the Committee Room" ends on an anticlimactic, inconsequential remark. "Grace" closes in the middle of a sermon. The ending of "Clay" skirts the irrelevant as Chekhov's "Vanka" does, the one with a remark about Balfe's music, the other with a dog wagging his tail.

The objectivity and impersonality of the two writers have often been misunderstood and ascribed to a lack of warmth and human understanding. Joyce and Chekhov have been pictured as unconcerned scientists, toying with their human specimens as with an exhibit under a microscope. But this appearance of hardness and detachment is a deliberate device of writers who felt intensely the pity and terror of the situations and the people whom they created, and yet could not [73] trust themselves to write without restraint of what was closest to them. An air of distance and matter-of-factness, even in recounting emotionally gripping events, would produce, they felt, more powerful effects.

Chekhov speaks for his own, and surely for Joyce's practice, when he lays down rules for the tone of a literary work: "The only defect . . . is the lack of restraint, the lack of grace. . . ." And again, "when you depict sad or unlucky people and want to touch the reader's heart, try to be colder—it gives their grief, as it were, a background, against which it stands out in greater relief." Finally, "You must be unconcerned when you write pathetic stories. . . . The more objective, the stronger will be the effect."[14] This is a rather crude expression by Chekhov of what later become Stephen's aesthetic theory. Ideally, the artist, "like the God of the creation, remains within or behind or beyond or above his handiwork, invisible, refined out of existence, indifferent, paring his fingernails." Like Joyce, Chekhov felt that "Subjectivity is a terrible thing. It is bad in this alone, that it reveals the author's hands and feet."[15] Both artists are alike in their ability to keep their hands and feet out of the picture.

Frequent parallels between the factual details of Chekhov's stories and of Joyce's demand more detailed treatment than can be offered here. It must serve now merely to point out the resemblance of the madman, Ivan Dmitritch, in "Ward No. 6" to Stephen Dedalus. Their families suffer financial reverses, they teach school at starvation wages, their mothers die. Chekhov's description of Dmitritch parallels that of Stephen, detail by detail:

Never . . . had he had the appearance of a strong man. He was pale, thin, and sensitive to cold. . . . His disposition impelled him to seek companion-

[14] Chekhov, in a letter to Gorki, quoted in Gerhardi, *Anton Chekhov*, pp. 146, 147.
[15] Evelyn May Albright, Introduction to Chekhov, *Short Stories*, trans. Constance Garnett (New York: The Macmillan Company, 1932), p. x.

ship, but thanks to his irritable and suspicious character he never became intimate with anyone, and had no friends. Of his fellow-citizens he always spoke with contempt, condemning as disgusting and repulsive their gross ignorance and torpid, animal life. He spoke in a tenor voice. . . . However he began a conversation, it always ended in one way—in a lament that the town was stifling and tiresome, that its people had no high interests, but led a dull, unmeaning life. . . . Of woman and woman's love he spoke passionately. . . . But he had never been in love.[16] [74]

Other instances of fictional resemblances abound. One might show how, in spirit at least, Gabriel Conroy is like the Greek Master of "The Man in a Case," who tries to ward off all the dangers of existence by physical shields—galoshes, preoccupation with ancient books, umbrellas —and finally, in his coffin, is thoroughly protected from natural hazards. Or how the hotel bedroom scene in "The Dead," in which Gabriel sees his real aging appearance in the mirror, finds its counterpart in Chekhov's "The Lady with the Pet Dog." In both tales the critical moment of revelation is rendered through the device of looking into a mirror to glimpse reality through the illusion. Whether or not Joyce knew Chekhov's work is fascinating speculation, but that they had much in common, artistically, is unquestionable.

Young Joyce probably learned about another Russian, Turgenev, from another Irishman, George Moore. In *Impressions and Opinions* (1891), Moore had lauded "Turgueneff" for his sketches, in which "the slightest events are fashioned into marvellous stories." These he hailed because they were "absolutely new in form as in matter. . . ." Each of the twenty-five stories in *A Sportsman's Sketches* is capable of independent existence.[17] But like the stories in *Dubliners,* Turgenev's simple sketches produce the over-all effect of a corrupt, dying, despairing country whose inhabitants are trapped in a system of their own making. Each story breathes that "special odour of corruption" that Joyce tried so hard to get in his own book. Yet it is probable that Turgenev's work came to Joyce at second hand through Moore's *The Untilled Field,* published in 1903.[18] In this volume of stories, the spirit and method of the Russian was successfully applied to Irish subjects. Moore, too, had found in the everyday concerns of petty folk a larger symbolic meaning, which carried beyond the characters to indict a whole nation.

Though Joyce could learn little from the diction and style of Moore, he may have picked up and used several themes that pervade *The Untilled Field.* Moore is fond of stressing the great influence of the none too scrupulous members of the clergy, the ignorance of the

16 Chekhov, *The Black Monk,* pp. 220–221.
17 Ivan Turgenev, *A Sportsman's Sketches,* trans. Constance Garnett (New York: The Macmillan Company, 1917).
18 George Moore, *The Untilled Field* (London: William Heinemann, 1915); the book was first published in 1903.

ordinary Irishman, and the necessity of flight by emigration. In "The Exile" a man must make up his mind to be either a priest or a police-man. The qualifications for the job seem to be very much the same in both professions. Joyce's "Grace," as we shall see, suggests a similar theme. Moore's descriptions of the priest's house [75] and of the youth's rejection of priesthood in this story remind one of "The Sisters." Further, the dozing priest in Moore's "Patchwork," "huddled in his armchair over the fire . . . the cassock covered with snuff . . . and the fat, inert hands," suggests Father Flynn. Whatever Joyce in his formative stage may have learned from Moore, he had only ridicule for Moore's refined, artificial style in later novels like *The Lake*.

The sources of Joyce's realism in *Dubliners* are difficult, and per-haps unnecessary or to trace. In spite of Mary Colum's emphasis on the relationship, he is no closer to Flaubert than most of the young writers of his day in English who admired what the better realists were doing and who sought to emulate their integrity in careful documentation and observation of the facts of life. From reading "A Simple Heart," Flaubert's chief contribution to the realistic short story, Joyce could have learned what every realist had to say—not only the Goncourts in *Germinie Lacertoux* (1864) and Zola in *Germinal* but even George Moore in *A Mummer's Wife*—that there are servants and masters in an unequal world, that scullery maids are notoriously faithful to their employers, that the lives of the poor are ugly and wretched but that love, even when unmerited, may justify existence. In Flaubert's effec-tive story, Joyce could have found the surface hardness and objectivity, in the face of terrible disclosures, that later distinguish his own short stories. Also, his strong bent for ironic fictional conversations may pos-sibly derive from Flaubert's *Bouvard et Pécuchet*.[19]

In this novel Flaubert deals with the level of society that Joyce considered his special province: the middle-class civil servant, the bourgeois salesman, shopkeeper, or clerk. He sees them very much as Joyce sees them, in their monotonous sameness, dressing alike, acting alike, thinking alike. The interminable account of matters on which Bouvard and his associate agree covers several volumes: "Mais la banlieue, selon Bouvard, était assommante par le tapage des guin-guettes. Peuchet pensait de même."[20] It is but a step to the ironic conversations of similar small men in Joyce's "Grace."

"I haven't such a bad opinion of the Jesuits," he said. . . .
"They're the grandest order in the Church, Tom," said Mr. Cunning-ham. . . .
"There's no mistake about it," said Mr. M'Coy, "if you want a thing well done and no flies about, you go to a [76] Jesuit. . . ."
"The Jesuits are a fine body of men," said Mr. Power.[21]

[19] Gustave Flaubert, *Bouvard et Pécuchet* (Paris, 1885).
[20] *Ibid.*, p. 2.
[21] James Joyce, *Dubliners* (New York: The Modern Library, n.d.), p. 208.

The tone that Flaubert took toward his environment, especially in *Madame Bovary*, creeps also into the work of his disciples and reaches its zenith in Joyce. Hard to define, it is perhaps a romantic debunking of a romanticism that has lost its power and needs pitilessly to be exposed. By displaying coldly a product of bourgeois education, bourgeois social standards, and bourgeois monetary vulgarity, he is able to convey to his audience the tragedy implicit in the gap between small-town reality and romantic illusion. The former brings death; the latter financial and social success. This hiatus between reality and illusion, as has been pointed out, is essentially Joyce's subject matter, and the trapped people of Dublin, educated by the priests, provincial in outlook, are his equivalents for the Flaubertian characters. The boy in "Araby," whose disillusion derives from his sudden realization of the difference between romance and reality, is a minor Madame Bovary.

Something should be said of the degree of accuracy of Joyce's naturalistic details in *Dubliners*. While there is no special virtue in slavish adherence to truth of environmental background, in a creative work, at the same time, Joyce's fidelity to the facts of Dublin as a physical entity should be recognized. Though the contest itself may not be the center of interest in "After the Race," it is exciting to recognize that not only did such a race take place but that young Joyce was commissioned to cover a like event for the local newspaper. His very pedestrian and uncomfortable account of it, unsigned, and in the form of an interview with the driver of one of the racing cars, has recently been found.[22] Again, Joyce sets one of his most memorable scenes in *Dubliners* in Corless' restaurant, where Little Chandler is made to feel more and more an outsider, a frustrated provincial, by his successful, cosmopolitan friend, Gallager. It has often been assumed that, for this scene at least, the writer had created the setting from his imagination. Yet examination of *Thom's Official Directory of . . . Ireland* for 1896 shows this item: "Corless, Thomas, wine merchant and proprietor Burlington dining rooms, 24, 26, and 27 St. Andrew Street" and later reference to the place as "Burlington Restaurant and Oyster Saloons." Since Joyce writes that "People went there after the theatre to eat oysters and drink liqueurs," it is [77] reasonable to suppose that once more he preferred to deal, like Zola, with a maximum of observable fact in his fiction.

The surface resemblance of the stories in *Dubliners* to some naturalist fiction has too often led to indiscriminate labeling of the book as a product of Zola's movement. It does indeed seem to conform to many of the criteria of naturalism that Vernon Parrington suggests: objectivity in the spirit of the scientist, frankness, an amoral attitude toward material, and a bias toward pessimism in selecting characters

[22] Unsigned interview in a Dublin newspaper, discovered by Richard M. Kain in the files of the National Library in Dublin.

and the details of environment. Yet what he designates the vital principle of naturalism, its philosophy of determinism, seems quite unimportant in Joyce's stories.[23] Not one of his characters may be accused of being a mere economic or social puppet, going through the motions of living so that the scientist-author may pull the strings and observe and record the results of his experiments in the area of heredity or environment.

Nor can it truly be alleged that Joyce's adherence to the tenets in Parrington's list of naturalist characteristics is more than superficial and accidental. Even Zola, the expounder of the gospel of scientific objectivity, found himself taking sides and becoming, in spite of himself, partisan to a cause. There is no doubt that he stands with Etienne in *Germinal* forcefully taking a position on the social system of the future, as he speaks darkly but exultantly of the "black avenging army, germinating slowly in the furrows. . . ." Similarly, through the smoke screen of random conversation in "Ivy Day in the Committee Room," one can see without difficulty the figure of the author condemning, cursing, comparing, hoping—though not a word of direct comment is recorded, certainly, with regard to frankness, he possesses all the qualifications of the naturalist group, but, in addition, he has, in *Dubliners,* a sense of refined reticence not available to Zola and his circle, who were forced to shock in order to dramatize their revolutionary position in nineteenth-century letters. As for Joyce's pessimism in selecting characters and setting, his position was determined for him by the only life he knew—a sordid, poverty-ridden, monotonous day-by-day existence in a city whose former greatness seemed in eclipse. Zola may have chosen his battleground, but Joyce was forced to fight on the streets of his home neighborhood. Paradoxically, however, Zola traveled to the scene of action of whatever novel he was preparing in order to do justice to his subject; while [78] Joyce, in order to work with artistic vision, had to separate himself physically from those scenes with which he was most deeply concerned as man and artist. Perhaps distance was for the Irish writer a necessary condition for the task of transforming living people and oppressive environment into mysteriously symbolic ingredients of literature. For, from first to last, Joyce was primarily a symbolist writer.

By nature and upbringing Joyce found himself drawn to presentation through indirection. From early childhood, his mind had been alert to hidden meanings—to the significance, for instance, of the maroon brush for Michael Davitt, and the green for Parnell. The symbolism of wine and wafer in the sacrament had thrilled him in his school days. The hidden fullness of details of the mass attracted and frightened him by their power. Allusions to the inexpressible, clothed

[23] Vernon Louis Parrington, *Main Currents in American Thought*, Addenda to Vol. III (New York: Harcourt, Brace and Company, 1927), pp. 323–327.

in images of Mary, the Sacred Heart, or the dark flames of Jesuit Hell, were his daily intellectual and emotional fare. There is much of the symbolist in every Catholic Irishman. Unlike most of them, however, Joyce put the technique to work in his books.

Like many distinguished contemporary writers—Eliot, Pound, Yeats—Joyce found what he needed in Dante. The familiar story of Dante and Beatrice, lovers on a spiritual plane, becomes a symbol of the unrealizable in an imperfect world. From Dante's quest, too, may have come additional support for the familiar theme of the symbolic quest in *Ulysses* and in the first few stories of *Dubliners*. In addition, much of the symbolism of Hell that appears impressively in *A Portrait* and unobtrusively in *Dubliners* is colored by Dante's classic representation.

Joyce came to maturity as a new wave of organized symbolism was making itself felt in English-speaking countries. Only Swinburne and a handful of Englishmen had previously recognized the importance of Baudelaire's strange poems and tortured pronouncements. Rimbaud was just a name to many literary people outside France. Arthur Symons's *The Symbolist Movement in Literature* (1899) gave formal standing to these foreigners. But earlier than that, according to William York Tindall, Joyce had turned to them because they gave him a way to express reality.[24] By suggestion, by mysterious images rich in symbolic associations, the reader might be made to feel the truth about Dublin, a truth deeper than any based on a lengthy, factual, naturalist survey. That Joyce had [79] earlier experimented with symbolic indirection in his poetry has already been demonstrated in what has been said of *Chamber Music*.

When Joyce turned from poetry to short fiction, he had before him the example of Yeats's early prose—filmy, misty, strangely spiritual and beautiful short stories. Because he admired so much the artistry behind them, Joyce committed several of them to memory and studied their technique.[25] Yeats's stories, like Chekhov's, deal almost poetically with the thin line that separates illusion and reality, spirit and matter, natural and supernatural. His "The Tables of the Law" tells of the quest of a man to achieve a mystical and direct communion with the powers above. He fails utterly, for he has ignored and alienated himself from the real world, thinking that he can create beauty in a void. He decides that only by tracing himself the human pattern of sin and redemption, only by intercourse with God's world on earth, can he hope to encounter reality. His misfortune, and he knows it, is that he

---

24 William York Tindall, *James Joyce: His Way of Interpreting the Modern World* (New York: Charles Scribner's Sons, 1950), p. 108 ff.

25 William Butler Yeats, "The Tables of the Law" and "The Adoration of the Magi," in *The Collected Works in Verse and Prose of William Butler Yeats* (Stratford-on-Avon: Shakespeare Head Press, 1908). These stories first appeared in 1897.

is so far removed from the things of the world that he is unable to sin.

The suggestive details—the symbolism—of the story probably interested Joyce much more than the familiar romantic theme. In the first paragraph, the quester, Aherne, is asked why he has at the last moment before ordination refused "the berretta."[26] As the question is asked, Aherne raises a glass of wine, but, without drinking, he replaces it on the table "slowly and meditatively" and holds it there. It is a safe bet that Joyce was aware of the symbolic rejection of priesthood in this action. The acceptance or rejection of priesthood becomes, in fact, an important symbolic situation in "The Sisters," in *A Portrait*, and certainly in *Ulysses*. Other suggestive details give evidence of how Yeats and Joyce manipulate symbols. Aherne's predilection for the painters of the Sienese school because they "pictured not the world but what is revealed . . . in . . . visions" is a symbolic reflection of his own character. Knowing this circumstance, the reader has no need of two or three pages of discursive exposition.

Yeats's story is heavy with additional symbolic details, which Joyce appears to have stored up for future use. There is the narrow door that leads to Aherne's chapel, the six "unlighted" candles on the altar, and the secret book of Joachim of Flora, whose writings receive mention in the "Proteus" episode of *Ulysses*. In the story, too, are traces of [80] the French symbolists. The confusion of senses in the final wild scene is familiar. "Faint figures robed in purple, and lifting faint torches with arms that gleamed like silver," burning gum, a "heavy purple smoke" might well have satisfied Rimbaud in his days as magician and alchemist. Finally, the "great bird made of flames," recalling the phoenix, the Holy Spirit, and Joyce's birds (especially in "An Encounter"), is as mysteriously symbolic as Baudelaire's albatross or Mallarmé's troubled swan.

From Yeats's stories Joyce learned how realistic detail could be wedded to symbolic evocation, how an insinuation could be more forceful than the statement of a fact. He saw the strength that derived from effective presentation of visions. These visions, dreams, or reveries dot the pages of his prose, with one significant difference. Yeats will present a delicate hint of the supernatural but is not content to leave it at that. He is more analytical of his visions, more discursive, and wonders: "I do not know if they were demons or evil spirits." Joyce lets the reader wonder. But Joyce appears to adopt Yeats's habit of associating with the dead and the spiritual a mélange of sensuous impressions. What the boy narrator of "The Sisters" smells and tastes and hears is given great stress as he kneels before the dead priest. The odor of wet ashes, the faint music, the rustle of funereal garments herald the vision of Stephen's dead mother throughout *Ulysses*.

Yeats impressed Joyce with the importance of symbol in a story.

[26] *Ibid.*, p. 143.

But Joyce worked out his own technique and called it *epiphany.* He explains it in *Stephen Hero.* Stephen Dedalus chances to hear snatches of a trivial, flirtatious conversation on a Dublin street. Inexplicably, it makes a deep impression on him, and he thinks of "collecting many such moments together in a book of epiphanies. By an epiphany he meant a sudden spiritual manifestation, whether in the vulgarity of speech or of gesture or in a memorable phrase of the mind itself."[27] To explain still further, Joyce must give Stephen's well-known analysis of the qualities of beauty: first, to be beautiful a thing must have wholeness, that is, it must be seen as separate from all other things. Second, it must have harmony, or symmetrical balance of part with part within the framework of the thing. Finally, and most important, it must have what he calls radiance. This radiance or whatness or *quidditas* is apparent in a work of art "when the relation of the parts is exquisite, when the parts are adjusted to the special point [so that] we recognize that it is *that* thing which it [81] is. Its soul, its whatness, leaps to us from the vestment of its appearance. The soul of the commonest object, the structure of which is so adjusted, seems to us radiant. The object achieves its epiphany".[28] This is a rather complicated way for Joyce to say that he would present beauty in symbolic form. In essence, it may be put thus: radiance equals epiphany equals symbol. He sees epiphany as a device of expression that, perfect in its wholeness and harmony, will show forth in an instant of illumination a meaning and significance greater than the words in another combination would carry. Thus, clay may be clay, but in Joyce's short story it becomes, through skillful arrangement of the total pattern, symbolically representative of impending death, and hence it lends meaning to the otherwise trivial narrative. [82]

[27] James Joyce, *Stephen Hero,* ed. Theodore Spencer (Norfolk, Conn.: New Directions, 1944), p. 211.

[28] *Ibid.,* p. 213; see also Tindall, *James Joyce,* p. 120.

PART TWO. THE STRUCTURE AND UNITY OF *DUBLINERS*

Virtues and Limitations

S. L. GOLDBERG

THE LIMITATIONS OF *Stephen Hero* ARE OBVIOUS ENOUGH AND IT IS EASY to see why Joyce eventually had to abandon it. But they also explain one of the conditions of his success in *Dubliners*, which was written more or less at the same time and reflects, obliquely, many of the same ideas. For one thing, he had to get rid of Stephen. Joyce's self-knowledge was still too slender for him to portray himself convincingly. But this also meant that he could not yet convincingly portray, specifically, in depth, his central values, what he could feel as genuine vitality of spirit. *Dubliners* succeeds because he found there a way of doing what he *could* do, but the limitations of that are the measure of its achievement.

Whatever influences may be detected in *Dubliners*—and Chekhov, Maupassant, George Moore, and Flaubert have all been mentioned[1]— and however easy it has since become to write the same kind of stories, it is nevertheless a remarkable achievement for a writer in his early twenties. The stories are by no means simple naturalistic sketches, as some have thought them; nor, on the other hand, are they structures of infinitely complex "symbolism."[2] Each brings a limited area of ex-

---

[1] M. Magalaner and R. M. Kain, *Joyce: the Man, the Work, the Reputation* (New York, 1956), pp. 58 ff.; Allen Tate, "Three Commentaries," *Sewanee Review*, LVIII (1950), 1. But cp. Ellmann, *James Joyce*, p. 171 n.

[2] See Magalaner and Kain, *Joyce: the Man, the Work, the Reputation*, pp. 68 ff. Other "symbolic" explications may be found in B. Ghiselin, "The Unity of James Joyce's *Dubliners*," *Accent* XVI (1956), 75 ff., 196 ff.; M. Magalaner, *Time of Apprenticeship: The Fiction of the Young James Joyce* (New York and London, 1959), ch. 3; W. Y. Tindall, *A Reader's Guide to James Joyce* (New York, 1959), ch. I; but as criticisms of *literature* most of these strike me as either irrelevant or unconvincing.

From S. L. Goldberg, "The Development of the Art: *Chamber Music* to *Dubliners*," in his *James Joyce*. Edinburgh and London: Oliver and Boyd Ltd., 1962. Pp. 29–46. Writers and Critics Series. Reprinted by permission of Oliver and Boyd Ltd.

perience to sharp focus, renders visible its "whatness," and does so with an economical, concentrated purposefulness that gives the realistic details their full metaphorical import. Joyce had learned his craft. What is more, [36] the stories are lightly but suggestively related, so that the book is something more than merely a sum of its parts.

The opening sentences of the first story, "The Sisters," as we gradually come to realise, are something like a statement of the major themes of the whole book:

There was no hope for him this time: it was the third stroke. Night after night I had passed the house (it was vacation time) and studied the lighted square of the window: and night after night I had found it lighted in the same way, faintly and evenly. If he was dead, I thought, I would see the reflection of candles on the darkened blind, for I knew that two candles must be set at the head of a corpse. He had often said to me: 'I am not long for this world,' and I had thought his words idle. Now I knew they were true. Every night as I gazed up at the window I said softly to myself the word paralysis. It had always sounded strangely in my ears, like the word gnomon in the Euclid and the word simony in the Catechism. But now it sounded to me like the name of some maleficent and sinful being. It filled me with fear, and yet I longed to be nearer to it and to look upon its deadly work.

The terms "paralysis" and "simony" (more discursively defined in *Stephen Hero*) suggest the pervasive moral condition, the "maleficent and sinful being," exposed in story after story.[3] "Gnomon" suggests their artistic method, by which the whole is suggested by the part or (as with the gnomon on a sundial) the light by its shadow: the simple but effective metaphor of light/darkness is used in many of the stories.

In this first story, the old priest's physical paralysis becomes the mark of his failure of courage before the divine mystery he had tried to serve, and of his consequent resignation to hopelessness and death. In "An Encounter," the paralysis is that of diseased obsession. The unruly, romantic, adventurous spirit of the boy, [37] seeking a larger freedom of life, encounters only the maleficent disorder of the old pervert; yet although he fears it, he outwits it: courage wins him his freedom. In "Araby," the boy's romantic longings at last collapse and yet triumph in the darkened hall of the bazaar; the chink of money and the inane chatter there come to represent the materialistic "simony" which (even in his own desires) at once betrays his foolish ideals and is itself exposed by their innocent "folly." And so on through the book. The stories become images: of paralysed automatism of the will, the paralysing hand of the past, a paralysing feebleness of moral imagination, a simoniacal willingness to buy and sell the life of the spirit, timidity, frustration, self-righteousness, fear of convention, fear of sin, hypocrisy, vulgarity, pettiness. Each, with a fine dexterity, vivisects its

[3] Cp. A. Ostroff, "The Moral Vision in *Dubliners*," *Western Speech*, XX (1956), 196 ff.

Vital

material to lay bare the moral disease that distorts it to its present shape.

The metaphor of vivisection is Joyce's own,[4] and it describes perfectly the art of such stories as "Two Gallants" or "Ivy Day in the Committee Room" or "Grace," an art swift, sharp, accurate, with every stroke deliberately measured. The tone is flat, grimly reticent; the style distant; the observation and metaphorical detail so consistently pointed that they achieve a kind of wit. Yet the success is not consistent. Some stories are too intent upon their analytical purposes. The formal neatness of "Eveline," "After the Race," "The Boarding House," and "Counterparts," for instance, is so obvious and oversimplifying, that the art comes to seem almost programmatic. These stories lack the vital detail pressing *against* the author's scalpel, and they also lack the author's rather malicious enjoyment both of his material and of his skill in dealing with it, which enliven "Two Gallants," "Ivy Day," "Grace," or even "A Little Cloud," "Clay," and "A Mother." But then, as all these images of spiritual decay succeed each other, we may well begin to question the mood of the book generally. Is not its tone, indeed its [38] whole attitude to life, perhaps too insistently, and too constrictingly, "vivisective"?

Our answer inevitably reflects our view of Joyce's work as a whole. To some critics, *Dubliners* is a dispassionate, morally realistic account of modern life, Joyce's discovery of his lifelong attitude (ironical exposure) to his lifelong subject ("paralysis" and alienation). To others, his irony is "romantic," built upon the contrast between the individual's desires or feelings and the sordid realities of the modern world. To others again, his irony is only a device (like Chekhov's) for heightening the pity and terror of life.[5] Clearly, there are grounds for each of these judgments; but we also have to remember Joyce's relative immaturity when he wrote *Dubliners* and not be surprised if the book betrays it. Even while recognising the artistic success, we must also appreciate its limitations—not least because both help to explain Joyce's further development. And, not unnaturally, the limitations are very much those revealed more blatantly in *Stephen Hero:* an uncertain grasp of the values by which others are criticised, a vagueness about the genuine "life" by which simony and paralysis are constantly measured, a tendency to oversimplify reality in the process of exposing it.

It is not that the stories fail to imply the importance of courage, self-knowledge, fulfillment, freedom, or even the plainer domestic virtues; nor do they lack pity of a kind. But the comparison with Chekhov (or *Ulysses* for that matter) shows how little these values mean in *Dubliners*, how little it reveals what they might *be* in the actual experi-

[4] *Stephen Hero* (New York, 1955), p. 186.
[5] E.g. Kenner, *Dublin's Joyce,* ch. 5; Levin, *James Joyce,* p. 41; Magalaner and Kain, *Joyce,* p. 62.

ence of ordinary people, how complacent is its superior viewpoint. Some of the stories do reach towards a more self-critical, more specific, and hence (to that degree) deeper insight: "Araby," for example, "The Boarding House," "A Painful Case," and (most notably) "The Dead"— each, incidentally, the last in its respective group (childhood, adolescence, maturity, and public [39] life.)⁶ But "Araby," for all its tone of mature wisdom, remains slightly evasive about how compromised the boy's romanticism really is; "The Boarding House" can only gesture vaguely towards the interconnexions between the mother's "simoniacal" plotting and the possibilities of life opening before her daughter as a result, symbolically suggesting only enough to make us realise how little the art realises (here and elsewhere) of the complicating paradoxes of life.

"A Painful Case" takes a rather longer step towards maturity. The stories immediately preceding it reveal an obvious pity for the frustrated lives they portray, but as Joyce's imagination is devoted less to the individual character than to the kind of situation he represents, so the pity is somewhat aloof, superior to its human object. "A Painful Case" deals with a related but deeper emotion: compassion. As many have pointed out, it portrays what Joyce felt he himself might have been (the central character, Mr. Duffy, is actually modelled on Stanislaus);⁷ it is also like a self-comment on the tone of much of *Dubliners*. For Mr. Duffy is locked, irretrievably, in the Hell of his egocentric superiority to life. He refuses ordinary conventions and even ordinary carnal love; he disdains "to live, to err, to fall," and therefore, despite his literary pretensions, can never "triumph, . . . recreate life out of life."⁸ Only the shock of Mrs. Sinico's destruction enables him to see anything of his "paralysis," and then only partially and too late. The ending of the story illustrates perfectly what Joyce's art could achieve at this stage and what it could not. The recumbent figures in the park, where Mr. Duffy stands at night, are still merely "venal and furtive loves" for him, though he despairs at his own loveless state. The subtle identification of the man and the "obstinate" and "laborious" engine disappearing into the darkness, his lapsing sense of reality, the perfectly silent darkness in which he feels himself alone, are precisely right. Nevertheless, the [40] repeated phrase—"outcast from life's feast"—remains, as it must in the very terms in which the situation is observed, only the merest "symbol" of a life fuller and richer than his "rectitude" or the "venal and furtive loves." The story gives it no more positive meaning than that. And what applies to "eating" here applies to a great many other "symbols" earnestly explicated by Joyce's critics; they are all *too* "suggestive" and therefore vague, too undefined dramatically. We could say that by

---

⁶ Richard Ellmann, *James Joyce* (New York, 1959), p. 216.

⁷ *My Brother's Keeper*, p. 165; cp. Ellmann, p. 39.

⁸ *A Portrait of the Artist as a Young Man* (New York, 1928), p. 200.

choosing to work through the limited consciousness of his characters, Joyce found the best way to make their limitations imaginatively real, and thus avoided the need to define his position, to give meaning to his own stance in or behind the narrative, except by oblique "symbols" of the relevant values. We could equally well say that while he had no fuller sense of those values than he shows here, he simply could not see more in his characters than their limitations. The strength of *Dubliners* is the formal clarity, the subtlety and precision of its art—qualities that derive partly from a finely sustained discipline but partly also from an immaturity of insight that made the formal problems relatively simple. Perhaps the most striking thing about the book, indeed, is the way Joyce turned his very limitations to account.

"The Dead," the last of the stories and the last written, is, I believe, the exception that proves the rule. It has been universally admired, and it is a minor masterpiece in its own right.[9] One important difference from the other stories is its protagonist. Gabriel Conroy is an intelligent and complex man, and Joyce's art is now at last capable of portraying him as such. In many ways he, too, represents a self Joyce might have been: a university teacher, a "man of letters" in a minor way, critical of Irish provincialism, sensitive to its frustrations—" 'O, to tell the truth, . . . I'm sick of my own country, sick of it!' " That sickness is diagnosed very subtly, and a [41] second important difference from the other stories is the kind of irony that emerges. For there are no simple black-and-white judgments here, but rather a delicate balancing of insights. In fact, that balance is the story's central theme, and it heralds the spirit of Joyce's major works.

Gabriel's "sickness" is partly that he aspires to the wider and more vital possibilities he sees in Europe; partly that his education makes him feel morally superior to others; partly that he is unable to imagine others' lives sympathetically, so that a touch of egocentricity mars all his personal relations and all his judgments. At his aunts' annual party he is a favoured and admired guest, but he shows himself awkward, slightly pompous, inclined to resent others and to impose on them his own attitudes and his own good opinion of himself. Yet beneath all this lies an uncertainty, a genuine goodwill, and at bottom a saving humility. During the party a number of little frustrations jar his self-esteem. His impulse is to retreat: out of the tangled involvements of life to the clean, abstract, simple, and solitary world of the snow outside. Significantly, we are made to perceive the bracing vigour which attracts him from the room, with its decaying echoes of once-vital social customs, as well as his evasion of the actual life the room contains. He is revealed as the

---

[9] Cp. David Daiches, *The Novel and the Modern World,* rev. ed. (Chicago and Cambridge, 1960), pp. 73 ff.; Tate, *Sewanee Review* (1950); Ellmann, pp. 252 ff.; Ghiselin, *Accent* (1956), pp. 207–211; Kenner, *Dublin's Joyce,* pp. 62–68; Magalaner and Kain, *Joyce,* pp. 92–98 (though the last two seem to me to distort various aspects of the story).

victim of his self-ignorance. Ironically, the drunkard he despises proves capable of a spontaneous grace he could never manage; he misses the ironical application to himself of his story about the old horse who could not break the habit of the treadmill; ironically, he cannot appreciate his own speech toasting his aunts. To him they are "only two ignorant old women"—like the old horse. What he says out of a mean and self-protective impulse expresses, beneath its sentimentality, a deeper truth than he realises: that traditions do live on and yet die, that life is choked and haunted by the dead and yet goes on. "We have all of us [42] living duties and living affections which claim, and rightly claim, our strenuous endeavours. Therefore, I will not linger on the past. . . ." The vividly evoked scene, the dramatically controlled symbolism, are created by a style now so responsive that it seems to disappear into the drama itself.

When Gabriel sees his wife on the stairs listening to an old ballad he asks himself what she is a symbol of. *"Distant Music* he would call the picture if he were a painter." And being the man he is, he takes the music and its strange effect on her for his own. Suddenly he desires her, impatiently, thinking of their long intimacy together, alone, living in the "cold" with their mutual flame: "Like distant music these words that he had written years before were borne towards him from the past. He longed to be alone with her." In truth, "he longed to be master of her strange mood." The last shattering blow to his complacency is the truth about her mood—that it is not for him but the memory of a young man she had known years before, who had sung that ballad and who had died, in the brightness of his passionate love, for her. Gabriel is not insensitive; he sees his own egotism; but the "shameful consciousness of his own person" that now floods over him is not (as it is sometimes taken to be) the climactic moment of insight. It is only the reverse side of his egotism. He is no more merely a "ludicrous figure," a "nervous, well-meaning sentimentalist . . . idealizing his own clownish lusts," a "pitiable fatuous fellow," than his fellow-Dubliners are merely ignorant and foolish, drunkards, moral paralytics, mere gibbering ghosts of the past. One of the dramatic triumphs of the story is that we realise already what Gabriel must come to realise, know already what his listening wife was a symbol of. For a moment Gabriel nearly fails, and the moment, though dramatically unstressed, is a crucial act of self-criticism on Joyce's part: [43]

'I think he died for me,' she answered.
A vague terror seized Gabriel at this answer, as if, at that hour when he had hoped to triumph, some impalpable and vindictive being was coming against him gathering forces against him in its vague world. But he shook himself free of it with an effort of reason and continued to caress her hand.

The sense of some *external* evil, some "maleficent and sinful being," threatening the inviolate self—the assumption that dominates and limits the stories from the very first page—is here at last purged. Reason and love, an unspectacular but visibly "unresentful" and "generous" love, replace it; the veiled kinetic "riot" of self-defensive emotion gives way to a real *stasis* of spirit. And only now is Gabriel free, able to feel what the whole story has enacted: the complex tangle of distance and presence, passion and decay, love and detachment, aspiration and limit, life and death, in every individual and every society. The snow no longer represents to him the purity of the withdrawn self; as he "swoons" into unconsciousness, it seems to fall "like the descent of their last end, upon all the living and the dead."

This story has often been compared with *Exiles* because of the personal and marital issues treated in both.[10] In more fundamental ways, however, it is prophetic of the end of *Ulysses*, where Leopold Bloom reaches at last a similar moral *stasis;* and perhaps also prophetic —in its rather equivocal "swooning" into the snow-world, a vast, undifferentiating state beyond all life and death—of *Finnegans Wake* as well. The swelling release of emotion is here just kept in control; with Molly Bloom and in *Finnegans Wake* it is more elaborately disguised and escapes. But "The Dead" is finally unshaken. Its deeply felt conviction, its originality, the range and subtlety of its drama, its complex yet assured ironies, its humility before life, place it apart from the rest of *Dubliners*. Fine [44] as they are, the other stories stand judged by this. In the six or seven years from the early poems, Joyce virtually found himself as a writer. [45]

10 *E.g.* Levin, *James Joyce*, p. 43; Kenner, *Dublin's Joyce*, pp. 68–69.

The Unity of *Dubliners*

BREWSTER GHISELIN

THE IDEA IS NOT ALTOGETHER NEW THAT THE STRUCTURE OF JAMES JOYCE'S *Dubliners*, long believed to be loose and episodic, is really unitary. In 1944, Richard Levin and Charles Shattuck made it clear that the book is "something more than a collection of discrete sketches." In their essay, "First Flight to Ithaca: A New Reading of Joyce's *Dubliners*," they demonstrated that like the novel *Ulysses* the stories of *Dubliners* are integrated by a pattern of correspondence to the *Odyssey* of Homer.

Brewster Ghiselin, "The Unity of Joyce's *Dubliners*," *Accent*, XVI (Spring 1956), 75–88, and XVI (Summer 1956), 196–213.

To this first demonstration of a latent structural unity in *Dubliners* must be added the evidence of its even more full integration by means of a symbolic structure so highly organized as to suggest the most subtle elaborations of Joyce's method in his maturity.

So long as *Dubliners* was conceived of only as "a straight work of Naturalistic fiction," the phrase of Edmund Wilson characterizing the book in *Axel's Castle*, its unity could appear to be no more than thematic. The work seemed merely a group of brilliant individual stories arranged in such a way as to develop effectively the import which Joyce himself announced, but did not fully reveal, in describing the book as "a chapter of the moral history of my country" and in suggesting that his interest focused upon Dublin as "the centre of paralysis." As Harry Levin explained in his introduction to *The Portable Joyce*, "The book is not a systematic canvas like *Ulysses;* [75] nor is it integrated, like the *Portrait*, by one intense point of view; but it comprises, as Joyce explained, a series of chapters in the moral history of his community; and the episodes are arranged in careful progression from childhood to maturity, broadening from private to public scope."

So narrow an understanding of *Dubliners* is no longer acceptable. Recent and steadily increasing appreciation of the fact that there is much symbolism in the book has dispelled the notion that it is radically different in technique from Joyce's later fiction. During the past six or eight years a significant body of critics, among them Caroline Gordon, Allan Tate, and W. Y. Tindall, have published their understanding that the naturalism of *Dubliners* is complicated by systematic use of symbols, which establish relationships between superficially disparate elements in the stories. Discussion of "The Dead," for example, has made it obvious that the immobility of snowy statues in that story is symbolically one with the spiritual condition of Gabriel Conroy turned to the wintry window at the very end of *Dubliners* and with the deathly arrest of paralysis announced on the first page of the book. In the light of this insight other elements of the same pattern, such as the stillness of the girl frozen in fear at the end of the fourth story, virtually declare themselves.

Such images, significantly disposed, give a firm symbolic texture and pattern to the individual stories of *Dubliners* and enhance the integrity of the work as a whole. But no constellation, zodiac, or whole celestial sphere of symbols is enough in itself to establish in the fifteen separate narratives, each one in its realistic aspect a completely independent action, the embracing and inviolable order of full structural unity. That is achieved, however, by means of a single development, essentially of action, organized in complex detail and in a necessary, meaningful sequence throughout the book. Because this structure is defined partly by realistic means, partly by symbols, much of it must remain invisible until the major symbols in which it defines itself are recognized, as too few of them have been, and displayed in their more significant relationships. When the outlines of the symbolic pattern have been grasped, the whole unifying development will be discernible as a sequence of events in a moral drama, an action of the human spirit struggling for survival under peculiar conditions of deprivation, enclosed and disabled by a degenerate environment that provides none of the primary necessities of spiritual life. So understood, *Dubliners* will be seen for what it is, in effect, both a group of [76] short stories and a novel, the separate histories of its protagonists composing one essential history, that of the soul of a people which has confused and weakened its relation to the source of spiritual life and cannot restore it.

In so far as this unifying action is evident in the realistic elements of the book, it appears in the struggle of certain characters to escape the constricting circumstances of existence in Ireland, and especially in Dublin, "the centre of paralysis." As in *A Portrait of the Artist as a Young Man,* an escape is envisaged in traveling eastward from the city, across the seas to the freedom of the open world. In *Dubliners,* none of Joyce's protagonists moves very far on this course, though some aspire to go far. Often their motives are unworthy, their minds are confused. Yet their dreams of escape and the longing of one of them even to "fly away to another country" are suggestive of the intent of Stephen Dedalus in *A Portrait* to "fly by those nets," those constrictions of "nationality, language, religion," which are fully represented in *Dubliners* also. Thus, in both books, ideas of enclosure, of arrest, and of movement in space are associated with action of moral purport and with spiritual aspiration and development.

In *Dubliners,* the meaning of movement is further complicated by the thematic import of that symbolic paralysis which Joyce himself referred to, an arrest imposed from within, not by the "nets" of external circumstance, but by a deficiency of impulse and power. The idea of a moral paralysis is expressed sometimes directly in terms of physical arrest, even in the actual paralysis of the priest Father Flynn, whose condition is emphasized by its appearance at the beginning of the book and is reflected in the behavior of Father Purdon, in the penultimate story "observed to be struggling up into the pulpit" as if he were partially paralyzed. But sheer physical inaction of any kind is a somewhat crude means of indicating moral paralysis. Joyce has used it sparingly. The frustrations and degradations of his moral paralytics are rarely defined in physical stasis alone, and are sometimes concomitant with vigorous action. Their paralysis is more often expressed in a weakening of their impulse and ability to move forcefully, effectually, far, or in the right direction, especially by their frustration in ranging eastward in the direction of release or by their complete lack of orientation, by their failure to pass more than a little way beyond the outskirts of Dublin, or by the restriction of their movement altogether to the city or to some narrow area within it.

The case of the boy in the first story, "The Sisters," is representative. [77] Restive under the surviving influence of his dead mentor Father Flynn, yet lost without him, and resentful of the meager life of the city, he only dreams vaguely and disturbingly of being in a far country in the East, and wakes to wander in the city that still encloses him. At the end of the story he sits among hapless women, all immobile and disconsolate, in the dead priest's own room, in the very house where the priest has died, near the center of the center of paralysis. His physical arrest and his enclosure are expressive, even apart from a knowledge of the rich symbolism which qualifies them in ways too complicated to consider at this stage in discussion. Bereft of spiritual guidance, and deprived of the tension of an interest that has been primary in his life, he sits confused and in isolation, unsustained by the secular world about him, unstirred by anything in the natural world, moved only by a fleeting sense of life still in the coffin in the room overhead, a doubt and a hope like a faint resurgence of faith, instantly dispelled.

It should be no surprise to discover in a book developing the theme of moral paralysis a fundamental structure of movements and stases, a system of significant motions, countermotions, and arrests, involving every story, making one consecutive narrative of the surge and subsidence of life in Dublin. In the development of the tendency to eastward movement among the characters of *Dubliners*, and in its successive modifications, throughout the book, something of such a system is manifest. It may be characterized briefly as an eastward trend, at first vague, quickly becoming dominant, then wavering, weakening, and at last reversed. Traced in rough outline, the pattern is as follows: in a sequence of six stories, an impulse and movement eastward to the outskirts of the city or beyond; in a single story, an impulse to fly away upward out of a confining situation near the center of Dublin; in a sequence of four stories, a gradual replacement of the impulse eastward by an impulse and movement westward; in three stories, a limited activity confined almost wholly within the central area of Dublin; and in the concluding story a movement eastward to the heart of the city, the exact center of arrest, then, in vision only, far westward into death.

Interpreted realistically, without recourse to symbol, this pattern may show at most the frustration of Dubliners unable to escape eastward, out of the seaport and overseas, to a more living world. An orientation so loosely conceived seems quite unsuited to determine a powerful organization of form and meaning. Understood in its [78] symbolic import, however, the eastward motion or the desire for it takes on a much more complicated and precise significance.

Orientation and easting are rich in symbolic meanings of which Joyce was certainly aware. An erudite Catholic, he must have known of the ancient though not invariable custom of building churches with their heads to the east and placing the high altar against the east wall or eastward against a reredos in the depths of the building, so that the celebrant of the mass faced east, and the people entered the church and approached the altar from the west and remained looking in the same direction as the priest. He knew that in doing so they looked toward Eden, the earthly paradise, and he may have felt, like Gregory of Nyssa, that the force of the sacramental orientation was increased by that fact. Perhaps he did not know that the catechumens of the fourth century turned to the west to renounce Satan and to the east to recite the creed before they stepped into the baptismal font, to receive the sacrament that opens the door of spiritual life. Probably he did know that Christ returning for the Last Judgment was expected to come from the east. And he must have shared that profound human feeling, older than Christianity, which has made the sunrise immemorially and all but universally an emblem of the return of life and has made the east, therefore, an emblem of beginning and a place of rebirth. Many times Joyce must have seen the sun rise out of the Irish Sea, washed and brilliant. He could not have failed to know that washing and regeneration are implicit in the sacrament of baptism, and he may have known that in the earlier ages of Christianity baptism was called Illumination. He could not have failed, and the evidence of his symbolism in *Dubliners* shows that he did not fail, to see how a multitude of intimations of spiritual meaning affected the eastward aspirations and movements of characters in his book, and what opportunity it afforded of giving to the mere motion of his characters the symbolic import of moral action.

In constructing *Dubliners*, Joyce must have responded to the force of something like the whole body of insights of which these are representative. For these insights, with some others closely associated with them, are the chief light by which we shall be enabled to follow the development of what I have called the unifying action of *Dubliners* and, through understanding the structure of the book, to penetrate to its central significance. The unity of *Dubliners* is realized, finally, in terms of religious images and ideas, most of them distinctively Christian. [79]

Among these the most important for the immediate purpose of understanding are the symbols, sacraments, and doctrines of the Catholic Church, especially its version of the ancient sacraments of baptism and the sacrificial meal and its concepts of the soul's powers, its perils, and its destiny. In terms of the religious ideas with which Joyce was most familiar the basic characteristics of his structural scheme are readily definable, and some of them are not definable otherwise. The unifying action may be conceived of, oversimply yet with essential accuracy, as a movement of the human soul, in desire of life, through various conditions of Christian virtue and stages of deadly sin, toward or away from the font and the altar and all the gifts of the two chief sacraments provided for its salvation, toward or away from God. In these ideas all the most essential determinants of the spiritual action which makes of *Dubliners* one consecutive narrative are represented:

its motivation, its goal and the means of reaching it, and those empowering or disempowering states of inmost being which define the moral conditions under which the action takes place.

The states of being, of virtue and sin, are doubly important. For in *Dubliners* the primary virtues and sins of Christian tradition function both in their intrinsic character, as moral manifestations and determinants of behavior, and structurally in defining the order of the separate stories and in integrating them in a significant sequence. Thus they are one means of establishing the unity of the book, a simple but not arbitrary or wholly superficial means, supplementing with structural reinforcement and with a deepening of import that more fundamental pattern of motions and arrests already touched upon.

Like the booklong sequence of movements and stases, the various states of the soul in virtue and sin form a pattern of strict design traceable through every story. Each story in *Dubliners* is an action defining amid different circumstances of degradation and difficulty in the environment a frustration or defeat of the soul in a different state of strength or debility. Each state is related to the preceding by conventional associations or by causal connections or by both, and the entire sequence represents the whole course of moral deterioration ending in the death of the soul. Joyce's sense of the incompatibility of salvation with life in Dublin is expressed in a systematic display, one by one in these stories, of the three theological virtues and the four cardinal virtues in suppression, of the seven deadly sins triumphant, and of the deathly consequence, the spiritual death of all the Irish. [80] Far more than his announced intention, of dealing with childhood, adolescence, maturity, and public life, this course of degenerative change in the states of the soul tends to determine the arrangement of the stories in a fixed order and, together with the pattern of motions and arrests, to account for his insistence upon a specific, inalterable sequence.

Although Joyce's schematic arrangement of virtues and sins in *Dubliners* does not conform entirely to the most usual order in listing them, it does so in the main. In the first three stories, in which the protagonists are presumably innocent, the theological virtues faith, hope, and love, in the conventional order, are successively displayed in abeyance and finally in defeat. In the fourth story, the main character, Eveline, lacking the strength of faith, hope, and love, wavers in an effort to find a new life and, failing in the cardinal virtue of fortitude, remains in Dublin, short of her goal and weakened in her spiritual powers and defenses against evil. In the fifth through the eleventh stories the seven deadly sins, pride, covetousness, lust, envy, anger, gluttony, and sloth, are portrayed successively in action, usually in association with other sins adjacent in the list. The seven stories devoted to the sins occupy exactly the central position in the book. The sequence of their presentation is the most conventional one, except for the placing of anger before gluttony, a slight and not unique deviation. And in the sixth place gluttony is defined in the attitudes and behavior of others than the main character, Maria, who is interested in food and much concerned with it rather than avid of it. Her quiet depression is more truly expressive of her essential state of soul; and in it another sin that appears rarely in lists of the seven is apparent, the sin of tristitia, or gloominess, sometimes substituted for the similar sin of sloth. Joyce's intent seems to have been to create here a palimpsest, inscribing three sins in the space afforded for two. The effect has been to reduce gluttony to secondary importance while giving it full recognition in both of its aspects as overindulgence in drinking as well as in eating. The sequence of sins completes Joyce's representation of the defeat of the soul in its most inward strength and prepares for its failure in the exercise of rational powers. Alienated wholly from God, it cannot act now even in expression of the natural or cardinal virtues, in the words of Aquinas "the good as defined by reason." In the [81] twelfth through the fourteenth stories, the subversion of the cardinal virtues of justice, temperance, and prudence, and the contradiction of reason, upon which they are based, is displayed in those narratives that Joyce intended to represent "public life" in Ireland. Justice, the social virtue regulating the others, comes first in the group. The placing of prudence or wisdom last instead of first, the commonest position, is perhaps influenced by the sequence of appearance in these stories of those hindrances of the spirit in Ireland, the "nets" of "nationality, language, religion." The order, moreover, is climactic. Certainly the culminating subversion of the three virtues is represented in the third story of this group, "Grace," in the sermon of "a man of the world" recommending worldly wisdom for the guidance of "his fellowmen." In the fifteenth and last story of *Dubliners,* no virtue or sin is given such attention as to suggest its predominance. Perhaps that virtue of magnanimity which Aristotle added to the group of four named by the Greeks is displayed in abeyance in Gabriel Conroy's self-concern, but recovered at last in his final self-abnegation and visionary acceptance of the communion of death. Perhaps merely the consequences of moral degeneration are to be discerned in the final story, the completion of spiritual disintegration, death itself.

The pattern of virtues and sins and the spatial pattern of motions and arrests in *Dubliners* are of course concomitant, and they express one development. As sin flourishes and virtue withers, the force of the soul diminishes, and it becomes more and more disoriented, until at the last all the force of its impulse toward the vital east is confused and spent and it inclines wholly to the deathly west. All this development is embodied, realistically or symbolically, in the experience of the principal characters as they search for vital satisfaction either in spiritual wholeness or in personal willfulness, apprehending the nature of their goal and their immediate needs truly or falsely, moving effectually toward the means of spiritual enlargement or faltering into meanness and withdrawing into a meager and spurious safety, seeking or avoiding the sacred elements of the font and the altar, those ancient Christian and pre-Christian means of sustaining the life of the spirit through lustration, regeneration, illumination, and communion. The unifying pattern of motions and arrests is manifested, story by story, in the action of the principal figure in each, as he moves in relation to the orient source and to the sacramental resources of spiritual life, expressing in physical behavior his moral condition of virtue or sin and his spiritual need and desire. His activity, outwardly [82] of the body, is inwardly that of the soul, either advancing more or less freely and directly eastward or else confined and halted or wandering disoriented, short of its true goal and its true objects the water of regeneration and the wine and bread of communion, the means of approach to God, and often in revulsion from them, accepting plausible substitutes or nothing whatever.

In *Dubliners* from first to last the substitutes are prominent, the true objects are unavailable. The priest in the first story, "The Sisters," has broken a chalice, is paralyzed, and dies; he cannot offer communion, and an empty chalice lies on his breast in death. The food and drink obtained by the boy whose friend he has been are unconsecrated: wine and crackers are offered to him solemnly, but by secular agents. Again and again throughout *Dubliners* such substitutes for the sacred elements of the altar recur, always in secular guise: "musty biscuits" and "raspberry lemonade," porter and "a caraway seed." Suggestions less overt are no less pointed. The abundant table in "The Dead," loaded with food and with bottled water and liquors but surrounded by human beings gathered together in imperfect fellowship, emphasizes the hunger of the soul for bread and wine that can nourish it, rather than the body, and assuage its loneliness through restoring it to the communion of love. The symbolism of baptismal water likewise enforces the fact of spiritual privation. In "The Sisters" the secular baptism of a cold bath is recommended by the boy's uncle as the source of his strength. Less certainly symbolic, but suggestive in the context, is the fact that the body of the priest is washed by a woman, a point that Joyce thought important enough to define by explicit statements in two passages. In the house where the priest has lived and died, his sisters keep a shop where umbrellas, devices for rejecting the rain of heaven, are sold and re-covered. The open sea, the great symbol of the font in *Dubliners*, is approached by many of the central characters, longed for, but never embarked upon, never really reached. Canal, river, and estuary are crossed; Kingstown Harbor is attained, but the vessel boarded in the harbor is lying at anchor. When, in fear of drowning, the reluctant protagonist of the fourth story, "Eveline," hangs back refusing to embark on an ocean voyage, she may be understood to have withdrawn as at the brink of the baptismal font, for by her action she has renounced that new life which she had looked forward to attaining through moving eastward out of Dublin Bay on the night sea. The idea of her deprivation is reinforced by her final condition, of insensate terror, the reverse of spiritual refreshment and illumination. [83]

Though the spiritual objects that are imaged in these substitutes represent the gifts of the two chief sacraments of the Church, baptism, the first in necessity, and the Eucharist, the first in dignity, there is no suggestion in *Dubliners* that the soul's needs can be supplied by the Church, in its current condition. The only scene in a church, in the story "Grace," implies exactly the opposite, for the sermon of Father Purdon is frankly designed to serve the purposes of those who "live in the world, and, to a certain extent, for the world." The Church is secularized, and it shares in the general paralysis. Its failure in the lives of Joyce's Dubliners is emphasized by the irony that although the nature of the soul has not altered and the means of its salvation retain their old aspect, its needs must be satisfied in entire dissociation from the Church.

Since those needs cannot be satisfied in Ireland, as Joyce represents it in *Dubliners*, the soul's true satisfaction cannot be exhibited in the experience of those who remain in Ireland. It can only be simulated and suggested, either in their relation to those secular substitutes for spiritual things that intimate the need for baptism and communion or in their turning toward the soul's orient, the symbolic east, variously imaged. Some of Joyce's dissatisfied characters, such as Little Chandler, suppose that they can change their condition by escaping from Ireland eastward across the sea to another life in a different place. Physically their goal must be another country; spiritually it has the aspect of a new life. The association functions symbolically. Throughout *Dubliners*, one of the symbolic images of the spiritual goal is a far country. Like the symbols of water, wine, and bread, the far country images the soul's need for life that cannot be attained in Ireland.

Apparently it is not easily attainable outside of Ireland either. Those Dubliners who have reached England or the Continent, characters such as Gabriel Conroy or Ignatius Gallaher, the journalist whom Little Chandler envies because he has made a life for himself in London, show by their continuing to behave like other Dubliners that to be transported physically overseas is not necessarily to find a new life, or to be changed essentially at all. No doubt their failure to change means that the whole of Europe is secularized, perhaps the whole world. Still more, it emphasizes the subjective nature of the attainment symbolized by arrival in a far country. A new condition of inward life is the goal; not a place, but what the place implies, is the true east of the soul. The far countries reached by the boy in [84] "The Sisters" and sought by the boy in "Araby," perhaps the same boy, are not in the world. In one story he dreams of being in an eastern land which he thinks, not very confidently, is Persia. In the other he goes to a bazaar bearing the "magical name" *Araby,* a word casting "an Eastern enchantment." In both stories the far country is probably the same, that fabulous Arabia which is associated with the Phoenix, symbol of the renewal of life in the resurrection of the sun. To the dreamer it suggests a journey and strange customs, but he cannot conceive its meaning. The meaning is plain, however, to the reader aware of the symbols: the boy has looked inward toward the source of his own life, away from that civilization which surrounds him but does not sustain him. The same import, with further meaning, is apparent in the later story. The response of the boy to the name *Araby* and his journey eastward across the city define his spiritual orientation, as his response to the disappointing reality of the bazaar indicates his rejection of a substitute for the true object of the soul's desire.

The sea too, like the image and idea of a far country, symbolizes the orient goal of life. It may of itself, as water, suggest the baptismal font. And in any case it must tend strongly to do so because of the sacramental import of water established by other water symbolism throughout *Dubliners.* The element itself is highly significant, and the great image of it is the sea, the water of liberating voyage and of change and danger, of death and resurrection. The sheer physical prominence of the sea eastward from Dublin colors the east with the significance of baptismal water. In turn the sea is colored by the significance of the east. The altar, even more immediately than the font, is implied in the concept of orientation.

Perhaps in the symbol of the sea in *Dubliners* the identification of the two chief sacraments should be understood. Their identification would not be altogether arbitrary. For the close relationship and even the essential similarity of the two sacraments is suggested in several ways, apart from their association with the east: by their interdependence in fulfillment of a spiritual purpose; by the invariable mixture of a few drops of water with the wine in the chalice; and above all by the concept of rebirth, in which the font is profoundly associated with the altar, the place where Christ is believed to be reborn at the consecration of the divine sacrifice. That Joyce could make the identification is plain from his having merged font with altar in *Finnegans Wake,* in the conception of the "tubbathaltar" of Saint Kevin Hydrophilos. [85] Going "west-from" toward a suitable supply of water, and showing his sense of the importance of orientation by genuflecting seven times eastward, Saint Kevin fills up his device of dual function, in "ambrosian eucharistic joy of heart," and sits in it. Though Joyce may not have been ready, so early as in *Dubliners,* to identify font with altar, he has developed a body of symbolism which intimately involves them, and possibly merges them, in the symbol of the orient sea.

In that spatial pattern in which the unity of *Dubliners* is expressed as an action the orient goal is no one simple thing. It is a rich complex of associated ideas and images, only outwardly a place or places, intrinsically a vital state of being, a condition of grace conferred and sustained, presumably, by all the means of grace. Perhaps the main aspect of the symbolic orient, however, is of the eastward sea, its richest and most constantly represented image. The sea is the image most clearly opposable to that deadly contrary of the symbolic orient in all its import of spiritual life, that deathly state of moral disability, which Joyce conceived to be dominant in Ireland and centered in Dublin. The opposition is basic and clear in *Dubliners* of the eastward sea to the westward land, of ocean water to earth, of movement to fixation, of vital change to passivity in the status quo, of the motion toward new life to the stasis of paralysis in old life ways.

Lesser symbols in *Dubliners* are understandable largely in terms of this opposition, the symbols of water, of color, of music, of clothing, and the various symbols of enclosure. Not even the predominant element of the sea, water itself, always implies the sea or its vital freedom. No doubt in its basic symbolic meaning water is conceivable truly enough in conventional terms as the water of life. But in *Dubliners* it is distinctly this only in a general sense, as it is also the natural water of the globe of earth and sky. For full understanding it must be viewed more exactly in terms of specific symbolism and associations. In the eastern sea, it is the water of the font and the chalice, toward which the soul is oriented. Sluggish in a canal beside which a wastrel walks with his tart, or as the ooze on the lavatory floor where a drunkard lies, at the opening of the story "Grace," it loses virtue. At the end of "Eveline," as the water of voyage which can carry the frightened girl from Ireland to a new life and to fulfilling love, it retains its basic meaning and values as well as those given it by its place in the symbolic complex of the sea.

The colors associated with the sea are established very emphatically in "An Encounter" by the boy narrator's finding to his surprise that [86] none of the foreign sailors has the green eyes that he expected; their eyes are only blue, grey, or "even black." Truly green eyes, "bottle-green," appear to him only when he encounters the demonic gaze of the pervert on the bank in Ringsend near the Dodder. Thus green is dissociated from the sea and associated with degeneracy in Ireland, with crippling spiritual limitations, and with the physical limitation of enclosure in a bottle, an image suggesting water, but not the water of the open sea. The symbols of the bottle and of green are effectively combined later in the book in the symbolic complex of the bottled water on the table in "The Dead," pure water appropriately "white," but precisely marked with "transverse green sashes," the cancelling strokes that declare the contents to be spiritually without virtue. Among the ten colors mentioned in description of the table, and the many more only suggested by the foods and drinks and the dishes and bottles that are described, blue and grey do not appear, black is mentioned once, and brown is markedly predominant. Brown, like green, is associated with the limitations of life in Ireland, but much more emphatically. It recurs many times in the stories. It is mentioned as the tint of Dublin streets and is found in the freckled face and in the eyes of Miss Ivors, in "The Dead," who wears a brooch with "an Irish device and motto" and is militantly Irish. Yellow and red, the colors of fire, are variable in meaning, being associable at one extreme with the vital orient, at another with the punishments of the pit, as at the end of "A Painful Case."

The symbol of music is more clearly related to the east than to the land, but it takes its meaning very largely from the context of association and symbol in which it is represented. In "Eveline," where it is associated with far countries and the sea, an Italian air played on a street organ, the singing of a sailor about a sailor, and the quayside whistle and bell of departure on an ocean voyage, music symbolizes the motion of the soul toward life or the call of life to the soul. As the remembered singing of Michael Furey in "The Dead," it is the call to the past life, to communion with the dead.

Since clothing is an expression of character or of personal preference, or an indication of occupation or other circumstance, its symbolic use is restricted by the requirements of naturalism, the need to conform to objective fact. Its symbolic meaning is given unequivocally only in images associated with it at the free will of the artist. The blackness of Father Flynn's clothing is less certainly symbolic than its green discoloration, but the "suit of greenish-black" worn by the [87] pervert in "An Encounter" is indubitably symbolic in both its hues, since Joyce was free in his choice of both. The "brown-clad" girl worshipped by the boy in "Araby" is a madonna emphatically Irish.

Certain images in *Dubliners,* of closed or circumscribed areas, such as coffin, confession-box, rooms, buildings, the city and its suburbs, become symbolic when they are presented in any way suggesting enclosure, as they frequently are; and by recurrence many of them are early established as conventional symbols. In general they express the restrictions and fixations of life in Ireland. Except for the city itself and its suburbs, the commonest of these symbolic images are the houses of the people of Dublin, which are so well characterized in *Stephen Hero* as "those brown brick houses which seem the very incarnation of Irish paralysis." Such is the home, no doubt, of Little Chandler in the story "A Little Cloud," who supposes himself to be a prisoner simply in the external circumstances of his existence, though really he is afflicted with the prevailing paralysis, the psychic limitation of his commitment to the ways of a society without vitality. Like Eveline of the story that bears her name, who leaves for a while the "little brown houses of her neighborhood," in one of which she lives, Chandler cannot escape the constriction which those houses symbolize. Surely his house too must be of symbolically brown brick, situated somewhere near those houses referred to in *Stephen Hero,* which are in Eccles Street, in the north central part of Dublin, at the very center of paralysis. [88]

II

Both the purpose and the length of this paper preclude discussion of all the symbolism of *Dubliners.* Enough of it has been defined in the preceding exposition, however, to make possible a brief and sufficiently clear account of the stories in sequence, as a means of displaying the outlines of the unifying action of the book in its essential character. To avoid reiteration, I will refrain from pointing out the import of the symbolism at every turn. The reader will no doubt find it preferable to bear in mind the meaning of the chief symbolic images and their main function in the symbolic pattern and to be constantly active in discernment. I will, however, make whatever interpretations may be required by the purpose of the discussion, to reveal the single action of *Dubliners* in the separate actions of the principal figures, story by story to trace in their diverse histories the symbolically significant motions and arrests and to discover in them the one composite movement of the agonistic soul of the Irish through stage after stage of its decline.

In the first story of *Dubliners,* "The Sisters," the sterility of Irish life is defined. As a naturalistic narrative, it is an account of a boy's deprivation of spiritual guidance and support, through the death of his friend the priest Father Flynn, a paralytic who has committed the ecclesiastical crime of simony, a sin implying worldliness, and has broken a chalice. His spiritual impotence even in life is made apparent by symbolic means. Sitting in a stupor, enclosed in his little dark room in his sisters' house that is also a shop, he spills through trembling fingers a powder of snuff. As odorous "clouds of smoke" it resembles incense, descending rather than rising. As "clouds" being "dribbled" in "showers," it has the aspect also of a liquid. Dropping from the hands that have broken a chalice, it is a dusty successor to the sacramental wine. Brown, like the earth of Ireland, it tinges his black garments with green.

When the priest is dead, his sisters Nannie and Eliza assume his place and functions in a significant scene. Nannie's name and the [196] appearance of her shoes "trodden down all to one side" suggest a goat, or worse. In the strangeness of her feet and in the clumsy way "her skirt was hooked at the back" she resembles the celebrant of the black mass in the Circe episode of *Ulysses,* who has "two left feet back to the front" and wears "a long petticoat and reversed chasuble." When the boy and his aunt visit the home of the dead priest and she performs the hospitable actions paralleling imperfectly the ceremony of the Eucharist, her evil aspect is a means of emphasizing the invalid character of the sacramental action. Essentially, however, she is a feckless old woman who does wrong in ignorance. Eliza, just as innocently usurping the position of the dead priest, is "seated in his armchair in state." She tells Nannie to pour the wine, and when she sits silent the others wait respectfully for her to speak. Her position, given force by her authority, suggests that of a bishop or pope, whose chair or throne can symbolize his state.

The futility of the spurious ritual is emphasized by two references to the empty fireplace, dark since the death of the priest. The symbolic import of the image is confirmed and defined by a parallel in *A Portrait of the Artist as a Young Man:* the dean of studies, seen kindling a fire, "seemed . . . a humble server making ready the place of sacrifice in an empty temple." The boy, moreover, refuses the ministration of the women. He rejects the crackers, the bread, the one element administered to the laity in communion, and takes up the wine from the table himself, the element reserved for the priest, as if he were sensible of the "great wish" that the priest has had for him, or as if he were conscious of the implications of his recent dream in which the priest has attempted to confess to him as to a priest. The suggestions in this dream of the assumption of spiritual responsibility by the boy and of his journeying to a churchlike place in the East, where there are "long curtains and a swinging lamp of antique fashion," define the need of Dubliners to seek out for themselves the spiritual life that is no longer available in Ireland.

In this story, however, the need for reorientation of the soul is no further defined than in these intimations. At the end, the boy and his companions are reminded of the priest in life, "in the dark of his confession-box" alone and laughing in his mild dementia, and they listen briefly for some similar token of life remaining in the coffin. Hearing no sound, the boy understands with apparent finality that the paralysis of Father Flynn is complete in death. Perhaps the death of God is intimated, for the priest lies overhead, and, moreover, in a stroke of wit Joyce has given him in the very first sentence of the book [197] an aspect of God, in stating that hope for his life was abandoned at the third onset of his malady, as if his death must be threefold. The surmise is made more plausible by the fact that, like that "half-witted God of the Roman Catholics" scorned by the Stephen of *Stephen Hero,* the priest has not been for some time wholly himself. Whatever we may wish to make of this, the fact remains that the boy, an orphan, is bereaved of his fatherly friend and is left without other spiritual authority to quide him than his own powers. Though these have been vaguely suggested in his dreams he has no reason to have faith in them.

In the first story of *Dubliners* the action takes place in or near the priest's home in Great Britain Street, near the center of Dublin, and though the boy dreams of a far country he does not conceive of going there or understand that he can move beyond the limits of his circumstances. The symbolic orient does not draw him. This is a story of the soul suspended in almost complete arrest, only vaguely sensing its orient and its powers.

In the second story, "An Encounter," a boy who lives in the northeast part of the city moves southeastward, across the Liffey, to wander in Ringsend. The expedition is a disorderly adventure of truants from a Catholic school, who "break out of the weariness of school-life for one day." Inspired by stories of the Wild West, they have spent their evenings in disorderly play that has seemed liberating but at last has become wearisome. The narrator begins to desire real adventures, but he understands that "they must be sought abroad." With another boy he plans to go along the Wharf Road until they reach the shipping by the quays, to cross in the ferry, and to visit the Pigeon House, a fort at the mouth of the Liffey, a mile east of Ringsend. The name of their eastward goal is symbolic, since the pigeon, or rock dove, is an emblem of the Holy Ghost. Accomplishing all but the last part of their plan, they admire a Norwegian vessel, observe the sea-colored eyes of the sailors, and remain in Ringsend to eat musty biscuits and chocolate and to drink pink Lemonade and to idle away their afternoon. Their hope of escape does not carry them so far eastward as they desire, but it brings them into contact with a pervert, green-eyed and dressed in "greenish-black," the hellish image of that spirit of disorder which has moved them. The implication is that in Ireland the choice for those who would have "real adventures" lies between degradation and conventional order. In this story, though the unsatisfied soul moves a little way eastward, in the hope of escape into life, it is quickly frustrated. [198]

In "Araby," the third story, as in the first, the absence of spiritual sustenance in Dublin is symbolized by the death of a priest. The enclosure of musty air in the house where he has died is suggestive of staleness in the very breath of life which he has ceased to animate, and the fact that he has been a "very charitable priest" is a reminder of that Christian virtue of love which in this story is portrayed as flourishing briefly before its dispersal. Outside, however, the evening sky has the liturgical color of violet and the air has a vital sting, the lamps of Dublin glow, there is music of shaken harness, and Mangan's sister stands on the doorstep. Her dress swings, the "rope of her hair" is "tossed." In this imagery there is vital motion and a slight suggestion of the sea, symbol of the soul's orient. If the Church lacks spiritual life, the natural life of man may be elevated to take its place. By his idealizing love, the boy narrator may restore the spiritual life of the secular city, worshipping his madonna in eucharistic rituals as if he would assume the powers of priest in a new faith. Leaving his home in the northeast part of Dublin, he journeys in an empty train across the water of the Liffey to a far place of eastern appearance and name, the bazaar *Araby,* where he hopes to obtain a gift for her, some confirmation of the life that exalts him. Hope, faith, and love itself are destroyed when, at his goal, he finds the bazaar about to close, silent like "a church after a service," and at its center the vulgar attendants conversing and counting money. The soul's energy has carried it across water but not to the sea, far eastward but to a secular goal, not to its true orient.

The central figure in the story "Eveline" lives in the state of deprivation determined by the failure of faith, hope, and love in the triad of earlier stories. She is the first of the characters in *Dubliners* to attempt, in the course of any story, to escape from Ireland and cross the water to a far country and new life; and she is the last. Her situation is unique: innocent of sin, yet old enough for independence, she is morally free enough to escape. But she lacks the necessary moral force. Offered a life in Buenos Aires by a young man, a former sailor, who loves her, she consents to leave her home and her drunken, abusive father. But at the North Wall, due eastward from the center of Dublin, the black ship appalls her, and she clutches the iron railing in frenzied fear of drowning. Her fiercely energetic action is symbolic of her moral paralysis, an inability to move to the baptism of the night journey over water and the communion of love in a new life. And at the same time it is actual arrest. At the end, Eveline is "passive, like a helpless animal," as if soulless, paralyzed by fear. Lacking the [199] virtue of fortitude that strengthens the soul for compliance with the dictates of reason, she must turn back from danger and from life. Her plight exemplifies the state of the soul enclosed in the barren homeland because it is too weak to cross the threshold of the east.

With "After the Race," the concourse of sins commences, inevitably with the sin of pride. The suppression of the soul that in "Eveline" caused its withdrawal from action and reduced the girl to the semblance of an animal, is seen in this fifth story to have opened the way for an extraordinary ebullience of material energy. The sweep of movement is greater than in any other story: it begins far to the west of Dublin and ends in Kingstown Harbor. Thus pride comes out of the west, the direction contrary to the vital east. Both physical and financial power are depicted in exaltation, most compellingly in the central symbol of the opening scenes, a costly motor car, "a swift blue animal," which by exacting response from "the machinery of human nerves" reverses the roles of man and machinism. The hero of the story, Jimmy Doyle, is a grey-eyed young man with a brown mustache, colors identified with the symbolic opposites of sea and land and defining precisely his spiritual condition, between the poles of good and evil. In him the state of the soul that has lost its virtue and stands at the threshold of sin is represented. His disposition toward pride is indicated early by his pleasure in the notoriety brought by his riding with wealthy foreigners in the car, and later by his feeling "the lack of an audience" when he finds himself in glittering circumstances aboard a yacht. His parents feel "a certain pride" because of his associations with the men and names of foreign cities. His triumph is accompanied by the sound of music: motor horns, gongs of trams, singing, and the piano music of a penniless Hungarian. It culminates in a night of card-playing and drunkenness aboard a yacht that rests nightlong on the symbolic waters of a harbor. The stationary voyage ends in stasis and stupor. Jimmy, like Eveline, resembles in the end a paralyzed animal.

The degradation of the soul continues in "Two Gallants," with a disreputable sexual adventure in which money is the primary object. As Levin and Shattuck have pointed out in their essay, the "fine decent tart" whom Lenehan covets and Corley enjoys is a debased Nausicaa, princess of a seagoing people and befriender of Odysseus. The tart wears clothing suggestive of the sea, a blue serge skirt, white blouse and sailor hat, and a black jacket with mother-of-pearl buttons; and her eyes are blue. The impression is complicated by other details: at her bosom are red flowers, stems up, inverted perhaps to symbolize [200] her barren nature, and her slack mouth with projecting teeth lies open, monstrously. She is not wholly a succoring princess, though Corley relies on her for goldpieces; she is no angel of the waters, but a gutter sprite. Corley's first encounter with her, began "under Waterhouse's clock," included a walk beside a canal and an excursion into a field in Donnybrook, through which flows the Dodder, of ugly associations in "An Encounter." Accompanied by Lenehan, Corley goes from Rutland Square, at the top of O'Connell Street, through the center of Dublin and southeast to Hume Street to meet her, then, leaving Lenehan, east with her to Merrion Square, where they board the Donnybrook tram that carries them southeast. Lenehan retraces his path across Dublin, turns west at Rutland Square, and circles back to his rendezvous with Corley. On the way he stops for a solitary meal of peas and ginger beer, and to meditate the possibility of marrying for money. He meets Corley, who displays in his hand what he has obtained from the tart, the gold coin, final object of his symbolic communion, the body and blood of the sacrifice counterfeited in gold. For both men the essential value in life is money, and their sin is avarice. The soul's primary movement in this story is southeastward to the debased substitute for communion and the symbolic waters, then westward in a partial return. Secondarily, as the movement of Lenehan, it is a circular motion about the center of the city.

The circular motion of Lenehan prefigures the confinement of movement in the next story, "The Boarding House," in which all the action takes place in the house, in Hardwick Street, just north of Rutland Square. There the soul is arrested, virtually at the center of Dublin. The object of his lust, the sin which he has confessed to a priest, is "a little perverse madonna" whose eyes are "grey with a shade of green." Glimpsed in her role of temptress, she wears a "loose open combing jacket," and the virgin white of her instep appears against the animal fur of her slippers. The symbolic indications of her relation to the spiritual orient are exact: her virginal aspect is vulgarized and contradicted, and her eyes tinged with pool-green symbolize at most the sea's ambivalent margins. She is the foam-born goddess of earthly love, a debased Aphrodite, as Levin and Shattuck have shown her to be in the Homeric parallel also. Her temple is a boarding house which is beginning to acquire "a certain fame" and which is managed by a woman referred to by the boarders [201] as "the Madam." Though her lover thinks of escape, he is constrained by social pressures, by concern for his business position, and by uneasiness about his sin. Longing "to ascend through the roof and fly away to another country," he descends to the parlor to agree to the marriage. The suggestion of upward motion toward the spiritual orient is countered by an actual downward movement toward the secular substitute.

The limitation of movement in this story is an emphatic expression of a new stage in the unifying action of the book. For the impulse to move eastward beyond Dublin is reduced to a fantasy, and it is never after this point restored, except in "A Painful Case," and then only to be suppressed in revulsion. In "A Little Cloud," the eighth and central story of *Dubliners*, the fantasy is continued in Little Chandler's brief dream of literary success, which is engendered by his envy of his friend Gallaher, who has become a journalist in London. Like the sun god of myth, Gallaher has blue eyes, though his are not perfectly blue, and his gold watch and "vivid orange tie," twice mentioned, suggest the glow of the god. Dazzled, and warmed by his heavily watered drink, Little Chandler timorously enjoys his brief communion, at the same time painfully considering the injustice of the contrast between himself and his friend. When the crying of the baby breaks into his reading of Byron, he rebels at his hopeless imprisonment in "his little house," and shouting at the child he frightens it into paroxysms. It is almost beyond doubt that he has come home to this defeat across O'Connell Bridge and past Rutland Square; for, as we have seen, the likeliest location of his home is in the neighborhood of Eccles Street.

A similar circling occurs in "Counterparts," the next story, when after leaving the office in Eustace Street the central character, Farrington, goes eastward to make the round of the bars, from Davy Byrne's south of O'Connell Bridge to Mulligan's somewhat east of it. The circling expresses his true desire, for he has come in anger and revulsion from the office, where he has been humbled by his superior, Mr. [202] Alleyne, and he goes home, eastward to the suburb of

Sandymount, with the bitterest loathing. The vital image toward which he is impelled, but without hope of attainment, is a woman with a London accent, wearing a peacock-blue scarf and gloves of bright yellow, the orient colors of sea and sun. But her eyes are brown, and he encounters her in Mulligan's in Poolbeg Street just east of the center of Dublin. Farrington's whole desire is concentrated upon central Dublin, where he hopes to restore his sensations of power and self-esteem, through drunkenness, sexual conquest, and a display of physical strength. But he is overcome in a show of strength, and his money runs out before he can accomplish his first two objects. In Sandymount he vents his anger and asserts his superiority by caning his little boy. His story shows the weakening of the disoriented soul as sin more and more alienates it from God.

In the next story, "Clay," the drift of the soul toward death begins. The central character, Maria, journeys away from the waters, symbolized by the *Dublin by Lamplight* laundry where she works. In this curious name, suggesting soiled water and artificial light, baptism both as washing and as illumination is implied. The barmbracks cut and served for tea by Maria are an intimation of the host, divided before the ritual and mechanically apportioned, exactly four pieces to each woman served. Both of the chief sacraments are represented in the symbolism of the false orient of the soul at which Maria's journey begins. The sacrament of marriage is represented by the ring mentioned by one of the laundresses, a Hallow Eve charm which Maria desires but never receives. Maria is a tiny, disappointed spinster with the grey-green eyes that combine the symbolic colors of sea and stagnant pools, appropriate for a laundress. Riding the tram from Ballsbridge to Drumcondra, she goes from the southeastern suburb, through the center of Dublin, to the northern suburb, stopping at the Pillar in O'Connell Street to buy gifts of food for her relatives. On the ride to Drumcondra, her spiritual inclinations are emphasized by her encounter with an ambiguous figure, a half-drunk elderly red-faced stout man with greyish mustache and brown hat. When he makes room for her to sit down she contrasts him with the young men, who have ignored her. The three topics of his conversation, Hallow Eve, the rain, and the food in her bag, are reminders of the three sacraments earlier represented. Maria's pleasure in him is misplaced, for she receives nothing from him. Instead, she suffers a loss. In her happy confusion, she forgets her package of plumcake. Or perhaps he actually steals it. The suspicion, coupled with his stoutness, his [203] drunkenness, and his talk of the enjoyment of food, is enough to associate him with the sin of gluttony. Amid the heavy emphasis upon food and drink throughout the story, Maria appears almost abstemious. Her downcast shyness and wistful disappointment in her lonely life seem evidence that her soul's defect is gloominess, the sin of tristitia. The impression is strengthened by her turning somewhat westward, away from the orient. She is ready for death, as her touching the clay in the Hallow Eve games intimates.

James Duffy, hero of "A Painful Case," actually lives in the far western suburb of Chapelizod, though he is a banker in Baggot Street in southeast Dublin. He lives "without any communion with others," withdrawn even from himself, thinking of himself in the third person and the past tense, somewhat as if he were no longer in life. His sin is sloth. Yet he interrupts his deathly abstraction by an intellectual intimacy that carries him eastward to Dublin concert halls and to the southeastern seaside suburb of Sydney Parade into the home of a Mrs. Sinico, blue-eyed, the neglected wife of a sea captain. When at Duffy's insistence upon the soul's loneliness she makes a gesture of affection, he withdraws from her in fear and rectitude and so deprives them both of the communion of life. Years later, reading of her drunken death, perhaps suicide, he hastens in revulsion from Dublin to Chapelizod, but is drawn eastward again to the western edge of Dublin, the scene of his last parting with her in Phoenix Park. It is a movement toward life, in yearning for contact, but though the name of the park suggests a resurrection, he finds there only a final realization that he is "outcast from life's feast," from communion. Aware of his responsibility for Mrs. Sinico's death under the wheels of a train, he wanders in his lonely night, turning his eyes first to the sea-grey river "winding along towards Dublin," eastward; then to its contrary image, a far freight train "winding out of Kingsbridge Station, like a worm with a fiery head winding through the darkness, obstinately and laboriously," westward. He hears its rhythm repeating her name. His sense of guilt, the image as of a worm of death and hell, and the heartlike thud of its noise in his ears, combine in an impression of his identification with the destroyer. Turning homeward he will go in the same direction as the train. It is a symbolic movement of the soul toward death, a suitable conclusion of the action in sin that began with a proud eastward plunge of mechanical energy.

Hereafter in *Dubliners* the disoriented, unregenerate, unnourished soul, alienated from God by sin, acts only at the center of paralysis and looks beyond it only toward death. The characters in the last four [204] stories move no farther to the east than the central areas of the city; they depend on the meager resources of life in Dublin, and their aspiration toward vital satisfaction beyond the present time and scene is directed to a future that has the aspect of the dead past.

In the three stories of public life that follow "A Painful Case," the culminating action occurs in one building or another within three quarters of a mile of O'Connell Bridge, approximately the center of Dublin. In "Ivy Day in the Committee Room," the uneasy canvassers for the Nationalist candidate Tierney assemble to wait for their uncertain payment at the headquarters in Wicklow Street just south of the

Bridge. Here the political life of the city and of the country as a whole is focused with symbolic force. The aged caretaker who tends the unwilling fire and sets out the bottles of brown stout has "moist blue eyes" and a mechanically munching mouth, and the canvasser O'Connor who sits with him has grey hair and a pimply face. Before the other canvassers return, a man with a brown mustache and raindrops on his hat, Joe Hynes, not of their group, steps into the room and twice asks, " 'What are you doing in the dark?' " Candles are lighted, the physical darkness is diminished; Mr. Henchy enters, and Hynes remains long enough to defend the right of the working-man to run for office and to condemn both Tierney, whom no one trusts, and the English King, whose visit to Ireland Mr. Henchy approves of because it will bring "an influx of money." The ambiguous figure of Father Keon appears, dubiously suggestive of priest and actor. His "very bright blue eyes" and rainwet face like "yellow cheese" give him the symbolic aspect of the orient god of the sun. Though the impression is modified by the quality of the yellow, it is strengthened by the "rosy spots" on the cheeks and by the shining of his buttons in the candlelight. His black clothing may symbolize the night sea, or the divine darkness, or the darkness of evil and death. He is called a "black sheep" and he goes to transact some business with a politician at the *Black Eagle*. His refusal of light on the dark stairs, where he "can see" to descend, suggests self-generated light, like that of the sun or of God. These and other indications in him of obscured divinity give him the aspect of a spiritual power in decline. Thus he is a symbolic apparition of a force supplanted by the present leader Tierney, by King Edward VII, and at the end of the story by Parnell, whom Hynes returns to praise in a poem as "Our Uncrowned King." Led by Hynes, all look to the political force of a life that has vanished in the past. Admired by all, Hynes' poem represents the hope of Ireland as dependent upon the resurrection of the betrayed leader, compared to [205] Christ and the Phoenix, in a world manifestly as barren of justice and as hostile to spiritual life as when he was "slain."

In the thirteenth story, "A Mother," the center of action lies somewhat farther to the east, in the Antient Concert Rooms on Great Brunswick Street, less than half a mile southeast of O'Connell Bridge. Mrs. Kearney, the main character, has lost all traces of an early superficial affinity for the east, symbolized by her "ivory manners" as a girl and by her habit of "eating a great deal of Turkish delight." She respects her brown-bearded husband for his solid fixity, which gives her a sense of security. She turns the Irish Revival to her daughter's advantage by having her taught Irish as a means of advancing her popularity. She cultivates Nationalist friends and musical friends, with the effect of establishing the girl's reputation in Dublin musical circles as a pianist with pleasing personality and the right outlook. When given an opportunity to manage her daughter's talent, she is energetic and able. But upon the esthetic and financial failure of a series of concerts for which her daughter has been engaged as an accompanist, she ruins the girl's career by an unreasonable, intemperate concern for money and a display of ill feeling, bad taste, and manners anything but ivory. The fecklessness of the management, the mediocrity of the performers, the indecorum of the audience, and the cupidity and uncurbed passion of Mrs. Kearney reveal the disabling deficiency both of force and of control among those concerned with the arts in Ireland. The esthetic life of Dubliners is symbolized by an apparition, the wraithlike figure of a soprano, Madam Glynn, imported from London to sing at the concerts. Her appearance as of one "resurrected from an old stage-wardrobe," the faded condition of her blue dress, and her "bodiless grasping voice" suggest the vanquished life of a former time. In the ghostly image the remoteness of the symbolic east and the feebleness of its influence are made apparent.

At the beginning of the fourteenth story, "Grace," which was for a time the final story of *Dubliners,* the principal character, Mr. Kernan, is seen at the end of a drunken bout, in degradation and immobility, "quite helpless," lying "curled up at the foot of the stairs down which he had fallen," on the filthy floor of a basement lavatory in a bar in south central Dublin. After his fall—not from grace, for that has occurred long before, but from the dead level of decency in Dublin—he lies as if paralyzed, or as if dead in the womb of earth awaiting a call to resurrection which he can hardly expect to profit by. The story ironically represents the futile efforts of Dubliners to elevate him. In the bar he is rescued by Mr. Power, a fair man in a yellow ulster, the [206] color of orient light, but without a trace of symbolic blue about him, and taken across Dublin to his home on the Glasnevin Road, the northwest outskirts. Glimpsed in his seat on the car, as it nears O'Connell Bridge at the heart of the city, Mr. Kernan appears as if in his original attitude on the floor, though set upright, "huddled together with cold" before the biting east wind that blows upriver from the sea. In his bedroom, two days later, he is seen in much the same position, "propped up in bed," while his friends plot to "make a new man of him" by persuading him to join them in a retreat, to confess his sins, and renew his "baptismal vows." His wife has denied him any of the stout served to his friends, but when he consents to join the retreat a neighbor, fair-haired like Mr. Power, suddenly appears with a bottle of "special whiskey," and all join in a round of drinks. The group look to the past, praising "the old, original faith" and old-fashioned education, and final plans are made for the retreat. Mr. Kernan refuses, however, to hold a lighted candle in the ceremony, and in doing so he symbolically rejects illumination. In the final scene, in the Jesuit Church in Gardiner Street, three quarters of a mile north of O'Connell Bridge, the friends are led by a priest, whom they rightly characterize as "a man of the world like ourselves," to the happy discovery that the attainment of grace requires of them no thought or act in the least contradictory of their worldly wisdom or more regular worldly behavior. While the casuist in the pulpit attacks the foundations of the cardinal virtue of prudence, or wisdom, Mr. Kernan and his friends kneel in the symbolic attitude first defined in his position amid the filth and ooze of the lavatory floor. Earlier Mr. Kernan, a former Protestant, having erred in a reference to the body of a church, has called it the "pit," as if he were thinking of a theater. But his tongue has found the word for *hell*. Obviously appropriate for the lavatory, it characterizes a church like that in which these Dubliners are last seen, kneeling in the polysymbolic attitude of drunken paralysis, of shrinking from the breath of the soul's orient, of the sickbed, and of supplication that we know to be hopeless because it is directed to the god of this world, the "mammon of iniquity" named in Father Purdon's text.

After this story, anything further might seem superfluous. The paralyzed soul has come to a dead halt, the end of its divagations, before a lifeless altar at "the centre of paralysis." Joyce may have asked himself, however, what would happen if the dead should recognize and accept their death. Whatever else the final story of *Dubliners* may be, it is an answer to this question. Recognition and acceptance [207] would bring liberation, though not into life, and movement, though not to the east and not of the body. This story, "The Dead," shows a new development in *Dubliners,* a mitigation of the punishment of the enclosed and paralyzed. The physical movement of the main character, Gabriel Conroy, from a house in the western part of the city eastward to a hotel at the very center expresses in spatial terms his commitment to the ways and the doom of his fellow Dubliners. His spiritual movement westward, in imaginative vision, symbolizes his transcendence of that doom through recognition of its meaning and acceptance of the truth of his inward nature.

But this is the conclusion of the action of a long story. When first seen, coming in from the night, his clothing dusted with that symbolic snow the deathly import of which has been noted often, Gabriel brings a "fragrant" breath of chill air. He seems to represent in a vivid image the "dead" of Dublin who are foregathering in a house on Usher's Island, nearly a mile west of O'Connell Bridge, the home of his aging spinster aunts and cousin, who are giving their annual party for their friends and their music pupils. Gabriel is dissatisfied and uneasy, and he longs for the pure snowy air on the quay. In part he is pressed by his responsibility as toastmaster with a speech to make in praise of the tawdry artificial little world of his cousin and his kindly, moribund aunts. In part he is pained by a sense of his own futility and falsity. Attacked playfully as a "West Briton" by brown-eyed, Irish-speaking Miss Ivors, because he is not enthusiastic about his country and plans a vacation in Europe rather than the Aran Islands, Gabriel answers,

"I'm sick of my own country, sick of it!" Like the characters in the earlier stories, he longs to escape out of Ireland. His difference is that his deep inclination is toward the west rather than toward the east. When he looks toward the snowy night or thinks of walking upriver from Usher's Island, in Phoenix Park and "the white field of Fifteen Acres" at its center, it is not only the night and snow that allure him but the west itself.

Galway and the Aran Islands are not far enough, however. They represent the goal of the one Dubliner, Miss Ivors, who will not be wholly identified with the group at the party. Though constricted by her insistent overemphasis upon Ireland, she is honest and warm. The symbolism of color discriminates her from those Dubliners who are not only constricted in their life but corrupted by it. Mr. Browne, tediously insisting that he is "all brown," is not really so: he wears a "green overcoat," the color associated with symbolically stagnant water, and its "mock astrakhan" trimmings further define his false [208] orientation. It is Miss Ivors who is "all brown," all Irish. Her refusal of supper is a rejection, symbolically, of communion in the house of the dead. Leaving the party early, she walks home, alone, up the quay, westward, going the way of Gabriel's desire, though not to his ultimate goal.

Gabriel remains to preside at his aunts' table and to praise the ladies of the household and their preservation of the old-fashioned Irish hospitality, and to discredit the present "less spacious age." Thus the past is opened before him as a pleasant prospect, sentimentalized, suggesting also, however, changes and "absent faces" of the dead, from which he feels it proper to turn again to "living duties and living affections," to the present scene that is dominated by the "Three Graces of the Dublin musical world." Gabriel's fulsome exaltation of this feeble trinity shows his insensitiveness to the life of the present.

The music of the past dominates the night, moreover. In conversation the guests have dwelt upon great singers of the past, Italian and English, performers hardly to be matched in the present day, except, as Bartell D'Arcy insists, in London, Paris, and Milan. And as the company disbands, toward dawn, the music of the past is sounded by D'Arcy's tenor voice, singing a song "in the old Irish tonality." For Gabriel and his wife Gretta it is arresting. He is "surprised at her stillness" as she stands listening. Shadow darkens the ruddy colors of her skirt to black and white, the earthly terra cotta, and the salmon pink that suggests, however obliquely, the sea and the return of life from the sea to the land. She is an ambiguous image. Colors of land and sea appear also in her bronze hair and blue hat. To Gabriel she suggests a picture, which he would entitle *Distant Music*. It calls him both toward her and to their past, their youth together. While they ride toward the hotel where they will pass the remainder of the night, waves of joy break upon his memory like "fire of stars," and he imagines the "old rattling box" of the cab is carrying them eastward out of Ireland "to catch the boat, galloping to their honeymoon."

Just before leaving his aunts' house Gabriel has revealed exactly the nature of the escape he is launched upon. Walking round and round in the hall, he has mimicked the action of an old horse, trained to the treadmill, that when driven in the streets has perversely circled around a statue. Gabriel has just finished a speech in praise of the past, to which all monuments are built. In the cab, which he believes will carry him to a renewal of old delight, he is going forward only to a travesty of the dead past, found as if by traveling in a circle. Such [209] movement, constricted by conventions of the soul, is really spiritual arrest, the psychic paralysis of the treadmill, in *Stephen Hero* aptly described as a "stationary march."

In their room, in the Gresham Hotel on the east side of O'Connell Street not far north of the Bridge, Gabriel dismisses the porter and sends the candle with him. Perhaps his wish is to be lighted only by the fire of his joy. But a "ghastly light" of the street lamp lays a long streak from the western window to the locked door; the blasting light of Dublin illumines the room. Turned there to the past, in hope of resurrecting his life by embracing his wife in the spirit of the early days of marriage, Gabriel does not understand that in having "escaped from their lives and duties" he has rejected the present and moved toward death. And he discovers too late that his wife has made a similar movement away from life, but not toward him. Stirred by D'Arcy's song to her own memories, Gretta like Gabriel has turned to the past and given herself to the image of love there. But what she remembers is a grave, that of the boy Michael Furey, who she believes died for her. Moving away from their present life, which has not sustained them spiritually, the living are not united, for their motion is toward diverse goals, not merely to the dead past but to separate graves.

Quieted by his realization of his own unimportance, in lonely shame and humility Gabriel stretches himself by his sleeping wife and, thinking of his aunts and their approaching death and of all the dead, he feels the fading of his own identity into vagueness. Looking westward from the window, watching the snowfall that covers Ireland with waters frozen to stillness, he feels that "his journey westward" is imminent. His thoughts carry him to the central plain and hills and the Bog of Allen, still, turf-colored water, and farther, in transcendence of that stasis, to the Atlantic ocean, "the dark mutinous Shannon waves" receiving the falling snow. As his soul swoons in his vision of a universe of snow, Gabriel senses in the oblivion of its descent the unity of the fate of "all the living and the dead." In recognizing that fate as universal, his also, Gabriel is restored to the community of men by his acceptance of the communion of the shades.

Though Gabriel's enlargement and liberation in his final vision is not a restoration to life, it is an achievement of true dignity and beauty. The one comparable attainment in *Dubliners* occurs in "Araby," where the way of release into life, as Joyce conceived it, is adumbrated in the only action of the book that is creative. By acts of invention, by transmuting an earthly love in worship and ritual, [210] a boy attains for a while some measure of religious satisfaction. But his experience is mainly compounded of imaginations and delusory expectations, and he is entirely alone and unsupported. Finding his idol inadequate to sustain him through all assaults and frustrations, he conceives of no other. He is like Gabriel, the potential artist confined and disempowered in Dublin.

The spiritual way of escape and attainment, only intimated in *Dubliners,* is fully defined in A *Portrait of the Artist as a Young Man,* in passages not unrelated to these stories. With a priest of the Church who is merely "schooled in the discharging of a formal rite," Stephen Dedalus contrasts himself, "a priest of the eternal imagination, transmuting the daily bread of experience into the radiant body of everliving life." The consummate act in the *Portrait* is Stephen's creation of a work of art. In a series of developments symbolized by images of generation and of sacred rites amid the cloudy flush and afterglow of a dream or vision of waves of light, the words of a poem flow into being in his mind. Here is the process whereby "the uncreated conscience" of his race will be forged. It is a ritual from which the work of art emerges, as the consecrated Host emerges from the ritual of the Mass, to be used for the redemption of the soul from death and the replenishment of the world with life.

The nature of this most vital action of the soul is made more fully apparent in the immediately following scene of augury. Watching the circling flight of swallows, Stephen is reminded of the flight of Daedalus out of captivity, symbol of his own escape from Ireland eastward over water. In the wanderings of the "birds ever going and coming, building ever an unlasting home under the eaves of men's houses," he seems to find a symbol of constantly renewed creative action and of that ceaseless motion of spirit like endless waters out of which invention comes and which beauty can evoke. Lines of Yeats about the wandering of the swallow over waters stir his life as in an earlier scene it was stirred by a girl—in her power not unlike the Irish madonna of "Araby"—standing beautiful, and birdlike, in midstream, stirring the water of the tide to motion and music. The meaning of that visionary image of beauty in action is disclosed in Stephen's dream that follows in response to it. The dream is of unfolding subjective light, flooding in waves, seeming to be simultaneously a world and a flower and a sea flushing with dawn, a complex of symbolic images like the orient goal of *Dubliners* that has the aspects both of another land than Ireland and of an eastern sea and that is at the same time a state of the soul in fullness of life. The vital condition of [211] the soul thus envisaged is the opposite of the soul's paralysis. It is a state of change in manifold movement, a flowing transmutation of multitudinous form as in the "hitherandthithering waters" of *Finnegans Wake* and in the tidestream stirred by the girl's "foot hither and thither."

Suggestions of such spiritual fulfillment in motion of a subjective light that is like water are to be found in *Dubliners* in Gabriel Conroy's joy, compared to a "wave," and in the images of his past delight that "burst like stars" and "broke upon and illumined his memory" while his illusion held that he and his wife were moving "with wild and radiant hearts to a new adventure." The parallel in the *Portrait* is striking: while Stephen, awaiting the augury, stood repeating the words of Yeats, "a soft liquid joy like the noise of many waters flowed over his memory. . . ." Gabriel's mind, like Stephen's, appears to have been stirring with the promise of life, before he turned to the past, away from the vital east. Perhaps even in the last moments of his decline he might have turned round and moved eastward if his spirit had been stronger. For as "his soul swooned slowly" into the vagueness of the snow and watery darkness, it was being freed of the "nets" of Irish ways, like that of Stephen Dedalus entering the dreamed watery light, whose "soul was swooning into some new world, fantastic, dim, uncertain as under sea. . . . Glimmering and trembling, trembling and unfolding, a breaking light, an opening flower. . . ." Failing to attain the freedom of that light, Gabriel escaped into darkness.

Clearly the escape from Dublin is not to be conceived of finally as a passage beyond physical enclosure, but as a transcendence of psychic constrictions, an attainment of that full mobility of the soul which is the reverse of its paralysis. The nature of Joyce's later works of fiction sustains this view. For the scene of all is Dublin, and all develop in one way or another the theme of wholeness in spiritual fullness and freedom. In the character and experience of Leopold Bloom, "allroundman," sensitive observer in whom there seems to be "a touch of the artist," wanderer and "waterlover," the attainment of wholeness is less approached than suggested. Not alone by Bloom, but in the very texture of *Ulysses,* is forefigured that universal being embodying our collective humanity which in *Finnegans Wake* Joyce represented in the forever renewed activity of a single character in whom all are comprised. In the interlinking formations and resolutions of meaning in flow that present the history of this being, Joyce offers to every reader, if only in the mode of esthetic understanding, a realization of life integrated in one continuing act of changing and inclusive vision, [212] a vast epiphany and a communion in which all may share. Thus in *Finnegans Wake* the resurrection and the life denied to almost all of Joyce's characters, found only briefly by the artists and the young, is discovered in the movement of the everliving spirit of humanity.

Ulysses approached this development. *Dubliners* began it, in a single
symbolic structure consubstantial with a full-bodied naturalistic narrative defining at once the symbolic method of Joyce's successive
masterpieces and the grounds of his mature vision. The revelation
thus presented is of the whole moral action of the soul in Dublin moving from the beginning to the end of its tortuous course between the
poles of life and death. [213]

Ibsen, Joyce, and the Living-Dead

JAMES R. BAKER

IN 1900 JOYCE WROTE TWO ESSAYS IN WHICH HE ANNOUNCED AN UN-
qualified admiration for Ibsen's later plays. The first, "Drama and
Life," dismisses the Greek and Elizabethan traditions as outmoded
and praises Ibsen for finding "the deathless passions" amid the com-
monplaces of modern bourgeois existence. "Ibsen's New Drama," the
second, is a eulogistic review of *When We Dead Awaken,* which concludes that appreciation is the only fitting response to the "perfect"
dramatist and "one of the world's great men." "The Day of the
Rabblement" and the famous letter to Ibsen, both written the following year, continue with unchecked enthusiasm. According to Richard
Ellmann's biography, Joyce carried his crusade to the Continent,
where he frequently defended Ibsen or sought to win new admirers.
As late as 1936 (during the last stages of work on *Finnegans Wake*)
we find him accepting with delight a comparison between Ibsen and
himself, on another occasion insisting that Ibsen is "head and shoulders"
above Shakespeare, and on still another arguing with James Stephens
over the merits of *Little Eyolf.*[1] [19]

The influence of Ibsen on the theme and structure of *Exiles* is a
long-established recognition in Joycean criticism.[2] In his chapter on
"The Backgrounds of 'The Dead'" Ellmann extends the range of

---

[1] Richard Ellmann, *James Joyce* (New York, 1959), pp. 701, 707, 709–710.

[2] James T. Farrell, "*Exiles* and Ibsen," in *James Joyce: Two Decades of
Criticism,* ed. Seon Givens (New York, 1948), pp. 95–131; Francis Fergusson,
"A Reading of *Exiles*" (Preface), *Exiles* (Norfolk, Connecticut, 1945), pp. v–xviii.

James R. Baker, "Ibsen, Joyce and the Living-Dead: A Study of *Dubliners,*"
in Marvin Magalaner, ed., *A James Joyce Miscellany,* Third Series. Carbondale,
Illinois: Southern Illinois University Press, 1962. Pp. 19–32. Reprinted by permission of the author and the publisher.

influence by sketching the presence of Ibsen's resurrection motif in a few of the stories of *Dubliners* and in all subsequent work, but the natural association of drama with drama continues to support the notion that the play is the only really blatant example of Joyce's debt.

By the end of 1914 Joyce had published *Chamber Music*, finished *Dubliners*, *Portrait of the Artist*, and *Exiles*, as well as the early plans for *Ulysses*. In a period of fourteen years, then, he conceived his basic subjects and techniques. It would be surprising to find that his regard for Ibsen had a significant function only in the case of the play. I wish to argue here that *Dubliners* affords not only an earlier but an even more radical example than *Exiles*. Like Ibsen's "social" dramas, *Dubliners* is an exposé of the paralysis of spirit which binds the urban bourgeois. Less obvious, the basic themes, the structural design, and symbolism of the stories parallel Ibsen's work in the group of plays beginning with *A Doll's House* and ending with *When We Dead Awaken*. The last play is most crucial because it provided for Joyce a neatly condensed version of the symbolic parable he was to repeat all his life, from *Chamber Music* through *Finnegans Wake*.

In his review of *When We Dead Awaken* Joyce notes that this play is the final member in a succession of eleven works dealing with "modern life," "a grand epilogue to its ten predecessors." For Ibsen it was the culmination of a theme which had occupied him at least twenty years—the vital ranges of experience beyond the lifeless region of the bourgeoisie and the problem for the artist of striking a balance between the dangers of rigid isolation and debilitating involvement. Joyce finds in it the embodiment of his own preoccupations: the problem of the artist's relationship to a [20] spiritually mean society, the penalties of aloofness from the common stream of life, and, most pertinent for the stories shaping in his mind, a comprehensive dramatization of the pitiful failure of men to awaken from the somnolence which holds them among the living-dead.

Joyce begins his summary of the plot by pointing out that it is composed of a series of dialogues in which the major characters, the sculptor Rubeck and his former model, Irene, produce in each other the realization that they have "forfeited" their lives: Rubeck, for the sake of his art; Irene, because she has held herself aloof in an unrequited passion for Rubeck. The result is that both are essentially "dead." The same failure is imminent in the psychology of the minor figures, Maia, Rubeck's young and bored wife, and Ulfheim, the bitter recluse who has been rejected by his beloved. The two sets of characters form a counterpoint built upon the single theme of resurrection. Joyce demonstrates his complete understanding by selecting for quotation the lines which most clearly define the burden of a complex and (at least in the William Archer translation) heavily sentimental play:

IRENE. We see the irretrievable only when [*breaks short off*].

RUBECK [*looks inquiringly at her*]. When?

IRENE. When we dead awaken.[3]

From the concluding scenes he adeptly chooses the following:

IRENE. The love that belongs to the life of earth—the beautiful, miraculous life of earth—the inscrutable life of earth—that is dead in both of us.

RUBECK [*throwing his arms violently about her*]. Then let two of the dead—us two—for once live life to its uttermost, before we go down to our graves again.

In his analysis of the characters the reviewer offers an interpretation of Rubeck which is something of a departure [21] from Ibsen's obvious projection of himself—the aging artist who realizes too late the price of isolation and dedication to aesthetic motives. "Arnold Rubeck," comments Joyce, "is not intended to be a genius, as perhaps Eljert Lövborg [in *Hedda Gabler*] is. Had he been a genius like Eljert he would have understood in a truer way the value of his life. But . . . the facts that he is devoted to his art and that he has attained to a degree of mastery in it—mastery of hand linked with limitation of thought—tells us that *there may be lying dormant in him a capacity for greater life, which may be exercised when he, a dead man, shall have risen from among the dead*"[4] (italics mine). Thus Rubeck's masterpiece, a statue called "The Resurrection," becomes the ironic symbol of the divorce between his art and his life. His personal resurrection comes too late, on the eve of his death. As he ascends the "Peak of Promise" with Irene, they are buried in the descending snow of an avalanche.

I have italicized the final portion of Joyce's comment on Rubeck because it defines with faultless precision the status of the characters in *Dubliners*. Most of them are summoned by these words: the boy of "The Sisters" and "Araby," Eveline, Little Chandler, Maria, Mr. Duffy, the wardmen of "Ivy Day in the Committee Room," and Gabriel Conroy. Each of these is "an outcast from life's feast," a member of the great host of the living-dead. For Joyce, as for Ibsen, "the timeless passions" are "lying dormant" in these drab lives. The Norwegian master offered eleven plays; Joyce offers fifteen miniature dramas on the same theme. Commenting on the relations between drama and modern life, the young essayist of 1900 formulates a statement of the aesthetic motives he was to pursue so consistently in *Dubliners*. "Still I think out of the dreary sameness of existence, a measure of dramatic life may be drawn. Even the most commonplace, the deadest among

---

[3] The passages from the play are cited by Joyce in "Ibsen's New Drama," in *The Critical Writings*, ed. Ellsworth Mason and Richard Ellmann (New York, 1959), pp. 59, 61.

[4] *Ibid.*, pp. 65–66.

the living, may play a part in a great drama."[5] Thus the real unity of *Dubliners* derives from the condensed symbolism of Ibsen's last play. The [22] technique of epiphany is only a means to an end, the pattern of eastward and westward movements[6] only an adjunct to the Ibsenesque juxtaposition of life and death, and the Homeric counterparts[7] (if they exist at all) are occasional analogies which function within the larger scheme provided by the dramatist's example.

When We Dead Awaken utilizes the same key metaphor which in one form or another appears in its predecessors—the comparison of the unawakened living with the dead. In *A Doll's House* Nora's existence is clearly a living death. Mrs. Alving of *Ghosts* adheres to a restrictive and Puritanical code of moral duties which prevents her from entering into a vital life. Paralyzed herself, she thus becomes responsible for the passionate indulgences of her husband and the consequent death of both husband and son. The dormant passions of Solness, the architect of *The Master Builder*, are awakened by the lively Hilda. In a strange final scene he escapes from the shroud which practical and moral demands have closed about him, and at the moment of his death rises to his former greatness.

It is obvious that Joyce adopted for *Dubliners* the basic metaphor which pervades this entire group of plays. But he also borrowed from them a device which is commonly traced to another source, his Catholic training. It was in Ibsen, however, that he found the basis for the technique of "epiphany." *When We Dead Awaken* is characteristic in its structure—a pattern in which the central character, through the stress of some unexpected crisis, is driven to an epiphanaic moment that reveals him as spiritually dead. The same structural design is typical of the stories in *Dubliners*. In "Araby" and "A Painful Case," for example, the initial vignette of paralysis is followed by an excruciating denouement in which reality rushes in upon the unprepared consciousness of the central character. Where the revelation is for the reader alone ("Two Gallants" or "Grace"), the persistent ironic metaphor emerges in a climactic scene. Conditioned [23] by his Christian education, Joyce calls the instant of perception "epiphany," and so underscores the saving quality of a revelation containing the seeds not only of suffering but resurrection. While his term is clearly borrowed from the Christian context, the applied technique of epiphany is an adaptation of the structural principle common to Ibsen's dramas. It is worth noting that Joyce wrote most of the short sketches he called "Epiphanies" in a three-year period beginning in 1900, at the very

---

[5] "Drama and Life," *The Critical Writings*, p. 45.

[6] Brewster Ghiselin, "The Unity of Joyce's *Dubliners*," *Accent*, XVI (Spring 1956), 75–88, and (Summer 1956) 196–213.

[7] Richard Levin and Charles Shattuck, "First Flight to Ithaca," in *James Joyce: Two Decades of Criticism*, pp. 47–94.

same time he was absorbing Ibsen's work. One of the "Epiphanies" is about Ibsen himself. And some of them image situations which foreshadow the stories in *Dubliners:* A "sudden spiritual manifestation" reveals the drabness or vulgarity of things, a latent passion for freedom, an abrupt awakening to life's possibilities.[8] Psychological suffering during the experience of epiphany and the promise of belated resurrection (so common in *Dubliners*) is stock Ibsen. One can imagine the delight with which Joyce discovered in the plays a convergence of the Christian, the secular, and the aesthetic.

He must have found equally appealing the rich irony which Ibsen develops again and again by allowing the voices of the dead to inform the living-dead. In *A Doll's House,* for example, the very presence of Dr. Rank in the Helmer household stresses the urgency of Nora's awakening. Rank is fated to live with the knowledge that he must soon die. Afflicted with a steadily advancing paralysis, a heritage from his father's indulgences, he adores beauty and vitality. On the eve of his death, he tells Nora of his love for her. Thus do the lost and ghostly passions of the dead become the agents of resurrection. Hedda Gabler's suicide follows quickly upon her recognition that the dead Lövborg embodies the passionate creativity which is foreign to the listless bourgeoisdom she inhabits. The device is characteristic, and the examples can be multiplied.

With ingenious variation Joyce employs in *Dubliners* the same means of achieving irony and pathos. And just as in [24] Ibsen the effect is to reinforce, either for the reader or a character suffering epiphany, the comparison of living and dead. In both "The Sisters" and "Araby" the frightening portent of paralysis and death is represented in the figure of a dead priest, and in each case it provokes in the child a bid for escape. Eveline, appalled by the fate of her dead mother, attempts to break out but fails. In "A Painful Case" the ghost of Emily Sinico illuminates for Duffy his outcast state and his status as one of the living-dead. A similar humiliation comes to Gabriel Conroy as his aerial and frigid soul is chastened by the visit of Michael Furey.

If we consider the problem which occupied Joyce's youth—his passionate quest for freedom from home, fatherland, and church—the appeal of Ibsen seems inevitable. In the invidious metaphor which dominates the later plays, and in the dramatic evolution designed to torture and expose bourgeois lassitude, Joyce found confirmation of his personal and aesthetic motives. On the very eve of exile, as he prepared to encounter "the reality of experience" and resolved to forge "the uncreated conscience" of his race, he found in Ibsen the techniques that were to carry him to fulfillment. Within the Ibsen framework he saw the possibility of indulging all his predilections: his delight

[8] See *Epiphanies,* edited with an introduction and notes by O. A. Silverman (Buffalo, New York, 1956).

in ironic humor, his nearly obsessive awareness of the pathos of smothered potentials and dreams, his Jesuit penchant for moral analysis and categorizing, and, under the aegis of dramatic "objectivity," an opportunity for persecution of "the most belated race in Europe."

Interpretation of *Dubliners* in the light of the Ibsen parable often resolves points of disagreement among the commentators.[9] The early dismissal of the collection as an example of pure naturalism has given way (and properly so) to close analysis and the search for a pervading and unifying symbolism. The usual conclusion is that the symbology stems mainly if not exclusively from Joyce's Catholic background. Some of the interpretations offered on this basis are useful, [25] but where Joyce utilizes the Christian paraphernalia it functions at a secondary level and within the dominant Ibsen scheme. The two converge in *Dubliners*, and they meet again in all the subsequent works. Every story in *Dubliners* depends to one degree or another on the Ibsen formula, but the most subtle uses of his example appear in stories where there is little or no consciously articulated epiphany. I would like to examine a few of these in order to suggest some of the modes of application.

In "An Encounter," "After the Race," "Two Gallants," "The Boarding House," "Counterparts," and "A Mother" there is little so immediately striking as the patterns found in "A Painful Case" or "The Dead." Yet these stories share the common pattern, and one has to shift the counters only slightly to see the Ibsen metaphor: Dublin is the realm of the living-dead, paralysis exists on every level of experience and at every stage of life. This same group is also typical in that the central characters fail to develop a conscious recognition of their state—even though their situation invariably offers the opportunity. The "epiphany" generally resides in a concatenation of events which is wasted upon the person most vitally concerned. The majority of Dubliners remain "dead" and pass by, like unimpressionable spirits, the very means of their resurrection.

"Two Gallants," ostensibly a bitterly realistic story of moral degradation, depends for its effects on a harmonious blend of atmosphere and characterization. Its ironies are far more subtle than those suggested by the title. The adventure begins as "the grey web of twilight" passes across "the large faint moon circled [portentously] with a double halo." As the two young men walk through the dim streets they hear the melancholy tones of "Silent, O Moyle," the air which later controls the movements of Lenehan in his lonely wandering. Characterized as a leech, Lenehan is prematurely gray and his face is "winnowed of vigour." Though he is only thirty-one he is "vanquished" and "weary." Unattached, jobless, [26] "a sporting vagrant" associated with "racing tissues," he lives for the most part off of loans and handouts from disreputable friends. His companion Corley is a burly automaton (his bearing a reflection of his egocentricity) who lives by informing the police and by the exploitation of prostitutes. Spiritually, both men are ghouls: Corley feeds upon the sterile souls of his "tarts," and Lenehan, volitionless himself, clings to Corley for subsistence. As Lenehan sits in the shop waiting for Corley's return, he participates vicariously: "In his imagination he beheld the pair of lovers walking along some dark road: he heard Corley's voice in deep energetic gallantries and saw again the leer of the young woman's mouth." He moves into the street and takes his stand in the shadow of a lamp where "he suffered all the pangs and thrills of his friend's situation as well as those of his own." When Corley returns in triumph, he stares "grimly before him" and "with a grave gesture" shows to his "disciple" the small gold coin he has taken from the girl. And so the imagery of death and the grave serves to symbolize the eerie and morbid exchanges in which the spiritually dead take from one another a corrupt and enfeebling subsistence. Corley's final gesture is made in confident pride and Lenehan, the leech, congratulates him. Neither youth is aware of the spiritual somnolence which their evening reflects.

Several of the commentaries on "Clay" have insisted upon an analogy between Maria, the virginal peacemaker, and Mary, the Holy Virgin. But in the case of Maria there has been no miraculous birth; she has no husband, secular or spiritual; she has been a nurse for Joe and Alphy, but never a mother. Maria has rejected marriage and takes pride in her sterile body and her sterile life. As she dresses for the Hallows Eve party she looks "with quaint affection at the diminutive body" and finds it "a nice tidy little body." And as she reviews her petty plans for the evening she thinks, "how much better it was to be independent and to have your own money in your pocket." This deadly pride in virginity and [27] independence is complemented by Maria's reputation as a "peacemaker." At the "Dublin by Lamplight" laundry she settles the disputes of the women, and at the Donnellys' home she smothers several of Joe's angry outbursts. In short, her reputation stems from her abhorrence of passion of any kind. She can endure no encroachment upon the drab and static sensibility which marks her as one of the living-dead. It is Hallows Eve. Ghosts, witches, goblins, all the spirits of the dead, are abroad. Maria is among them: the ghost of a woman, an ugly witch (traditionally the epitome of sterile and morbid femininity) from the realm of the dead.

The ring, the prayerbook, and the clay itself have a common symbolic function. They form a trinity, and the order of their occurrence traces the line of Maria's evolution. The ring is a symbol of the secular or profane passion which Maria has rejected; the prayerbook is a symbol of a passionate spiritual marriage (such as the nun's union with Christ), but Maria is incapable of fruitful sacrifice and devotion. When she touches the clay a double irony emerges, for the clay is simultaneously the symbol of her life and her imminent physical death. When the prayerbook is quickly substituted and Mrs. Donnelly announces merrily that Maria will enter a convent, the irony is not diluted but increased: to enter the convent is to continue her death in life. So deep is her paralysis, the twice-repeated verses of the song fail to do their work, and "no one tried to show her her mistake." Maria's irretrievable mistake is the rejection of passional life, a rejection so habitual that it nullifies every revelatory suggestion, the hints by the laundry women, the sarcasm of the shopgirl, the attentions of the tipsy gentleman on the tram, the clay, the song, and Joe's tearful scrabbling for the corkscrew.

The insensibility of the child, the adolescent, and the adult is duplicated in the "public life" of the community. "Ivy Day in the Committee Room," "A Mother," and "Grace" constitute an ironic trilogy exposing the lifelessness of politics, art, and religion. In comparison with its companion [28] pieces, "A Mother" has received very little critical attention. Yet the episode it presents is a richly symbolic comment on the fate of aesthetic values in Joyce's Dublin. The three members of the Eire Abu Society suggest something of the spirit behind the concert series. Holohan, the assistant secretary, is crippled and ineffectual. The chief secretary, Mr. Fitzpatrick, is "a little man with a white, vacant face," a "flat" accent and a "vacant" smile. When the first concert fails Mrs. Kearney observes that Fitzpatrick "seemed to bear disappointments lightly." Miss Beirne has "an oldish face which was screwed into an expression of trustfulness and enthusiasm." Taken together, these three spell out the community attitudes toward the arts.

Mrs. Kearney takes upon herself the task of infusing life and efficiency into this listless group, and in the attempt she becomes the spiritual "mother" of art. Her qualifications are implicit in the sketch of her girlhood and her marriage. As a young woman she was taught the social graces in a convent. Pale and unbending, she developed "ivory manners" and "sat amid the chilly circle of her accomplishments, waiting for some suitor to brave it and offer her a brilliant life." But the rescuer fails to appear. She is forced to suppress her romantic fancies and marries an older man "out of spite." The marriage is as passionless as the wooden souls of husband and wife, but Mrs. Kearney "never put her own romantic ideas away." Thus when the Irish Revival becomes popular she sees in it an opportunity for genteel indulgence of her suppressed romanticism. And in this respect she represents the motives which in Joyce's mind characterized the movement—the attempt by a staid and essentially paralyzed people to capitalize on the safely remote passions of the dead.

The graceless mediocrity of the concerts (which awaken very

little response in the city) is symbolized by Madam Glynn, the ancient soprano. She is a "solitary woman" with "a pale face." A "faded blue dress is stretched upon her [29] meagre body," and as she stands waiting her turn "The shadow took her faded dress into shelter but fell revengefully into the little cup behind her collar bone." The younger ladies wonder where they dug her up. When she sings *Killarney* "in a bodiless gasping voice" she appears to have been "resurrected from an old stage-wardrobe."

As the first concert "expires" Mrs. Kearney senses the ultimate collapse of the series and takes steps to protect the eight-guinea contract which her daughter Kathleen holds for her work as accompanist. The last scene, in which Mrs. Kearney demands payment, involves multiple irony. Like her fellow citizens, she allows her instinctive material values to supersede the repressed romantic and aesthetic impulses, thus indicating the shallowness of these motives. Thwarted in her bid for a safe, vicarious fulfillment, she bursts into an angry passion over a small sum of money, and, resuming her role as natural mother, leads the willess doll, Kathleen, from the hall. The committee, in its refusal to pay, evidences the same meanness of spirit. Mr. O'Madden Burke, representative of the public press, offers a concluding remark which sums up (like a post-mortem) the prevailing opinion: "You did the proper thing, Holohan."

"The Dead" was apparently written last, but it was certainly not "appended" to the volume merely for the purpose of toning down the biting judgments of the earlier pieces. Its great quality lies in the nearly perfect manipulation of the basic metaphor and technique which function throughout the volume. It is the culmination of a sustained and unified effort. With "The Dead" Joyce's skill comes to maturity, and we have a fully realized prose drama that equals or excels the art of his master. This is not to say that all of the other stories are inferior, but the characters who inhabit them constitute a limitation which inhibits the complete realization of possibilities latent in Joyce's subject. Since the characters do not achieve a significant degree of self-awareness, the epiphany cannot be fully articulated. And in keeping [30] with the restraint of "dramatic" presentation, it must be rendered by the arrangement of ironies inherent in the various situations. These facts account for the obscurity and ambiguity in some of the stories. The effects are often over-subtle, the suggestions too frail to bear a maximum of implication. Thus most of the characters are pathetic but not tragic creatures. The young boy of the first three sketches merely intuits the nature of his environment; the adolescents of the next four either capitulate at the moment of crisis or remain unconscious of their peril; among the adults only Mr. Duffy and Gabriel Conroy drink a full measure of bitters; and all the participants in community affairs (from the priests and politicians down to the *artistes*) are hopelessly impervious.

"A Painful Case" and "The Dead" are notable exceptions because the two intelligences which dominate them make it possible for Joyce to arrive at a dignified and explicit articulation of the tragic dimension implicit in his design. For the same reason they contain the most obvious applications of the Ibsen theme and technique. "A Painful Case," however, is inferior to the final story. Though Mr. Duffy comes to realize his blindness and his guilt, his epiphany does not carry him beyond the borders of his own life; it leaves him an "outcast," living utterly alone, cut off even from the communion of suffering. The superior range and development of "The Dead" is possible because Gabriel Conroy has the intelligence and the imaginative vision to extend the implications of his own epiphany and so perceive the universal tragedy involving "all the living and the dead." His provincial ego dissolves, and in the twilight of that demise he sees that the indifferent snow descends over the entire cosmos of souls. In Gabriel's evolution one can measure the widening arc of Joyce's own perspective, the fruit of his studied apprenticeship to Ibsen. [31]

The Perspective of Joyce's *Dubliners*

GERHARD FRIEDRICH

"I AM WRITING A SERIES OF EPICLETI—TEN—FOR A PAPER," JAMES JOYCE confided to Constantine Curran sometime in 1904. "I have written one. I call the series *Dubliners* to betray the soul of that hemiplegia or paralysis which many consider a city." The paper to which Joyce referred was *The Irish Homestead,* and the first of the *Dubliners* stories published in its pages was "The Sisters." Only two other Joyce stories, "Eveline" and "After the Race," were also printed in that journal. But the idea of a *Dubliners* sequence soon developed into a book of fifteen "epicleti," and "The Sisters" proved of special importance, retaining its position as the opening story, in considerably revised form. The most noteworthy revision occurred in the opening paragraph of "The Sisters," which came to assume the function of a thematic prologue or overture for the entire collection, just as the concluding paragraph of the last story, "The Dead," serves as a general

Gerhard Friedrich, "The Perspective of Joyce's *Dubliners,*" *College English,* XXVI (March 1965), 421–426. Reprinted with permission of the National Council of Teachers of English and Gerhard Friedrich.

coda. Indeed, only in the course of revising "The Sisters" did the key term "paralysis" enter into the book itself, though Joyce—besides using it in his letter to Curran—stressed its crucial appropriateness by explaining to his publisher: "My intention was to write a chapter of the moral history of my country and I chose Dublin for the scene because that city seemed to me the centre of paralysis."

The central consciousness of "The Sisters" (at least in its revised version) is that of a perceptive schoolboy, apparently orphaned, whose disturbing involvement in the life and death of a priest is narrated from hindsight in adult language. The decline of the priest is referred to as "one of those . . . peculiar cases," and the narrator remarks in the opening paragraph: "the word paralysis . . . filled me with fear, and yet I longed to be nearer to it and to look upon its deadly work." This statement, which may be autobiographical of Joyce, has much in common with Hawthorne's comment in *The Scarlet Letter*: "A strange case! . . . I must needs look deeper into it. A strange sympathy betwixt soul and body! Were it only for the art's sake, I must search this matter to the bottom!" The boy is drawn to, and seeks to look in upon and to comprehend, the destruction of the Rev. James Flynn, his supposed friend, yet he is at the same time puzzled by feeling "as if I had been freed from something by his death." Since the paralytic condition with which Joyce was concerned is symbolic and [421] pervasive, he could not through the minds and mouths of children—big or little—give more than hints toward a diagnosis of the real disease. The unfinished sentences of the story reflect an incomplete understanding, not only on the part of the boy, but also on the part of the priest's sisters, Nannie and Eliza, and of the boy's foster parents and the visiting, garrulous Old Cotter. Yet, though the story ends vaguely and with ellipsis points, concluding only that "there was something gone wrong with him . . . ," the reader may complete the analysis by contemplating a number of clues, such as the faded and snuff-stained priestly garments and the priest's massive, truculent face, or the observation: "It was that chalice he broke. . . . That was the beginning of it."

Father Flynn is presented as a figure of unspiritual decadence, dead of a stroke in 1895 (when Joyce himself was 13 years old), but stricken long before that by the paralyzing sin of simony. He had, however queerly, cause to be "sitting up by himself in the dark in his confession-box, wide-awake and laughing-like softly to himself." While he is pointedly associated with empty and idle and broken chalices, the high mystery of the mass had come for him to be replaced by snuff-packets of High Toast. As to his learning, impressive like that of Gabriel Conroy in the last story in *Dubliners*, the most that could be said was that "education is all very fine and large," for it did not clarify or strengthen a spiritual awareness and commitment, but produced instead an eroding skepticism. And like Gabriel Conroy also,

Father Flynn had apparently no roots of loyalty in his own land, having moved from his native Irishtown to Great Britain Street. All normal human relationships—those of family, country, and religious communion—have in "The Sisters" suffered serious and bewildering dislocation; thought, feeling, and will are afflicted. It is a momentous fact that the light of life has been extinguished in the window of the priest's room, that the warming glow has died in his fireplace, and Joyce aims in story after paralytic story to sensitize the reader to the overwhelming, cumulative darkness.

Not only the disastrous condition to be probed, but also the method to be employed, is indicated by Joyce in his curious revision of the opening paragraph of the book. As a nimble linguist he became later notorious for his verbal chain reactions and short circuits. Here he insisted on linking the word "paralysis" with the words "gnomon" as used by Euclid and "simony" as used in the Catechism, by its sup- posedly similar sound, adding that it sounded also "like the name of some maleficent and sinful being." Since Euclid defined a gnomon as a parallelogram from a corner of which a parallel portion has been taken, and since paralysis and parallelogram share the characteristic of being loosened or disabled at the side, the following word-chain is suggested: paralysis-parallelogram→gnomon (implying no-man)- Simon-demon. None of these linked phenomena is solid, upright, and foursquare: they share a major lack. If paralysis may be regarded as the physical counterpart to the benumbed spiritual state of simony, then the gnomon may be viewed as perhaps the aptest geometric or structural equivalent of such a pathetically partial existence. The actual value of the gnomon lies, however, in its use as the index of a sundial, indicating the time of day by casting a shadow-line on a sun- brightened background. The world of the Dubliners Joyce chose to portray is, by contrast, a benighted world, so that Joyce had to invert the gnomonic technique, indicating Ireland's predicament by throwing a shaft of illumination into the obscure of wrongnesses with which he was preoccupied. Thus the adoption of the term "epiphany" for the enlarged perspective of those "instantaneous intensities" in which, to quote Melville, [422] "every revelation partook more of significant dark- ness than of explanatory light."

It should be noted that the term "epicleti" mentioned above is at least as important to the understanding of Joyce's story-telling art, and in particular of "The Sisters," as his explanation of the literary-spiritual technique of "epiphany" in *Stephen Hero*. "Epiclesis" refers to the invocation of the Holy Spirit for the purpose of consecrating the eucharistic elements of bread and wine, at the point where these are to become the body and blood of Christ the Redeemer. The paralyzing guilt of chalice-breaking lies in that spiritual and physical corruption which prevents sacramental fulfillment. It is a comprehensive ailment, of which all of Joyce's stories are symptomatic, and his "epiphanies" are therefore not so much manifestations of the spirit of redemption in mundane and trivial situations as they are occasions for a momentary acknowledgment of the very pathos of mundaneness and triviality. No new and better priest provides a happy ending to "The Sisters." Furthermore, the narrator's second memorable episode, "The Encounter," merely accentuates a bewildered anxiety, while puff-faced Leo Dillon, who "had a vocation for the priesthood," proves confused and unreliable. And the parent-less boy in "Araby," bearing the empty chalice of his romantic notions to an alluringly named temple of money-changers, knows at last only the grueling sensation of utter disillusionment. Beginning with a reference to an uninhabited house at the blind end of a street in which a priest had died, the terminology and the context of "Araby" become appropriately and inescapably religious or quasi-religious.

If the boy's three oppressive recollections from his own childhood experience have thus distinctly a priestly reference point, the subsequent third-person stories enlarge the sense of pathos by an assortment of gnomonic men and women no less grotesque than the troubled citizens of Sherwood Anderson's *Winesburg, Ohio.* Joyce's instances of Old World hemiplegia are, however, conditioned by the decline of an ancient city civilization, and they are much more subtly drawn than Anderson's small-town Americans. The sterile spinsterhood of "Eveline" as of "Clay," the failure of playboyish excitement in "After the Race," the sordid satisfactions of pseudomaster and disciple in "Two Gallants," the calculated entanglement of an eligible male in "The Boarding House," the ineffectual outbursts of domesticated clerks in "A Little Cloud" and "Counterparts," and the old-maidish obtuseness of Mr. Duffy in "A Painful Case"—these are all seen against a decadent Dublin, exhausted and exhausting. To highlight these debilitating influences, Joyce follows up with three stories in which patriotism has become a politician's memorial game ("Ivy Day in the Committee Room"), interest in art is vain and mercenary ("A Mother"), and the Church has withdrawn into innocuous retreat ("Grace"). Such, in brief, is the diagnosis of "dear dirty Dublin," as Joyce later called it in *Ulysses.* The full import of these stories, and of many of their nuances, depends however upon seeing their progressive interrelationship, and their absolute culmination in the subtlety and sweep of "The Dead." The final instance of human failing among the brownstone houses of Joyce's city demands therefore particularly detailed analysis.

II

The last and longest story in the *Dubliners* sequence is all-encompassing in its ironic tensions. The title-term, "The Dead," stands like a headstone above a buried world and applies to anything and everything in it—certainly to every one of the many characters introduced or only alluded to. With varying shades of meaning, it becomes the collective [423] verdict with which Joyce concludes: "all the living and the dead."

The story opens with a young girl, appropriately named Lily, for whom the possibility of pure love has died in disillusionment, and ends with oblique reference to crucifixions in a doomed universe ("crooked crosses . . . spears . . . barren thorns"). Along the way we encounter hospitable monks who, silently, remind us of our physical and spiritual "last end" by sleeping in their coffins. The pointed explanation "that the monks were trying to make up for the sins committed by all the sinners in the outside world" and the uncomprehending question whether "a comfortable spring bed [wouldn't] do them as well as a coffin" help to generalize and domesticate the existential problem of imperfect being and imperfect communion, of life in death and death in life. The central character, Gabriel Conroy, and his nominal wife Gretta also live in Monkstown, however unaware of Joyce's implication.

The range of comic touches in "The Dead" is masterful, including a superb parody of after-dinner speeches, but the paralyzing effect of human limitations must essentially be a matter for serious and solemn assessment. The individuals engulfed by the cosmic snow register the physical and metaphysical winter in psychological and ethical terms. The displaced existences of "The Dead" belong thus with Eliot's later "The Hollow Men" and "The Love Song of J. Alfred Prufrock" as well as with Arnold's earlier "The Buried Life" and "Dover Beach" and with Hawthorne's "The Haunted Mind." They suffer from the paralysis of cowardly incompetence as much as from paralyzed vision. Their blindness being habitual, they have accumulated apparently meaningless, still-born experiences, and the tomb-womb of memories will not yield anything except in startling moments of sudden rebirth.

The paragraphs of this sophisticated story aimed at self-discovery are shot through with cumulative hints and ironic multiple *entendres*. Words and sentences echo through the pages so that the entire narrative, told in retrospect with third-person omniscience, becomes a haunting, thought-tormenting, distant music which crescendoes into shocks of recognition. When we are told at the beginning of the Misses Morkan's annual dance that "never once had it fallen flat . . . as long as anyone could remember," we may suspect but do not know yet that not merely the party but a whole world will cave in, once somebody really remembers. When the aunts remark upon Gretta's arrival that "she must be perished alive" and ask whether "Gabriel [was] with her," and when Gabriel—"as right as the mail"—calls from the dark: "Go on up. I'll follow," the innocuous conversation is charged with all the tragic truth as the chain of events will reveal them. If what the spinster sisters Kate and Julia Morkan seem to believe in is eating well, the pathetic substitute is common enough, but Joyce proceeds to suggest the cause by directing attention to the balcony scene in *Romeo and Juliet* and Shakespeare's two murdered princes in the Tower which Aunt Julia (!) has rendered in needlework. And when Gabriel speaks of "absent faces that we miss here tonight" and admonishes his captive audience to "cherish in our hearts the memory of those dead and gone great ones whose fame the world will not willingly let die," the ghost of Michael Furey is evoked before he is ever mentioned. Joyce employs this technique of the flash-forward as freely as Shakespeare did oracles and omens, his literary determinism is worked to the point of obvious diagnosis, as when the nationalistic Miss Ivors criticizes Gabriel Conroy for not "visiting your own land . . . that you know nothing of, your own people, your own country." As story-teller, Joyce is simultaneously realistic [424] and symbolic, notably in the following passage:

> He stood still in the gloom of the hall, trying to catch the air that the voice was singing and gazing up at his wife. There was grace and mystery in her attitude as if she were a symbol of something. He asked himself what is a woman standing on the stairs in the shadow, listening to distant music, a symbol of. If he were a painter he would paint her in that attitude. Her blue felt hat would show off the bronze of her hair against the darkness and the dark panels of her skirt would show off the light ones. *Distant Music* he would call the picture if he were a painter.

Parallel to Gabriel's perpetual failures and annoyances, half-guesses and evasions, and to his unshared passionate recollections, there runs the portentous undercurrent of Gretta's unfulfilled attraction for the boy Michael Furey, who was apparently consumed by love ("I think he died for me"). Gretta has not been able to acknowledge and accommodate the vitality of her idealized past, but in this miraculous Christmas and New Year's season of her soul the mention of a place name (Galway) and the singing of a song ("The Lass of Aughrim") associated with the person of Michael Furey coincide to give to memories an unusual vividness and urgent voice, and to their confession an extraordinary illuminating power. While she, exhausted from the ordeal, is submerged in sleep, it is Gabriel who sees Gretta and himself honestly at last, amid the transitoriness of all earthly things. The supreme irony lies of course in the paradoxical fact that Gabriel's ultimate insights are so unnerving as to disable him: the snow melts and yet does not melt within the confines of the story. So there is need for Easter in Joyce's snowbound Christmas, the one implying the other. While the spirit of Michael Furey has risen from the grave to walk overpoweringly among the survivors, the living dead remain to be resurrected.

Since "The Dead" is a story of such penetrating self-realization, windows and mirrors are important to it—in contrast with closed doors and with Gabriel's "glimmering gilt-rimmed eyeglasses." Even more important is the breaking-in of unaccustomed light into the recesses of obscured privacies, ironically just when illumination is least desired. "We don't want any light. We have light enough from the street," says Gabriel jovially to the hotel porter. Yet, away from home and rid of electric light and candle, the Conroys take in quick succession these Joycean steps toward revelation:

> A ghastly light from the street lamp lay in a long shaft from one window to the door. Gabriel . . . crossed the room towards the window. He looked down into the street in order that his emotion might calm a little. Then he turned . . . his back to the light. She . . . was standing before a large swinging mirror. . . . She turned away from the mirror slowly and walked along the shaft of light towards him. . . . She went on to the window and stood there, looking out; . . . he did not hear her come from the window. . . . As he passed in the way of the cheval-glass he caught sight of himself in full length. . . . She looked away from him along the shaft of light towards the window in silence.

We are told incidentally: "No, it was not the moment yet," the moment of epiphany unlocking a heart heavy with memories, the gnomonic instant measuring precisely the nighttime of two who have lived beside one another in ignorance, and unfolding their convenient lies. That moment is the predetermined goal, and all sorts of "moments" (the term is used prominently in "The Dead") lead up to it. When it is reached, Joyce projects the conclusion of an earlier story, "Araby," to the adult level: "He saw himself as a ludicrous figure. . . ." Moreover, [425] he converts the dubious financial generosity of Gabriel Conroy, of which several examples have been given, into genuine humaneness: "a strange friendly pity for her entered his soul. . . . Generous tears filled Gabriel's eyes."

That Gabriel Conroy, a college teacher, is particularly given to the complexities of Browning's dramatic monologues is then not surprising, but symptomatic. The experience to which he is driven may be analogous to Rabbi Ben Ezra's, but is more aptly summarized in Thoreau's lines:

> I hearing get, who had but ears,
> And sight, who had but eyes before;
> I moments live, who lived but years,
> And truth discern, who knew but learning's lore.
>
> ("Inspiration")

The perspective opened up to Gabriel and to the reader is certainly universal and religious. As to the universality, there are in this final *Dubliners* story references to Belgium, England, France, Germany, Scotland, and America, to Glasgow, London, Milan, Paris, and Smyrna, and more significantly to the Aran Isles out in the Atlantic as opposed to the continent, and to such figures as Lucrezia Borgia and Mignon as well as to Shakespeare's tragedies of love and social corruption and to Browning's psychological verse portraits. As to the religious import of "The Dead," the story is a parable of love versus lust, personified primarily in Michael and Gabriel, and also an allegory in which these influences modeled after the two highest archangels contend for Gretta, to whom grace is first attributed and then denied.

Since the incomplete existences of the sisters Kate and Julia Morkan, who are the party-givers among "The Dead," may be regarded as crucial to the story, like their counterparts Nannie and Eliza Flynn in the first story of the *Dubliners* sequence, and since in that first story the death of the priest is in fact the main event, the titles of "The Sisters" and "The Dead" could conceivably be interchanged. This possibility suggests that the first and the last stories overlap significantly, and that the *Dubliners* sequence moves as a spiral, widening inward and outward, toward awareness and purgation. The paralysis and death of the priestly role which fascinates the boy in the first story indicates the cause of all the derangements that follow, for wherever vision is troubled and decadent, there the harmonies of spirit and flesh give way to naturalistic case studies. [426]

PART THREE. CRITICAL
ANALYSIS OF THE STORIES

Joyce's "The Sisters"

THOMAS E. CONNOLLY

OF THE STORIES IN *Dubliners*, ONLY "THE DEAD" AND "CLAY" HAVE received more critical attention than "The Sisters," but, among these stories, "The Sisters" is distinguished by the fact that it has received the most fanciful, contradictory, and frantic interpretations of all. Depending upon which critic one reads, Father Flynn is either the God of Ireland or a homosexual, or, with his lolling tongue, a gargoyle. Most critics seem fairly well agreed that he is sacrilegious. The broken chalice may be, according to the critics, the symbol of the loss of integrity that results from simony or the symbol of the "great friendship" that exists between the boy and Father Flynn. At either extreme lies absurdity. At least two critics ask us to believe that paralysis is the *natural* result of simony.

Invoking a principle known since the fourteenth century as *Occam's razor* ("entities must not be unnecessarily multiplied"), I suggest that a simple reading of the story is in order after all the wild and speculative guessing that has gone on [189] about it. Why leap over the real thing to seek either the symbol or the far-fetched when the real thing makes very good sense and a very good story by itself?

The theme of this story is the response that the boy makes to the death of his old friend, Father Flynn. In making his response, the boy reacts violently in the early part of the story; later, he becomes a calm, objective narrator of events. Initially, he does not like Old Cotter, and, even before he learns that Cotter has brought news of Father Flynn's death, the boy thinks of him in a hostile fashion: "Tiresome old fool!" After his uncle relays the news of Father Flynn's death and after Old Cotter makes insinuating and derogatory remarks about the priest, the boy is angry, partly because Cotter referred to him as a child and partly in defense of his former friend: "I crammed

Thomas E. Connolly, "Joyce's 'The Sisters': A Pennyworth of Snuff," *College English*, XXVII (December 1965), 189–195. Reprinted by permission of the National Council of Teachers of English and Thomas E. Connolly.

my mouth with stirabout for fear I might give utterance to my anger. Tiresome old rednosed imbecile!"

While the priest was alive, the boy had been attracted to and repelled by him. His first angry response to Cotter's remarks after the news of Father Flynn's death reflects the attraction. By the following morning, anger yields to a feeling of relief. "I found it strange that neither I nor the day seemed in a mourning mood and I felt even annoyed at discovering in myself a sensation of freedom as if I had been freed from something by his death. I wondered at this for, as my uncle had said the night before, he had taught me a great deal." The final state of the boy's feelings, when, on Tuesday evening, he and his aunt visit the dead priest's sisters, is quite calm and objective. He is now the observant narrator who, without personal involvement (except for fear that he may make too great a noise while munching his cream crackers), relays the words of Eliza and allows them to fill in the gaps in the history of the removal of the priest from the active ministry. It seems to me to stretch the story beyond its limits to make the cream crackers and sherry the bread and wine of the Mass as one critic has done.[1] The serving of refreshments at an Irish wake is too familiar to allow me to go beyond realistic detail. Furthermore, Father Flynn as the Irish God, as he has been called by the critic who transubstantiated crackers and sherry into the Eucharistic elements,[2] seems equally beyond my grasp.

Most critical discussions of this story have concentrated on Father Flynn's lapses as a priest. The two offenses that have been presumed to have caused his removal are hinted at only very sketchily. First, the boy implies that Father Flynn committed simony, and second we learn from Eliza that her brother had broken a chalice during Mass. The implication that the priest committed simony is introduced very early in the story: "Every night as I gazed up at the window I said softly to myself the word paralysis. It had always sounded strangely in my ears, like the word gnomon in the Euclid and the word simony in the Catechism. But now it sounded to me like the name of some maleficent and sinful being. It filled me with fear, and yet I longed to be nearer to it and to look upon its deadly work." Not only is there a strangeness about these words, but there is also an unusual linkage in the boy's mind between bodily illness and sin, and this linkage, it will be noted, is accompanied by the conflicting feelings of attraction and revulsion. Fritz Senn has commented very significantly on the [190] substitution in the boy's mind of the word for the disease.[3]

J. B. Kaye, in his article, "Simony, the three Simons and Joycean

[1] Marvin Magalaner, *Time of Apprenticeship: the Fiction of Young James Joyce* (London, 1959), pp. 79–81.

[2] Marvin Magalaner and Richard Kain, *Joyce: the Man, the Work, the Reputation* (New York, 1956), p. 73.

[3] Fritz Senn, " 'He Was Too Scrupulous Always': Joyce's 'The Sisters,' " *James Joyce Quarterly*, 2 (Winter 1965), 67–68.

Myth," may be right in tracing the gift of snuff as a continuing act of simony, although I doubt it. But he stretches matters when he confuses simony with the breaking of the chalice: "What he is trying to confess is the mysterious sin of Simon Magus—the sin of simony. It is simony that causes the loss of integrity—symbolized by the broken chalice—which turns the man into a gnomon, a shell of himself. Paralysis ensues as a natural consequence."[4] How paralysis ensues "as a natural consequence" of either breaking a chalice or practicing simony is not entirely clear.

John Kuehl also sees a relationship between simony and the broken chalice. He makes a more detailed linkage between the two acts than does Kaye, and, in addition, he introduces the notion of homosexuality into the relationship between the priest and the boy:

Ultimate adult betrayal in "The Sisters" has to do with Father Flynn's perverted attraction to his protégé, an attraction Old Cotter's enigmatic statements, iterative oral imagery and, above all, the boy's thought, dream and actions establish. The priest grown paralyzed, incomplete, through trafficking in sacred things, through using a holy office to perpetuate covert homosexuality. Having *sensed* this, the boy caused the chalice—symbol of their great friendship—to be broken and feels much hostility toward Father Flynn during his illness and after his death. The crisis of Joyce's drama of the unconscious occurs in the boy's room, which, like the "dead-room" later, is probably upstairs. Here, during a dream—"some land where the customs were strange"—the priest makes his indistinct confession and the boy smiles his absolution. Now Father Flynn, whose perverse desires have cut him off, may commune again with God (new chalice) and the boy with him (Eliza's sherry).[5]

In addition to the question of whether this particular boy can be linked to the broken chalice, it is very hard to see the chalice as a "symbol of their great friendship." The fact that Father Flynn teaches the boy the Mass responses *after* his retirement indicates that this boy was not the altar boy serving at the time the chalice was broken. Once again I am hard put to understand how one becomes paralyzed as a result of simony, "trafficking in sacred things."

William Bysshe Stein pushes matters rather far when he sees Father Flynn's lolling tongue, which reminds him of a gargoyle on Notre Dame in Paris, as "an unconscious reflex of guilt stemming from the priest's sacrilegious act."[6] The most damning thing that can be said,

---

[4] Julian B. Kaye, "Simony, the three Simons and Joycean Myth," *James Joyce Miscellany* (1957), p. 23.

[5] John Kuehl, "A la joyce: The Sisters Fitzgerald's Absolution," *James Joyce Quarterly*, 2 (Fall 1964), 5–6.

[6] William Bysshe Stein, "Joyce's 'The Sisters,' " *The Explicator*, 20 (March 1962), Item 61. W. F. Gleeson has written a sane note on this story. See *The Explicator*, 22 (December 1963), Item 30. Mr. Gleeson and I are in essential agreement at several points, especially about the absence of sacrilege.

in all fairness and honesty, and I venture to say in canon law, about Father Flynn's breaking of the chalice is that it was an unfortunate accident. To commit a "sacrilegious act" one must *deliberately* violate or profane a sacred person or thing. In breaking the chalice, Father Flynn committed no sacrilege. Furthermore, serious as the spilling of the consecrated wine might be, and even the breaking of the chalice, these acts would not in themselves be sufficient to cause the involuntary retirement of a priest from his priestly duties. The act of [191] simony, however, would be cause for removal, as would mental deterioration.

William A. Fahey[7] disagrees with Magalaner and Kain,[8] and presumably he would disagree with Kaye also, about the "undue service" to the priest constituting the sin of simony, but he, too, tends to place the act of simony after Father Flynn's retirement from the active ministry. He says, "I think that 'undue service' was rendered not by Stephen [note that Fahey as well as Magalaner identifies the boy of this story with Stephen Dedalus of the *Portrait* and *Ulysses*] but by the sisters. For they have ministered to the acting priest, *qua* priest, without believing in him." Irish sisters might very well be expected to "minister" to their brother, especially if he is a priest, or at least they might have been expected to do so in Joyce's time in Ireland. It is also particularly difficult for me to understand just what Fahey means by saying that the sisters ministered to Father Flynn "without believing in him." I find no such lack of belief in him in the story. Certainly they "believed" in him insofar as they continued to accept him as a priest and so did all the neighbors with the possible exception of Old Cotter. Finally, how can Father Flynn be called "the acting priest" when he is just exactly the opposite of an acting priest, a retired priest? The ordination service includes these words: "Thou art a priest *forever* [italics added] according to the order of Melchizedek."

It is important at this point to discriminate between the retirement of a secular priest from the active duties of a parish and the defrocking of a priest. Some commentators treat Father Flynn as though he were a defrocked priest, and this, I believe, is wrong. There is never a hint in the story that Father Flynn has been defrocked. The retired priest who lives quietly on a side street of a parish is fairly common. The most serious thing that can be said about Father Flynn in this respect is that he has been involuntarily retired, probably because, after mental de-

---

[7] William A. Fahey, "Joyce's 'The Sisters,'" *The Explicator*, 17 (January 1959), Item 26. Incidentally, Fahey's interpretation of *gnomon* as the pin of a sundial ignores the boy's own statement in the story that the world *paralysis* sounded strangely in his ears, "like the word gnomon in the Euclid." It may appear to be quibbling to point out that Kaye's interpretation of gnomon as a "shell" is not quite accurate either. See footnote 19 below for a definition of *gnomon* taken from the Euclid that Joyce must probably used.

[8] Magalaner and Kain, p. 73.

terioration, he acted strangely in the confessional. One might note here that, in the original version of the story, Father Flynn was laid out "in his brown habit." The color of the habit suggests that originally Joyce intended Father Flynn to be a member of the regular clergy (a Franciscan, for example) but in the final version he became a secular parish priest. The requirements of the story dictated this change to Joyce, for when a member of one of the orders (regular clergy) retires, he usually remains within the walls of the monastery or abbey. He ordinarily does not return to live with his relatives.

Now let us come to the simple, straightforward reading of the story. The first clue to the effect on Father Flynn of the breaking of the chalice comes when the boy, after his feeling of relief at the news of the priest's death, thinks of the hours he spent with Father Flynn: "His questions showed me how complex and mysterious were certain institutions of the Church which I had always regarded as the simplest acts. *The duties of the priest towards the Eucharist and towards the secrecy of the confessional* [italics added] seemed so grave to me that I wondered how anybody had ever found in himself the courage to undertake them. . . ." The italicized lines in this excerpt point up the two offenses of Father Flynn. [192] The old man, who had failed in his own duties toward the Eucharist—at least toward one half of the Eucharistic sacrifice—dwells on those duties, for, as his sister says, "He was too scrupulous always. . . . The duties of the priesthood was too much for him." Immediately after making this comment, Eliza reveals his first offense, the breaking of the chalice which led eventually to his mental deterioration. "It was that chalice he broke. . . . That was the beginning of it"; and then she repeats the obviously false phrases that the sisters have been using to conceal their brother's offense. "Of course, they say it was all right, that it contained nothing, I mean. But still . . ." Her very hesitancy in speech and her conscious effort to make excuses for her brother argue that the chalice in all likelihood was not empty. After her pregnant comment, "But still," she attempts to shift the blame to the altar boy: "They say it was the boy's fault." Her second attempt at covering up the offense is no better than the first.

Anyone who has closely observed altar boys or who has himself served at Mass knows that, after the altar boy pours the wine into the chalice before the Offertory (and before the Transubstantiation), he does not come near the chalice again nor near the center of the altar where the chalice rests until after the contents have been consumed by the priest. He then, at the end of Mass and after the congregation has received Communion (the Host for individuals), offers water and wine to the priest to cleanse the chalice. The only way the altar boy (Joyce always used the Irish term *massboy*) could cause the priest to break the chalice while it contained the consecrated wine would be to jerk hard on the chausible (the priest's outer garment) which he raises while the priest elevates the Host and chalice immediately after the

Consecration of the Mass, or to perform some other equally outlandish action. What Eliza says to excuse her brother merely points up, to those who are familiar with the Mass service, the priest's responsibility for breaking the chalice and, most likely, spilling its contents. The effect of this accident was disastrous. Eliza says, "But poor James was so nervous. . . . That affected his mind. . . ."

Both William Bysshe Stein[9] and Florence L. Walzl[10] note that July 1, the day on which Father Flynn died, is the Feast of the Most Precious Blood in the calendar of the Roman Catholic Church. It is not beyond belief that Joyce was aware of this fact when he chose to have Father Flynn die on that day, for he changed the date from July 2 in the earlier versions and he substituted in his final version of the story, as Magalaner has pointed out, a cruelly ironic "idle chalice" for a rosary and a crucifix which Father Flynn held in his coffin in the two earlier versions.[11]

None of those who have commented on this story have noted, with respect to Father Flynn's alleged priestly lapse, that there are three distinct points of view about that lapse. First, there is the public view expressed initially in the vague and tantalizing incomplete sentences of Old Cotter. From these implied charges one may conclude anything or nothing about Father Flynn's flaw, and this very vagueness may account in part for the boy's annoyance with the "tiresome old fool." Second, there is the sisters' point of view of their brother's lapse. They alone seem to know that their brother broke a chalice. Neither the boy nor his aunt knew of this event until Eliza offered her own halting account [193] of it.[12] The sisters knew of Father Flynn's strange action in the confessional, but the boy's aunt did not. (The boy might have known of the strange confessional behavior. This point is discussed below.) Finally, there is the point of view of the boy, the one who has been closest to the priest. The boy, who narrates this story, is the only one who applies the terms *simony* and *simoniac* to the priest. None of the others, not even the openly hostile Cotter, accuses the priest of simony. The boy associates the term *simony* with both *paralysis* and *gnomon,* and the term *simoniac* with *paralysis* alone.[13] When these two terms pass through his mind, the boy feels an attraction to and a revulsion from Father Flynn. On the second application of the term to the priest, the boy associates it, in a dream, with the confessional, and the confessional is the link back to the breaking of the chalice, for

[9] Stein, *The Explicator,* 21 (September 1962), Item 2.

[10] Florence L. Walzl, "A Date in Joyce's 'The Sisters,'" *Texas Studies in Literature and Language,* 4 (Summer 1962), 183–187.

[11] Magalaner, *Time,* p. 85. Stein and Walzl clarify the "mystifying set of changes" that Magalaner has noted.

[12] In the first version of this story, the aunt knew of the charge of his having broken the chalice prior to Father's Flynn's death. Magalaner, *Time,* p. 180.

[13] For an interesting biblical association of these two words, see Senn, p. 69.

Eliza informs the boy and his aunt that, after he broke the chalice, Father Flynn began to act strangely in the confessional, and this behavior led to his removal from active parish duties. To assume, as do Magalaner and Kain,[14] that the priest actually did try to confess to the boy is again, it appears to me, to push what Joyce says too far. This confession took place in a dream and the "velvet curtains and swinging lamp of antique fashion" are part of the furniture of the dream confessional. (It must be noted, however, that Magalaner in *Time of Apprenticeship* treats the confession of the priest to the boy as a dream.[15])

If a simoniacal act was committed, Joyce leaves its exact nature vague, although there is enough of a hint to connect it with the confessional. I think that it is wrong to link the act of simony to the gift of snuff and the Latin lessons, for these acts, which take place after the removal of the priest, provide almost no basis for the charge of simony, the details of which I shall soon examine. The final emphasis is on the deranged priest sitting in the confessional "wide-awake and laughing-like to himself. . . ." Eliza says, "So then, of course, when they saw that, that made them think there was something gone wrong with him." In the final version of the story, the mental breakdown began after Father Flynn broke the chalice,[16] and the simony, if it occurred at all and in whatever form it occurred, followed. Magalaner, speaking of the indefiniteness of the simony, says: "In the specific context of this story, simony may be involved simply in the superior relationship of Flynn to the boy, since the Church defines simony as an exchange of spiritual for temporal things. It can take the form of having the applicant pay homage 'which consists in subserviency, the rendering of undue service.'"[17] This argument, persuasive as it is, implies a very sophisticated knowledge of Church definition on the part of the boy, who alone associates the term *simony* with the priest and who is just learning the responses at Mass. It is doubtful that simony could have existed between the priest and the boy on the basis of service rendered. There are three types of [194] simony: conventional, real, and mental. Both conventional and real simony require the expression of mutual agreement to be either completely or partially carried out

14 Magalaner and Kain, p. 72.

15 Magalaner, *Time*, p. 77.

16 In the earliest version of the story, it should be noted, Father Flynn's sister and the boy's uncle and Old Cotter speak openly about Father Flynn's sanity (or lack of it), using such phrases as, "Upper storey—(he tapped an unnecessary hand at his forehead)—gone," and "Not that he was anyway mad, as you know yourself, but he was always a little queer." Magalaner, *Time*, pp. 175 and 179. It should also be noted that the mental breakdown started long before he became a priest in the first version of the story.

17 Marvin Magalaner, " 'The Sisters' of James Joyce," *University of Kansas City Review*, 18 (1952), 259.

by both parties. Even mental simony, which alone could be applicable here, requires "approval on the part of the person to whom a proposal is made."[18] There is no evidence whatsoever that the boy approves of the simony.

I rather think that Father Flynn, in his mental deterioration, committed simony in the confessional, *if he committed this sin at all*, by offering some spiritual forgiveness to the boy in return for some temporal favor, but even to go that far is to write a part of the story that Joyce never wrote.

More probable still is that no act of simony was committed at all. All we know for certain is that a scrupulous priest broke a chalice, suffered mental deterioration that caused him to sit laughing in an empty confessional, and was involuntarily retired from the active ministry. We know further that a boy, born with an interest in language, has picked up three vaguely understood terms, two from his schoolbooks, *gnomon* and *simony*, and one from neighborhood gossip, *paralysis*. Two of these terms, *paralysis* and *simony*, he associates with the ailing priest; the third he leaves to Joyce to use symbolically (if Joyce did so) and to Joyce's critics to use imaginatively (as they have).

The exact nature of the alleged simoniacal act seems not so important as the fact that the priest has drifted from the activity of the spiritual life and has become a "remainder after something else has been removed," a gnomon.[19] In a very real sense a *gnomon*, therefore, is a type of paralysis, an incompleteness, and the hulk of Father Flynn spiritually and physically paralyzes the society which he dominates. He has become an example of paralysis to which society continues to pay respect, even if it is the respect only of pious clichés uttered by ignorant old women and vaguely felt by one small boy.[20] [195]

---

[18] *The Catholic Encyclopedia*, ed. by Charles G. Herbermann, *et al.* (New York, 1913), XIV (1).

[19] The edition of Euclid that Joyce most likely knew is *The First Six Books of the Elements of Euclid and Propositions I–XXI of Book XI. etc.*, by John Casey, published in Dublin by Hodges, Figgs & Co. Ltd., and in London by Longmans, Green & Co. By 1894 this book was in its thirteenth edition. There *gnomon* is defined as follows: "In any parallelogram the figure which is composed of either of the parallelograms about a diagonal and the two complements . . . is called a gnomon. Thus, if we take away either of the parallelograms AO, OC from the parallelogram AC, the remainder is called a *gnomon*" (p. 78).

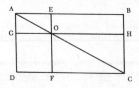

[20] I am grateful to the ever-helpful and gracious Adaline Glasheen for hints and promptings in the development of this paper.

The Wings of Daedalus

JULIAN B. KAYE

IT IS NOW TIME TO TAKE ANOTHER LOOK AT *Dubliners*. RECENT TEXTUAL studies of *Ulysses* and *Finnegans Wake* have tended to make *Dubliners* look thin, simply because it has not been "read" with the same critical attention. Moreover, Hugh Kenner's founding of a "Stephen-hating" school of Joyce criticism has led inevitably to the depreciation of *Dubliners*. The critics who hold that Joyce portrays the Stephen Dedalus of *Ulysses* as a hopeless failure must, willingly or unwillingly, give the impression that the stories Stephen is writing are inferior Joyce. Consequently, there has been a tendency to make two Joyces —one for *Dubliners* and *A Portrait*, the other for *Ulysses* and *Finnegans Wake*—and to see the first Joyce as a mere literary apprentice.

I believe this view of Joyce's career to be both unfortunate and— more important—untrue. Although Joyce's prose in *Dubliners* is conventional in syntax and vocabulary, it often has the richness of texture of that of *Ulysses* and *Finnegans Wake*. By giving it the same kind of attention, I hope to demonstrate that even so uncomplicated a story as "An Encounter"—one of the first stories Joyce wrote (1903)—is *echt* Joyce and that by the time Joyce wrote "The Dead" (1906) he was already at the height of his powers.

The only explication of "An Encounter"—that of Marvin Magalaner in *Joyce: The Man, the Work, the Reputation*—treats the excursion of two truant schoolboys as an attempt to escape from the paralysis of Dublin life by visiting the Pigeonhouse Fort, which is interpreted as a religious and paternal symbol. "The Pigeonhouse, then, is identified in Joyce's mind with the 'father' of Christ and with fathers in general" (p. 77). The pervert whom the boys encounter after they have abandoned their attempt to reach their destination is, according to this interpretation, both a perverted God and a perverted father. [31]

This excellent reading is solidly based not only on the story itself but on Joyce's treatment of Stephen Dedalus's search for a father and for religious faith in *A Portrait* and *Ulysses*. Nevertheless, I feel that a detailed re-examination of the text is necessary if we are to appreciate

From Julian B. Kaye, "The Wings of Daedalus: Two Stories in *Dubliners*," *Modern Fiction Studies*, IV (Spring 1958), 31–41. Reprinted by permission of the Purdue Research Foundation.

the rich ambiguity of Joyce's symbolism and the dramatic intensity of the story.

"An Encounter" is a story of escape. The boys who play hooky are weary of the routine of school life; and we are prepared for their adventures by three pages (one quarter of the story) about their previous attempts to vary the monotonous routine of their days, all of which were unsatisfactory because, in the words of the boy narrator, ". . . I wanted real adventures to happen to myself. But real adventures, I reflected, do not happen to people who remain at home: they must be sought abroad."

Therefore, it is not surprising that the boys plan to "go along the Wharf Road until we came to the ships, and then to cross in the ferryboat and walk out to see the Pigeon House." When they reached the ships they feel an impulse to run away to sea. Instead they cross the Liffey in a ferryboat and the narrator looks about for a foreign sailor with green eyes, "for I had some confused notions . . ." The narrator breaks off and does not tell us what his confused notion was, perhaps because he cannot verbalize it. At any rate, his expectations are not fulfilled: the only sailor with green eyes whom he sees does not seem to be foreign and the boy does not reach the Pigeonhouse because "it was too late and we were too tired. . . ."

For a long time I did not understand why a visit to the Pigeonhouse should be the climax of a day spent in seeing foreign ships; I then learned that in the late eighteenth and early nineteenth century the Pigeonhouse was the Irish terminus of the Irish-English packet service.[1] Certainly some one so well informed about Dublin local history as Joyce must have known the history of the landmark that so strongly stimulated his imagination. The fact that the packet service had been established at Kingstown and the North Wall before Joyce's birth is not significant. For one thing, children distinguish past from present much less exactly than adults. The boy narrator of "An Encounter" may very well have read an old story which mentions the landing of a packet at the Pigeonhouse—e.g., The Absentee of Maria Edgeworth—and may have assumed the Pigeonhouse was still used as a terminus.

More important, it seems to me, is the theme of belatedness that pervades all the fictional representations of Joyce as child and adolescent. [32] In "The Sisters" we see the boy narrator with the dead Father Flynn and his two aged and decrepit sisters. He seems bound to them and to the dead and dying past which they represent. In "Araby" he arrives at a bazaar—the object of another enthusiastic expedition—just before closing time on the last day; and he sees only the winding up of things in the almost deserted and half-darkened hall.

---

[1] See Weston St. John Joyce, The Neighborhood of Dublin (Dublin, 1912), pp. 1–8, for an account of the history of the Pigeonhouse.

Stephen Dedalus, his *alter ego,* is wounded to think that his ". . . monkish learning . . . was held no higher by the age he lived in than the subtle and curious jargon of heraldry and falconry" (*Portrait,* Modern Library edition, p. 209).

Thus, much of the pathetic futility of the boys' attempt to escape lies in the fact that they try a path 'that had been closed before they were born. Also to be noted is the relevance of the name as well as the function of the Pigeonhouse to the Daedalus myth of *A Portrait* and *Ulysses.*[2]

The boys, although they are unable to attain their goal, do have an adventure. We may say that, unable to escape, they are confronted with Ireland itself. Instead of the green-eyed sailor, who represents the romance of the exotic, they encounter the green-eyed pervert (green for Ireland).

The perversion of love into cruelty is one of the most common themes in *Dubliners.* To Joyce it is one of the characteristics of Dublin life. The working out of this theme is explicit in "Counterparts" and is implicit in such stories as "The Boarding House," "Two Gallants," and "A Little Cloud." In Irish political life the bitterness and personal animosity of the battle that followed the Bishops' condemnation of Parnell, described so powerfully in *A Portrait,* is an analogous example of disappointed love delighting in the infliction of pain.

The sterile autoeroticism and sadism of the pervert is an excellent symbol of Joyce's view of political Ireland after Parnell—the Ireland of "Ivy Day in the Committee Room." It may be significant that the narrator insists that he and his friend give the pervert the false names of Smith and Murphy if he should ask their identity. Beyond psychological realism and the primitive superstition that plays an important role in the Lohengrin legend and in the Cyclops episode of the *Odyssey,* there is Joyce's fear of Ireland's hatred of its artists—a fear which he often voices.

There is yet another level—in my opinion, the most important one —on which the symbols of the story function. Stanislaus Joyce [33] has pointed out that the first three stories of *Dubliners* are about early adolescence. Of all three "An Encounter" deals most explicitly with sex. One may say that the three principal characters—the boy narrator (Joyce), his friend Mahony, and the pervert—are defined by their attitude towards sex. The restlessness and desire for adventure and escape that motivate the day's "miching" are principally puberty. The narrator is facinated by the "unkempt fierce and beautiful girls" of American detective stories. At about the same age (Stanislaus

[2] See Ovid's *Metamorphoses,* VIII, 183 ff., for the story of Daedalus's escape from Crete after King Minos has refused him permission to depart by the regular sea route. "An Encounter" records the defeat of an early attempt of a fictional surrogate of Joyce to escape from Ireland by sea.

Joyce, in his "Background to *Dubliners*," says that his brother was about fourteen at the time of the incident recorded in "An Encounter") Stephen Dedalus is impelled to restless wandering and romantic fantasy: "He returned to Mercedes and, as he brooded upon her image, a strange unrest crept into his blood. Sometimes a fever gathered within him and led him to rove alone in the evening. . . . He wanted to meet in the real world the unsubstantial image which his soul so constantly beheld. . . . They would be alone, surrounded by darkness and silence: and in that moment of supreme tenderness he would be transfigured. . . . Weakness and inexperience would fall from him in that magic moment" (pp. 70–71).

Joyce quite explicitly connects Stephen's fantasy with the desire to escape to foreign lands which is stimulated by roaming around the docks of Dublin:

He [Stephen] passed unchallenged among the docks and along the quays. . . . The vastness and strangeness of the life suggested to him by the bales of merchandise stocked along the walls or swung aloft out of the holds of steamers wakened again in him the unrest which had sent him wandering in the evening from garden to garden in search of Mercedes. . . . A vague dissatisfaction grew up within him as he looked on the quays and on the river and on the lowering skies and yet he continued to wander up and down day after day as if he really sought someone that eluded him. (pp. 72–73)

Thus the itinerary of the boys' trip may be viewed as an attempt to find an object that will assuage their restlessness. Experience itself— i.e., the foreign, the exotic—seems to be an abstraction of that object.

Marvin Magalaner has observed that the Pigeonhouse may function as a phallic image of fatherhood as well as a religious symbol of God as father and as paraclet. W. Y. Tindall has pointed out that some of the historic functions of the Pigeonhouse ("successively a fort, a lighthouse, and a power station") may be interpreted symbolically (*James Joyce*, p. 26). All these themes are part of the meaning of the Pigeonhouse to the narrator. Since he lives with his aunt and uncle, he is presumably an orphan; and he seems anxious to find a father. Significantly, Stephen Dedalus thought of himself as an orphan when he was the narrator's age (p. 111).

We know from *A Portrait* that Stephen's adolescence was extremely [34] painful because of his family's decline from affluence to scarcely genteel shabbiness and that he held his father responsible for the family misfortune; and we may guess that Stephen's diffidence about sex was partially due to the feeling of insecurity caused by his family's loss of wealth and his father's loss of status.

In "An Encounter" the insecure and diffident narrator is contrasted with the aggressive and self-confident Mahony, who accompanies him on the outing. Mahony does not care about reaching the Pigeonhouse; instead, he wants to have some fun with his catapult.

"While we were waiting he brought out the catapult which bulged from his inner pocket and explained some improvements which he had made in it." He intends "to have some gas with the birds," from which one may surmise that Mahony and the narrator have widely differing conceptions of the Pigeonhouse. We do not, however, hear anything about Mahony shooting birds; instead, "he chased a crowd of ragged girls, brandishing his unloaded catapult. . . ." The next independent action he performs is to chase a cat. When the boys decide that they will have to give up the expedition to the Pigeonhouse, Mahony seems concerned only because he has not been able to use his catapult. During the boys' conversation with the pervert, Mahony answers the pervert's questions about their sweethearts by saying that he has "three totties," while the narrator answers that he has none. Later Mahony goes off to chase a cat and leaves the narrator alone with the pervert.

The reiteration of the images of brandished catapult and pursued cats, the pursuit of birds and girls, the bold assertion that he has three sweethearts, the insouciant indifference to the pervert—this is essentially all we are told about Mahony, and it is all we need to know. His character, for this story, is his aggressive sexuality, which is conceived primarily as a contrast to the confusion and tortured uncertainty of the boy narrator. Mahony does not seem to need the support of a father —earthly, heavenly, or national—to confirm his manhood. Living for instinctual satisfactions, he remains unperturbed by the paralysis of family, church, and state that is the theme of *Dubliners*. He is the first of a series of males whom Joyce contrasts with his fictional surrogates: Cranly in *A Portrait* and Buck Mulligan in *Ulysses* with Stephen Dedalus; and Shaun the Post with Shem the Penman in *Finnegans Wake*.

Unlike the happy-go-lucky Mahony, the boy narrator *is* disappointed by his failure to reach the Pigeonhouse and to find the green-eyed foreign sailor. It is therefore significant that the pervert is dressed in greenish-black (like another symbol of unsuccessful paternity, Father Flynn of "The Sisters") and has green eyes. When he begins talking about "Sir Walter Scott and Lord Lytton," the [35] boy narrator, who is of course literary, attempts to impress his interlocutor by pretending that he has read every book the former mentions. He is therefore presumably pleased when the pervert says of Mahony: " 'Now . . . he is different; he goes in for games.' " When Mahony asks a question which the narrator thinks is stupid, he is both ashamed of his friend and afraid "the man would think I was as stupid as Mahony."

The pervert then changes the subject to girls, and the narrator, detecting the lack of conviction in the pervert's praise of normal sexuality, begins to feel vaguely uneasy about his new friend. Then the pervert walks across the field away from the boys and performs the un-named act which the boy narrator—unlike Mahony, who observes the pervert's exhibitionism with scientific curiosity: "'I say . . . He's a queer old josser!'"—refuses to acknowledge that he has seen. He immediately, however, insists that they give the pervert false names; and we can infer, from the horror and guilt that Stephen Dedalus feels about his autoeroticism when he is about the same age,[3] the painfulness of the narrator's observation, in the man with whom he momentarily hoped to identify himself, of a perverse form of the behavior he detests in himself.

The pervert returns to the boys and Mahony runs off in pursuit of a cat, leaving the boy narrator and the man together. The pervert again begins talking about sex, but this time he says what he believes —sex is cruelty. Here he speaks not only as a priest instructing a catechumen—as, for example, Father Flynn in "The Sisters" instructing the same boy narrator—but also as a father telling his son about life: "He described to me how he would whip such a boy as if he were unfolding some elaborate mystery. He would love that, he said, better than anything in this world; and his voice, as he led me monotonously through the mystery, grew almost affectionate and seemed to plead with me that I should understand him."

The mystery—and the word is applicable to sex as well as religion —disgusts the boy narrator, who is now anxious only to escape the father whom he has been seeking and by whom he has been welcomed. He calls for the recently disavowed Mahony. When the latter responds immediately to his summons, he feels ashamed of himself. "And I was penitent; for in my heart I had always despised him a little."

The words of penitence with which the narrator concludes the story measure his loss of hope, of which the story is the record.[4] The [36] narrator hoped for escape, hoped for a father who would give him the counsel and companionship he needs; instead he encounters the epitome of all he detests. He is obliged to ask for help not from the superior being for whom he is searching but from Mahony, whom he has thought his inferior. He is reduced to accepting the friendship of a commonplace contemporary for the fostering love and wisdom of a father.

Thus "An Encounter" is a symbolic history of the boy narrator's rejection of the authority of father, church, and state as perverted and degenerate and his despairing substitution of the friendship of a contemporary who, although mediocre, can assuage his loneliness.[5] [37]

---

[3] See *Portrait*, pp. 131–132, 100–102, 111.

[4] See Brewster Ghiselin, "The Unity of Joyce's *Dubliners*," p. 81, for a corroborating opinion: "In the first three stories . . . the theological virtues faith, hope, and love, in the conventional order, are successively displayed in abeyance and finally in defeat."

[5] Our awareness of this substitution is important not only in itself but because it helps us to understand why the commonplace Cranly is perhaps the least shadowy character in *A Portrait* next to Stephen himself and why the rather unattractive Buck Mulligan is the closest associate of the proud and fastidious Stephen of *Ulysses*.

The Chalice Bearer

CLEANTH BROOKS, JR., AND ROBERT PENN WARREN

ON WHAT MAY BE CALLED THE SIMPLEST LEVEL ["ARABY"] IS A STORY
of a boy's disappointment. The description of the street in which he
lives, the information about the dead priest and the priest's abandoned
belongings, the relations with the aunt and uncle—all of these items,
which occupy so much space, seem to come very naturally into the
story. That is, they may be justified individually in the story on realistic grounds. But when one considers the fact that such material constitutes the bulk of the story, one is led to observe that, if such items
merely serve as "setting" and atmosphere . . . , the story is obviously
overloaded with nonfunctional material. Obviously, for any reader
except the most casual, these items do have a function. If we find in
what way these apparently irrelevant items in "Araby" are related to
each other and to the disappointment of the boy, we shall have defined
the theme of the story.

What, then, is the relation of the boy's disappointment to such
matters as the belongings of the dead priest, the fact that he stands
apart talking to the girl while his friends are quarreling over the cap,
the gossip over the tea table, the uncle's lateness, and so on? One thing
that is immediately suggested by the mention of these things is the
boy's growing sense of isolation, the lack of sympathy between him and
his friends, teachers, and family. He says, "I imagined that I bore my
chalice safely through a throng of foes." For instance, when the uncle
is standing in the hall, the boy could not go into the front parlor and lie
at the window; or at school his ordinary occupations began to seem
"ugly monotonous child's play." But this sense of isolation has, also,
moments which are almost triumphant, as for example is implied when
the porters at the station wave the crowds back, "saying that it was
a special train for the bazaar" and was not for them. The boy is left
alone in the bare carriage, but he is going to "Araby," which name involves, as it were, the notion of romantic and exotic fulfillment. The
metaphor of the chalice implies the same kind of precious secret
triumph. It is not only the ordinary surrounding world, however, from
which he is [420] cruelly or triumphantly isolated. He is also isolated
from the girl herself. He talks to her only once, and then is so confused

From Cleanth Brooks, Jr., and Robert Penn Warren, *Understanding Fiction.*
New York: F. S. Crofts & Company, 1943. Pp. 420–423. Reprinted by permission
of the authors and the publisher.

that he does not know how to answer her. But the present which he hopes to bring her from Araby would somehow serve as a means of communicating his feelings to her, a symbol for their relationship in the midst of the inimical world.

In the last scene at the bazaar, there is a systematic, though subtle, preparation for the final realization on the part of the boy. There is the "improvised wooden platform" in contrast with the "magical name" displayed above the building. Inside, most of the stalls are closed. The young lady and young men who talk together are important in the preparation. They pay the boy no mind, except in so far as the young lady is compelled by her position as clerk to ask him what he wants. But her tone is not "encouraging." She, too, belongs to the inimical world. But she, also, belongs to a world into which he is trying to penetrate: she and her admirers are on terms of easy intimacy —an intimacy in contrast to his relation to Mangan's sister. It is an exotic, rich world into which he cannot penetrate: he can only look "humbly at the great jars that stood like eastern guards at either side of the dark entrance to the stall. . . ." But, ironically, the young lady and her admirers, far from realizing that they are on holy, guarded ground, indulge in a trivial, easy banter, which seems to defile and cheapen the secret world from which the boy is barred. How do we know this? It is not stated, but the contrast between the conversation of the young lady and her admirers, and the tone of the sentence quoted just above indicates such an interpretation.

This scene, then, helps to point up and particularize the general sense of isolation suggested by the earlier descriptive materials, and thereby to prepare for the last sentence of the story, in which, under the sudden darkness of the cheap and barnlike bazaar, the boy sees himself as "a creature driven and derided by vanity," while his eyes burn with anguish and anger.

We have seen how the apparently casual incidents and items of description do function in the story to build up the boy's sense of intolerable isolation. But this is only part of the function of this material. The careful reader will have noticed how many references, direct or indirect, there are to religion and the ritual of the church. The atmosphere of the story is saturated with such references. We have the dead priest, the Christian Brothers' School, the aunt's hope that the bazaar is not "some Freemason affair," her remark when the uncle has been delayed, [421] to "this night of Our Lord." These references are all obvious enough. At one level, these references merely indicate the type of community in which the impressionable boy is growing up. But there are other, less obvious, references, which relate more intimately to the boy's experience. Even the cries of the shop boys for him are "shrill litanies." He imagines that he bears a "chalice safely through a throng of foes." When he is alone the name of Mangan's sister springs to his lips "in strange prayers and praises." For this reason, when he speaks of his "confused adoration," we see that the love of the girl takes on, for him, something of the nature of a mystic, religious experience. The use of the very word *confused* hints of the fact that romantic love and religious love are mixed up in his mind.

It has been said that the boy is isolated from a world which seems ignorant of, and even hostile to, the experience of his love. In a sense he knows that his aunt and uncle are good and kind, but they do not understand him. He had once found satisfaction in the society of his companions and in his school work, but he has become impatient with both. But there is also a sense in which he accepts his isolation and is even proud of it. The world not only does not understand his secret but would cheapen and contaminate it. The metaphor of the chalice borne through a throng of foes, supported as it is by the body of the story, suggests a sort of consecration like that of the religious devotee. The implications of the references to religion, then, help define the boy's attitude and indicate why, for him, so much is staked upon the journey to the bazaar. It is interesting to note, therefore, that the first overt indication of his disillusionment and disappointment is expressed in a metaphor involving a church: "Nearly all the stalls were closed and the greater part of the hall was in darkness. I recognized a silence like that which pervades a church after a service. . . . Two men were counting money on a salver. I listened to the fall of the coins." So, it would seem, here we have the idea that the contamination of the world has invaded the very temple of love. (The question may arise as to whether this is not reading too much into the passage. Perhaps it is. But whatever interpretation is to be made of the particular incident, it is by just such suggestion and implication that closely wrought stories, such as this one, are controlled by the author and embody their fundamental meaning.)

Is this a sentimental story? It is about an adolescent love affair, about "calf love," a subject which usually is not to be taken seriously and is often the cause of amusement. The boy of the story is obviously investing [422] casual incidents with a meaning which they do not deserve; and himself admits, in the end, that he has fallen into self-deception. How does the author avoid the charge that he has taken the matter over-seriously?

The answer to this question would involve a consideration of the point of view from which the story is told. It is told by the hero himself, but after a long lapse of time, after he has reached maturity. This fact, it is true, is not stated in the story, but the style itself is not that of an adolescent boy. It is a formal and complicated style, rich, as has already been observed, in subtle implications. In other words, the man is looking back upon the boy, detachedly and judicially. For instance, the boy, in the throes of the experience, would never have said of himself: "I had never spoken to her, except for a few casual words, and yet her name was like a summons to all my foolish blood." The man knows, as it were, that the behavior of the boy was, in a sense, foolish. The emotions of the boy are confused, but the person telling the story, the boy grown up, is not confused. He has unraveled the confusion long after, knows that it existed and why it existed.

If the man has unraveled the confusions of the boy, why is the event still significant to him? Is he merely dwelling on the pathos of adolescent experience? It seems, rather, that he sees in the event, as he looks back on it, a kind of parable of a problem which has run through later experience. The discrepancy between the real and the ideal scarcely exists for the child, but it is a constant problem, in all sorts of terms, for the adult. This story is about a boy's first confrontation of that problem—that is, about his growing up. The man may have made adjustments to this problem, and may have worked out certain provisional solutions, but looking back, he still recognizes it as a problem, and an important one. The sense of isolation and disillusion which, in the boy's experience, may seem to spring from a trivial situation, becomes not less, but more aggravated and fundamental in the adult's experience. So, the story is not merely an account of a stage in the process of growing up—it does not merely represent a clinical interest in the psychology of growing up—but is a symbolic rendering of a central conflict in mature experience. [423]

Eveline

MARTIN DOLCH

"EVELINE" IS ONE OF JOYCE'S EARLIEST STORIES AND "MAY HAVE SET the theme and tone"[1] of *Dubliners*, in which it was to be incorporated. It was written in Paris in 1903 shortly after Joyce's elopement with Nora Barnacle, and was first published in an agricultural newspaper, *The Irish Homestead*, in 1904. In the final edition of *Dubliners* (1914) it appeared with some slight alterations, the fourth of fifteen stories. In a letter of May 5, 1906, Joyce said that in these stories it had been his intention "to write a chapter of the moral history of my country and I chose Dublin for the scene because that city seemed to me the

---

[1] William York Tindall, *A Reader's Guide to James Joyce* (New York, 1959), p. 21.

From Martin Dolch, "Eveline," in John V. Hagopian and Martin Dolch, eds., *Insight II*. Frankfurt: Hirschgraben-Verlag, 1964. Pp. 193–200. Reprinted by permission of the editors and the publisher.

centre of paralysis. I have tried to present it to the indifferent public under four of its aspects: childhood, adolescence, maturity and public life. The stories are arranged in this order. I have written it for the most part in a style of scrupulous meanness and with the conviction that he is a very bold man who dares to alter in the presentment, still more to deform, whatever he has seen and heard."

While the first three stories in *Dubliners*, which deal with an adolescent boy, are told in the first person, thus indicating an autobiographical element, the following twelve are told by an objective narrator. But the point of view throughout this story is Eveline's, and the style of the prose, in describing her thought process, is strictly in keeping with the shifts in her emotions and the simplicity of her mind. For example, in the beginning the prose style embodies as well as expresses fatigue: "She was tired. Few people passed." Later, "in a sudden impulse of terror," she flees the house in such a panic that the next thing she knows she is at the dock—and that is also the next thing the reader knows. Since her mind is a blank during her flight and since the story is a presentation of her stream-of-consciousness, there is nothing the narrator can say. And at the very end, when she is so frozen with a paralysis of the will while Frank is calling to her to follow him aboard ship, the author says, "He was shouted at to go on . . ."—*the only use of the passive voice in the entire story!*—before revealing her condition explicitly: "She set her white face to him, *passive*, like a helpless animal."

As Eveline never thinks of her outward appearance, the narrator does not pay any attention to it, but concentrates on developing her state of mind within the last hour at home and the following crucial minutes at the dock. The thought process is simple: first, impressions from outside the window, such as the view of the avenue and the sound of the street organ, evoke associations with the past; then, looking within her room she recalls her present situation; finally she examines her own judgment. Everything seems settled, she has consented to go away with Frank and marry him, and has written two letters of farewell. But the nearer the moment of departure comes the more her strength [194] fails her. The development of her crisis and failure is magnificently rendered in her physical motions: "She sat at the window . . . she looked round the room . . . she continued to sit by the window . . . she stood up . . . she stood among the swaying crowd . . . she gripped with both hands at the iron railing . . . she sent a cry of anguish . . . she set her white face to him, passive . . ."—this is the helplessness of a paralytic.

Furthermore, the movement of the story to the climax of her collapse is symbolically connected with the passing of time; after an excellent initial foreshadowing in the first sentence: "She sat at the window watching the evening *invade* the avenue," darkness increases outside the house and inside her heart: "The evening deepened in the avenue. . . . Her time was running out. . . . A bell clanged upon her heart."

As so often with Joyce, particularly in *Dubliners*,[2] escape is the theme of this story. It must have occupied his mind a great deal, and it is indeed a problem that has long been of central importance to the Irish nation. Eveline is faced with the question whether or not to escape by emigration from a life that has been full of hardship and bitterness, with a tyrannical father inclined to violence and meanness, and nagging superiors in her job. It is a kind of life that drove her mother crazy,[3] and when "the pitiful vision of her mother's life laid its spell on the very quick of her being" she tries to break out in a sudden impulse of terror: "She must escape! . . . she wanted to live . . . she had a right to happiness." Frank has successfully ventured to the new world. Even the priest whose photograph has been hanging on the wall as long as she can remember is in Melbourne. Emigration, it appears, offers the only way to salvation.

Eveline has experienced the excitement of having a "fellow" courting her and has come to like him. He offers her a home of her own, happiness, love and respect. "He would save her." So she has consented to go with him, and he has booked their passage. She has written the letters of farewell to her father and her brother. In an impulse of terror she flees to join him at the North Wall where their ship is lying ready to depart. But when she finds herself "among the swaying crowd," she feels lost in "a maze of distress," and at the last barrier she breaks down, unable to throw off the chains tying her to Dublin.

The diagram [below] may help to visualize the conflicting forces affecting Eveline's mind. The left half represents the life to which she is accustomed, to which she clings in the end, and which, in its sterility, decay and horror is really DEATH. The right half contrasts the chances that lie before her, freedom, and happiness in a married LIFE. Given such a choice, the decision seems simple, and it was clear to Eveline as long as her escape was only imaginative. But the nearer she comes to its realization, the more the prospect begins to frighten her. All her likes and dislikes become painfully conflicting and ambiguous. [195] This is first foreshadowed when she feels that however monotonous and joyless her Dublin life, however bitter and depressing her sacrifice for her family may be, "now that she was about to leave it she did not find it a wholly undesirable life." Change is already beyond her

___

[2] In "A Little Cloud," e.g., Little Chandler realizes, "if you wanted to succeed you had to go away. You could do nothing in Dublin."

[3] The puzzling "Derevaun Seraun" is perhaps corrupt Gaelic for "the end of pleasure is pain," cf. Tindall, p. 22. But whatever it means, it shows the mother's insanity.

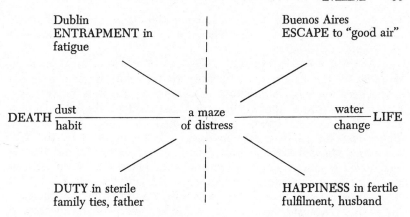

capacity and fills her with a crazy fear which mistakes salvation for destruction.

Joyce employs various symbolic details which underline his moral valuation. Most prominent is the dust which pervades the room where she is sitting as well as her life: "she had dusted [the furniture] once a week for so many years, wondering where on earth all the dust came from." The first paragraph explicitly states the effect on her: "in her nostrils was the odour of dusty cretonne. *She was tired.*" Dust suffocates, it is a product of decay and stagnation. Eveline has been poisoned by it, her powers of motion seem paralyzed as by a drug, for "her time was running out, but she continued to sit by the window, leaning her head against the window curtain, *inhaling* the odour of dusty cretonne." She is so worn out with her hard work .that she lacks the strength for a break, the courage "to explore another [real] life."

Contrasted to the dust of Dublin is, of course, the good air promised by *Buenos Aires,* and in a deeper sense, the water that is the way of escape and symbolizes the life that lies beyond it. At the North Wall, which is an appropriate name for a place that proves a barrier to freedom and love, she feels that "the seas of the world [and of life] tumbled about her heart," and her timid and tired heart is not able to stand the stress of freedom, she "fears what alone could save her" (Tindall) and is afraid of being drowned in "the seas of the world"—so she clings to the railing for support, not realizing that she clings to the bars of her prison. Magalaner[4] sees "an unnecessary waste of a carefully built-up symbol" in Eveline's fear of death by drowning (which is echoed in Madame Sosostris' advice "Fear death by water" in T. S. Eliot's *The Waste Land*) after

[4] Marvin Magalaner, *Time of Apprenticeship: The Fiction of Young James Joyce* (New York, 1959), pp. 118–128, 152–153.

the dust imagery. But he does not get the irony—she is not afraid of *death* by water but of life. The dust = death, water = life equation holds consistently.

Another recurrent symbolic element is music, which seems to embody all the beauty and sexuality that Eveline is missing in her life. There is still a harmonium in her home, but it is broken now. Frank is "awfully fond of [196] music," and she feels the lure of a new life and distant, unknown countries when he takes her to see *The Bohemian Girl* (a long popular opera, written in 1843 by the Irish composer Michael William Balfe) and when he sings "about the lass that loved a sailor." An organ-grinder had played "a melancholy air of Italy" the night before her mother was finally released from Dublin by death, but her father significantly had ordered the player to go away. When she hears the same tune again, the recollection of her mother's pitiful end drives her out of the home, but ironically it also serves "to remind her of the promise to her mother, her promise to keep the home together as long as she could," and thus increases the conflict in her. When she finally approaches the ship, there is no band playing in the sunshine, but instead "the boat blew a long mournful whistle into the mist," and in vain she prays to God "to show her what was her duty." But no heavenly Father answers her prayer, only her real father is brutally present in Dublin.

Reviewing all the familiar objects in the room, Eveline also notices two religious pictures above the broken harmonium. One is a yellowing photograph of a priest who had been a school friend of her father and later went off to Melbourne, possibly in renunciation of his calling; this would explain why her father does not like to talk about him. Australia, in the late 19th century, was a haven for disreputable exiles from the British Isles. So it appears that he had succeeded where Eveline fails. The other picture is a coloured print of the promises made to Blessed Margaret Mary Alacoque.[5] The latter was a French nun (1647–1690) who became paralyzed because of the tortures which she inflicted upon herself, but was miraculously cured when she vowed to consecrate herself to a holy life. In some way Eveline's fate resembles hers as she is paralyzed by her suffering, renounces her happiness and puts up with a "life of commonplace sacrifices" and with a celibacy which is implicitly condemned by Joyce.

Eveline cannot throw off the chains of convention and habit as she cannot bear freedom, she is "too moribund to abandon the dust of her native city for the good air of exile. . . . The end is not a coming to awareness but an animal experience of inability" (Tindall). "Dublin has won. Given a chance of life, Eveline has chosen sym-

[5] The name also appears in *Ulysses,* where Mulligan prays to "Blessed Margaret Mary Anycock," and makes the bawdy blasphemy clear with the word-play.

bolic death. She has refused to set forth over the water" (Magalaner).

Dublin not only provided Joyce with an inexhaustible source of material for a life-long writing, it also stirred up deep emotions in him, "the fury of a lover at the hideous flaws in his sweetheart," as Gorman says. In his letters he called Dublin a moral and spiritual "dunghill" or even saw it as "the fat sow that eats its young." But while his mind was occupied with *Dubliners*, Joyce also wrote, in a letter to his brother in 1906: "Sometimes thinking of Ireland, it seems to me that I have been unnecessarily harsh. I have reproduced (in *Dubliners*, at least) none of the attraction of the city . . . I have not [197] reproduced its ingenuous insularity and its hospitality . . . I have not been just to its beauty . . . And yet I know how useless these reflections are. For was I to rewrite the book . . . I am sure I should find again what you call the Holy Ghost sitting in the ink-bottle and the perverse devil of my literary conscience sitting on the hump of my pen." It was not his intention to give a just portrait; in selecting his material he was guided by a moral purpose. With regard to his countrymen he saw his book as a chapter of the "moral history" of his country and a first step toward its "spiritual liberation"; in a personal way *Dubliners* also gave Joyce an opportunity to state his reasons for exile and to justify it before himself and before the world. [198]

A Study in Weakness and Humiliation

ROBERT M. ADAMS

"AFTER THE RACE" DOES NOT OFFER VERY MANY KNOTTY PARTICULARS. It is a study in weakness and humiliation—Irish weakness and Irish humiliation—in the face of Continental assurance. Jimmy Doyle is a lightweight carried along by a swift current of factitious excitement with perhaps a suggestion of sharp practice behind it. All the consequences of his folly are hinted at rather than spelled out. We have the suggestion of a frightful hangover, the assurance that his [64] father the ex-butcher will be furious, and that carefully undefined and so all the more ominous cloud—how much money has he really lost? The story boils and bubbles along until all these awful consequences have begun to impinge on Jimmy Doyle's wretched consciousness, and then, as if shrugging off what is already obvious enough, closes on a tableau.

How much contempt does Joyce feel for Jimmy Doyle? How much liking is mingled with this contempt?—for the two emotions by no means exclude one another, particularly in Joyce. The wild oats which Jimmy is sowing are familiar and unimaginative enough; they do not seem even to involve any real pleasure for him, being hectic and gassy, as it were. Joyce as an old Dublin reprobate knew the wisdom of the world on this score: let a boy run a bit wild in his youth because he is bound to settle down later on. The old ex-butcher from Kingstown is clearly following that program and the evidence is that it will succeed admirably with Jimmy who has neither the energy nor the intelligence for any sustained revolt. Indeed, we are reminded that his father was too sensible to play the rebel for long; having "begun life as an advanced Nationalist, [he] had modified his views early." Now he sends his son to "a big Catholic college" in England, and to "Dublin University to study law." Dublin University is of course Trinity College, under its other name, and Jimmy is plainly expected to make friends with the scions of the Establishment. All these little details serve to mark out Jimmy Doyle as a characteristic "shoneen," a breed aptly described in "Ivy Day in the Committee Room" as "always hat in hand before any fellow with a handle to his name." Petty squires and successful bourgeois, such people may call themselves "Nationalists" (like Tricky Dicky Tierney), but they can be trusted to want what is best for the business community, i.e., themselves. Young Jimmy Doyle, when he is "under generous influences" [65] —drunk—feels "the buried zeal of his father wake to life within him." But it is not much life—Joyce never had anything but contempt for muzzy, sentimental, barroom patriotism—and Jimmy is managed out of his sentiments, as out of his money, by "friends" who really despise him.

He is a feeble figure, then, but in his puppyish way, not altogether unlikeable. And there are even grounds for thinking that he may, in certain respects, have a buried relation with Joyce himself. The names, for one thing, are very similar: James Joyce and James Doyle. Joyce had gone to Clongowes Wood, very often referred to, by those not friendly to it, as a school for training up "shoneens." His father was not a butcher, of course, or financially successful, but he had lived at Kingstown, and had he had a few of the butcherly qualities (which in "The Boarding House" for example enable Mrs. Mooney to deal "with moral problems as a cleaver deals with meat") he might have been a financial success like Mr. Doyle. Jimmy Doyle has some of the physical mannerisms which Joyce persistently attributed to characters whom he associated with himself: like Little Chandler of "A Little Cloud," Gabriel Conroy of "The Dead," and Richard Rowan of *Exiles*, he has a soft mustache and innocent-looking—i.e., weak—eyes. Joyce got the idea for the story after going to an automobile race,[1] and when he wrote it he was fresh from a visit to Paris, where he had felt much humiliated by his own poverty and innocence, as contrasted with the sharp and knowing manner of Parisians. He had, further, a persistent notion that when he got drunk with people like Gogarty, they were encouraging him to drink from malicious motives, in the hope of ruining his talent. Finally, Jimmy Doyle rather fancies himself as a turner of phrases, and he makes a fawning one, in not very good taste, about the Frenchman and the Englishman. Jimmy is not only Joyce, he is all Ireland in this context [66] "—which reminds us of that quiet, ironic phrase in the opening paragraph, "the cheer of the gratefully oppressed." The Irish, like Jimmy, are only fleeced but grateful. The game of cards, which lies between Routh the Englishman and Segouin the Frenchman, and in which Farley the American and Doyle the Irishman are the heaviest losers, is a thumbnail sketch of Irish history. "It was a terrible game," thinks poor lost Jimmy Doyle. Indeed it was.

Lastly, though with apologies and reservations, I am afraid something will have to be said about Jimmy Doyle's last name. It had a special fascination for the later Joyce, who included a section in *Finnegans Wake*[2] where a trial takes place in which the defendant, the prosecutor, and all the members of the jury seem to be named Doyle. What is the point of this foolery? Elijah, preaching a degenerate gospel in the brothel scene of *Ulysses*, implies that under the religion of humanity, everyone is Christ—"Florry Christ, Stephen Christ, Zoe Christ, Bloom Christ, Kitty Christ, Lynch Christ."[3] Stephen, speculating what various characters would be called if their names were translated into English (pp. 622–623), concludes that Jesus would be Mr. Doyle (Christ = the anointed = oiled = Doyle). This identification of Christ with Doyle may have been helped or suggested by a well-known Dublin baritone of the turn of the century, who figures in both *Ulysses* and *Finnegans Wake;* his name was J. C. Doyle.[4] Thus, by making a series of far-fetched identifications with characters in other Joyce books and people from his biography, we may establish still another, rather grotesque ground for thinking that Joyce viewed Jimmy Doyle [67] with secret sympathy, as an aspect of himself, and Christ, and everyman.

[1] See Joyce's interview of the French racing-car driver, Henri Fournier, reprinted under the title "The Motor Derby" in *The Critical Writings of James Joyce,* ed. Ellsworth Mason and Richard Ellmann (New York, 1959), pp. 106–108. [Eds.]

[2] New York: Compass Books, 1958, pp. 574–576.

[3] New York: Modern Library, 1961, p. 507.

[4] Cf. also *Finnegans Wake* where the 12 patrons of Earwicker's pub are "doyles when they deliberate but sullivans when they are swordsed" (p. 142).

Now the reader himself at this point is no doubt feeling outraged; and if I may venture to interpret for him, he is muttering: "But if we have to read even a little short story like this, a bare sketch, in terms of Joyce's entire career, if we have to make such elaborate transpositions and macaronic puns, so that everything is something else and nothing is itself; if we have to do this, well . . ." Well, what will happen? We shall have an infinite number of possible relationships to investigate; we shall be so busy fighting our way through riddles and cross-references that we shall have little occasion to appreciate Joyce's work as literature. Unhappily, the fact seems to be that Joyce was very often guided in his writings by these private patterns of word-association, these intimate attitudes, so that from time to time, we shall and must have recourse to some rather strained and exotic exegetical constructs. We shall have to bring his often maddeningly private patterns of association, and the peculiarities of his private attitudes, to bear on the reading of the texts. On the other hand, this procedure is chiefly justified where the text by its own peculiarities requires such treatment. In the example at hand, "After the Race," there are some reasons why the figure of Jimmy Doyle is not simply contemptible, contemptible though he doubtless is. Our "esoteric" reason is no doubt unnecessary in view of the many simpler ones; but it illustrates a sort of critical method which cannot be altogether ruled out, and if it has the effect of rendering the story richer, and the final balancing of attitudes more satisfying, it may well have a claim to our serious consideration. [68]

Epiphany in "Two Gallants"

WILLIAM T. NOON, S.J.

BETWEEN THE HALF-WORDLESS AND LARGELY PARENTHETICAL TRANSCRIPtions of Joyce's earliest Epiphanies, and the highly compressed, many-visioned verbal formulations of the *Wake*, a complicated series of linguistic experiments was to take place. From *Dubliners* onward, Joyce's style shows a steady development in the direction of symbolic verbal notation. Levin has compared *Dubliners* to the collection of epiphanies which Stephen, as he walked along the beach in *Ulysses*,

Excerpted from William T. Noon, S. J., *Joyce and Aquinas*. © 1957 by Yale University Press. Pp. 83–84. Reprinted by permission of Yale University Press.

had lost hope of ever recording in words.[1] The fact that Joyce succeeded in recording some of them in *Dubliners* is a sign that Joyce had come to see that the "sudden spiritual manifestation" was not in itself enough to constitute a poem or a story. The radiant structure of the object in literature is not self-adjusting. Only insofar as the poet or storyteller can turn the symbolic resources of his language to advantage will the literary experience "epiphanize," "seem to us radiant."[2] If *Dubliners* is the turning point in Joyce's attitude toward the epiphany, it appears reasonable to assume that his independent study of Aquinas during the period when he was writing these stories would have been one of the influences inducing him to a higher degree of symbolization in his art.

A brief look at one . . . of the *Dubliners* stories may help to show how this new epiphanic strategy operates. The moment of "sudden spiritual manifestation" for the reader of "Two Gallants"[3] occurs at the very end, when Corley with a grave gesture extends his hand toward the light and opens it to the gaze of Lenehan: "A small gold coin shone in the palm." So far as the incident might have been viewed by a spectator in the Dublin streets that evening, who was aware of what Corley had been up to, as Lenehan certainly was, this wordless "vulgarity of gesture" would be deeply and horribly illuminating of the ironic perversion of romantic gallantry in twentieth-century Dublin. But for the reader of a story to be thus enlightened a strategic psychological preparation is necessary, which the writer has no other means to effect except through the calculated arrangement of words so as to achieve the right adjustment of symbolic insight. How does Joyce, the "Spickspookspokesman of our specturesque silentiousness,"[4] manage this? The [83] central image elaborated by the language of the story is that of the harp whose mournful music struck silent the two gallants. This image of the harp with her covering about her knees is also made to suggest, through an allusive verbal recall, Moore's treatment of the harp as a symbol of poor, paralyzed, charmed Ireland, "Lir's lonely daughter." The naked harp of Joyce's story is mournful with reason, since in Corley the reader sees her ignored, despised, and sold for a gold coin. But besides the symbolism of the harp image, Joyce negotiates a further insight through language by

[1] This reference is to Harry Levin's *James Joyce: A Critical Introduction*. See bibliography, item 33. [Eds.]

[2] *Stephen Hero*, ed. Theodore Spencer (New York: New Directions, 1946), p. 213.

[3] My remarks here on "Two Gallants" are largely a parapharse of an excellent unpublished interpretation of this story by Robert R. Boyle, S. J. [This interpretation has since been published: Robert R. Boyle, S. J., " 'Two Gallants' and 'Ivy Day in the Committee Room,' " *James Joyce Quarterly*, I (Fall 1963), 3–9. Eds.]

[4] *Finnegans Wake* (New York: The Viking Press, 1957), p. 427.

his development of the imagery of the moonlight and of the rain. The faint romantic light of the moon is represented as gradually fading as the story develops, and as completely disappearing behind the rain clouds at the end, to be replaced by the hard glitter of the shining gold coin, become thus the emblem of the "base betrayer." It is in this way that the success of the gallants "epiphanizes" as the betrayal of gallantry: "the object achieves its epiphany"—but within the symbolic dimensions of language and not as a depressing vulgarity of nonliterary fact. [84]

The Boarding House

WILLIAM YORK TINDALL

COMPARED WITH "TWO GALLANTS," THIS STORY SEEMS SIMPLE—SIMPLE maybe but admirably handled. The style is fittingly ignoble, the [25] revelation of human nature disheartening and funny. We are confronted here with a butcher's daughter, who solves moral problems with a cleaver, with her somewhat common daughter, Polly, and with their conspiracy against poor Bob Doran, whose subsequent decline is recounted in *Ulysses*. For a plot at once so full of guile and so guileless comment seems unnecessary. It is as plain to us as to poor Bob Doran that "he was being had." That all men and all women are implied adds to the fun.

Our interest, aside from pity, fear, and laughter, must be with kind. For the first time in *Dubliners* we encounter a story that can be called naturalistic—more or less. Even with this qualification, "The Boarding House" affords comfort to those who think Joyce loyal to Zola. Never was pressure of environment more obviously displayed. Bob Doran's fall, determined by Dublin's moral conventions and hypocrisies, seems exemplary. The theme, like that of any naturalistic story, is this pressure, within which the "Madam" and her daughter work.

Yet "The Boarding House" lacks the overabundance of observed detail that Zola delighted in; and the end, with action off stage or interior, seems more or other than naturalistic. What links this story with the earlier stories of *Dubliners* is the yielding of Polly's absence of mind to awareness. A difference is that this awareness is less of self (though at her moment of truth she looks at self in mirror) than of conquest. Polly is Corley's female counterpart. [26]

"A Little Cloud": Joyce's Portrait of the Would-Be Artist

JAMES RUOFF

STANISLAUS JOYCE HAS RECENTLY SCOLDED CRITICS FOR READING ALtogether too much into his brother's early work. It may be legitimate to scrutinize *Ulysses* or *Finnegans Wake*, but it is "pernicious," he claims, to probe into *Chamber Music* or *Dubliners*.[1] He is especially incensed about the way critics have treated *Dubliners*, finding as they have the Virgin Mary symbolized in "The Sisters," homosexuality covertly ensconced in "An Encounter," etc. As if to scotch this recondite quibbling once for all, he urges that "A Little Cloud" in *Dubliners* ought to be read as "nothing more" than a simple story about matrimony, "with the figure of a successful and impenitent bachelor in it to cause discord and cast a little cloud over married life."[2] There is reason to believe, however, that Joyce's "A Little Cloud" suggests a great deal more than is framed within Stanislaus Joyce's description of the story, that it does, in fact, deserve to be studied with *Stephen Hero* and *A Portrait of the Artist* as a statement of Joyce's ideas regarding the nature of the artist and his relation to society.

That some of the aesthetic principles set forth in *Stephen Hero* and *A Portrait of the Artist* are foreshadowed in "A Little Cloud" may be the result of the fact that in March, 1906, when Joyce was [256] at

---

[1] See "The Background to 'Dubliners,'" *The Listener* (March 25, 1954), pp. 526–527. Stanislaus Joyce has always been vehemently critical of the obscurity of his brother's later work, and this article may well be an attempt to vindicate *Dubliners* from what he considers the stigma of complexity. Partly as a result of his objections to *Ulysses*, he and Joyce were not on friendly terms after 1920. (Cf. Herbert Gorman, *James Joyce* [New York, 1939], p. 271. Gorman's was the biography Joyce read and approved.)

[2] Stanislaus Joyce, p. 526.

James Ruoff, "'A Little Cloud': Joyce's Portrait of the Would-Be Artist," *Research Studies of the State College of Washington*, XXV (September 1957), 256–271. Reprinted by permission of the publisher.

work on the story,[3] he was also busy entering notes on aesthetics into his commonplace book and beginning *Stephen Hero*,[4] the first draft of what was later to become *A Portrait of the Artist*. Whereas the autobiographical novels depict a genuine artist's victorious struggle to liberate himself in a world he never made, "A Little Cloud" describes a would-be artist's pathetic failure to transcend a narrow existence of his own creation. Padraic Colum once observed that the most memorable stories in *Dubliners* are those which have to do with people touched by death.[5] In "The Sisters" the boy is confronted with the death of his neighbor, an aged priest; in "Eveline" the heroine is haunted by the memory of her dead mother; in "Clay" Maria is sheltered from an omen that portends her death; in "Ivy Day in the Committee Room" the memory of the dead Parnell hovers over the company like a forlorn ghost, and in "The Dead" Gabriel Conroy cannot shake off the accusing presence of a romantic young lover who died years before.[6] Like these other stories in *Dubliners*, "A Little Cloud" is also concerned with death, but with the purely metaphorical, living death of creative impotence and frustration, a protracted form of death which for Joyce the artist was as terrifying in its finality as any organic dissolution.

"A Little Cloud" is a character sketch delineated in three episodes. In each of these, the character of the protagonist, Little Chandler, is revealed by three separate but thematically related [257] conflicts. In the first episode, at King's Inns and in the streets of Dublin, Little Chandler is shown in conflict with himself; in the second, at Corless's restaurant, in conflict with Gallaher, and in the third, at Little Chandler's home, in conflict with his child. The title of the story functions as an anagrammatic device suggesting the close affinity of these three scenes—A Little Chandler, A Little Cloud (Gallaher), A Little

[3] Referring to "A Little Cloud," Joyce wrote to Grant Richards, March 13, 1906: "I shall send you in a week or so the last story which is to be inserted between 'The Boarding House' and 'Counterparts.'" (Quoted in Gorman, p. 148.) As it turned out, Joyce wrote one more story for *Dubliners*, "The Dead," which he did not complete until much later, sometime in 1907. (*Ibid.*, p. 188.)

[4] *Ibid.*, p. 148.

[5] Introduction, *Dubliners* (Modern Library, 1926), p. xii.

[6] In writing about "The Dead," David Daiches touches briefly on a subject related to that discussed in this essay. According to Professor Daiches, "The Dead" was added as "an after-thought" to *Dubliners* to illustrate the aesthetic theories expounded by Stephen Dedalus in *A Portrait of the Artist*. Like Stephen, Gabriel Conroy is shown to move away from "the lyrical," or subjective, attitude and toward the impersonal, "which for Joyce was the proper aesthetic attitude." (See "James Joyce: The Artist as Exile," in *Forms of Modern Fiction*, ed. William Van O'Connor [University of Minnesota, 1948], p. 66.) Professor Daiches' theory is, I believe, based on a misunderstanding of Gabriel Conroy's character. If anything, Gabriel Conroy becomes progressively more personal and emotional, until at the end of the story he is able to feel profoundly the emotions of his wife and her dead lover, and, more significantly, the shallowness of his own emotional life. Moreover, "The Dead" has to do with Gabriel's domestic life, not with his life as a potential artist.

Child.[7] As the story begins, Little Chandler, a clerk in Dublin's King's Inns, looks up fretfully from his "tiresome writing" to gaze out of his office window at the panorama of life in the streets—aged men dozing in the sun, children playing, young men and women hurrying about their affairs—a scene which stirs in Little Chandler "a gentle melancholy," for his own life is soured by a sense of futility: "He watched the scene and thought of life; and (as always happened when he thought of life) he became sad. A gentle melancholy took possession of him. He felt how useless it was to struggle against fortune, this being the burden of wisdom which the ages had bequeathed him." His spirits rise, however, when he recalls his rendezvous at Corless's restaurant with Gallaher, an old friend who has returned for a brief visit to Dublin after becoming, in Little Chandler's words, "a brilliant figure on the London Press." (As we shall see, it is very much to Joyce's purpose that both Little Chandler and his friend are "writers.") When, on his way to meet Gallaher, Little Chandler encounters a throng of urchins, he again reveals himself to be insensitive to the life around him:

A horde of grimy children populated the street. They stood or ran in the doorway or crawled up the steps before the gaping doors or squatted like mice upon the thresholds. Little Chandler gave them no thought. He picked his way deftly through all that minute vermin-like life and under the shadow of the gaunt spectral mansions in which the old nobility of Dublin had roystered. No memory of the past touched him. . . .

In contrast to the squalor and faded grandeur of historic old Henrietta Street is the swank, tinsel world of Corless's, where the after-theatre crowd gathers to eat oysters and the waiters speak French and German. It is a world Little Chandler has always viewed timidly and resentfully: "He always passed without turning [258] his head to look." His self-imposed isolation is absolute: he has cut himself off from the young and the old, the past and the present, the poor and the rich. In poetry he seeks an assuasive remedy for the torment of his isolation from others. In his desire to articulate the mysteries of his troubled nature, he has often wanted to read poetry to his wife, but "shyness had always held him back; and so the books had remained on the shelves. At times he repeated lines to himself and this consoled him." Little Chandler's habit of finding solace in remembered quotations recalls a similar practice of Stephen Dedalus, who "consoled himself" in a dreary tavern with his father by repeating some lines from Shelley,[8] and, while walking the streets of Dublin, sought to relieve

[7] As far as I know, this is Joyce's first use of a device he employed liberally in his later work, as in Finnegans Wake, for example, where H. C. Earwicker's name signifies "Here Comes Everybody."

[8] A Portrait of the Artist as a Young Man, in James Joyce (Viking Portable, 1948), p. 346. All references are to this edition.

his dissatisfaction with life by meditating on Aristotle's *Poetics* and the psychology of St. Thomas Aquinas.[9] During his restless peregrinations through the main streets and back alleys of the city, Stephen invokes memories of his reading of Gerhart Hauptmann, Newman, Guido Cavalcanti, and Ibsen, repeating to himself Ben Jonson's refrain "I was not wearier where I lay"[10] or disciplining his mind to "summon back to itself the age of Dowland and Byrd and Nashe" by savoring the poignant sweetness of Nashe's line from *Summer's Last Will and Testament:* "Brightness falls from the air."[11] Like Little Chandler's Stephen's literary recollections serve as palliatives to mitigate the pain of loneliness and unfulfillment; they signify the efforts of the romantic temperament to transcend its environment in search of a reality of pure imagination. In Stephen's aesthetic essay in *Stephen Hero,* he defines that temperament as one which seeks to escape from a world of extended reality. "The romantic temper," Stephen states, "is an insecure, unsatisfied, impatient temper which sees no fit abode here for its ideals and chooses therefore to behold them under insensible figures."[12]

But there are some noteworthy differences between Stephen's studied detachment and Little Chandler's puerile escapism. Where Little Chandler's timid evasion of life is a disorderly retreat into [259] himself, Stephen's detachment is a meaningful ritual in his worship of art. Paradoxically, Stephen's dissatisfaction with life enables him to come back to it at last on his own terms, with a fuller awareness of its meaning. It is Stephen's fretful walking—a symptom of his discontent with life—which causes him to explore his environment, to widen his circle of contact with reality. And this physical activity of walking, accompanied by the mental exercise of linking literary phrases and impressions into coherent unities of thought, creates a coalescence of apprehended reality and intellectual vision which prepares Stephen Dedalus for what Joyce called "the epiphany,"[13] a spontaneous insight into the normally imperceptible totality or unity of a person or situation. In ironic contrast to the manifestation which dazzled the Magi, Joycean "epiphanies" throw out their revelations to the sentient observer through the humblest and most mundane details—a haggard face in a crowd, an inane tune whistled in the street, a crane-like Irish girl wading in a stream—which becomes bright fragments illuminating the dark and chaotic world of sense experience. What Stephen is unconsciously searching for in his roaming through the Dublin streets is the most personal and elementary form of "epiph-

9 *Ibid.,* p. 437.

10 *Ibid.,* p. 439.

11 *Ibid.,* p. 502.

12 *Stephen Hero,* ed. Theodore Spencer (New Directions, 1944), p. 78.

13 Cf. Dorothy Van Ghent, *The English Novel: Form and Function* (New York, 1953), pp. 263–270.

any,"[14] a perception of the Thomistic *quidditas*, the "whatness" of things and people which can be known only through identification or empathy.

It is Stephen's inability to relate himself to others which temporarily inhibits his religious development, a phase which, together with its renunciation, constitutes a necessary and crucial stage of his artistic life. Of Stephen at sixteen, Joyce observes: "To merge his life in the common tide of other lives was harder for him than fasting or prayer, and it was his constant failure to do this to his own satisfaction which caused in his soul a sensation of spiritual dryness together with a growth of doubts and scruples."[15] Although at the end of his first year in college, Shephen is "disquieted and cast down by the dull phenomenon of Dublin," some benign compulsion drives him out of his cloistered self into the teeming life of the city: [260]

In the beginning he contented himself with circling timidly round the neighboring square or, at most, going half way down one of the side streets: but when he had made a skeleton map of the city in his mind he followed boldly one of its central lines until he reached the Customs House.[16]

Stephen's distaste for the squalor, shoddiness, and sloth of Dublin is emphasized everywhere in *A Portrait of the Artist*, but it is an ambivalence which Joyce is always careful to qualify:

He met the eyes of others with unanswering eyes for he felt that the spirit of beauty had folded him round like a mantle and that in reverie at least he had been acquainted with nobility. But, when this brief pride of silence upheld him no longer, *he was glad to find himself still in the midst of common lives, passing on his way amid the squalor and noise and sloth of the city fearlessly and with a light heart.*[17]

In *A Portrait of the Artist,* as in "A Little Cloud," Dublin is pictured as "dreary," "dirty," "squalorous," a city of cultural atrophy, political imbecility, and philistinism—a faded relic of a half-remembered, more glorious past—but it is part of the essential world nevertheless, and for Stephen Dedalus it holds in its fullness of life the indispensable human materials the artist must have to work at his craft. In its quest of epiphanies, the vision of the artist is fixed outward into "the common tide of other lives." In contrast, Little Chandler, the would-be artist, lives insecurely within himself because he fears and shuns life. His explorations of Dublin, unlike Stephen's, are anything but fearless:

[14] Concerning its various stages, see Irene Hendry, "Joyce's Epiphanies," in *James Joyce: Two Decades of Criticism,* ed. Seon Givens (Vanguard Press, 1948), pp. 38–40.

[15] *A Portrait of the Artist,* p. 409.

[16] *Ibid.,* p. 326.

[17] *Ibid.,* p. 437. Italics mine.

It was his habit to walk swiftly in the street even by day and whenever he found himself in the city late at night he hurried on his way apprehensively and excitedly. . . . He chose the darkest and narrowest streets and, as he walked boldly forward, the silence that was spread about his footsteps troubled him; and at times a sound of low fugitive laughter made him tremble like a leaf.

Little Chandler longs to be a poet. On his way to meet Gallaher at Corless's, he pauses on Grattan Bridge to "weigh his soul to see if it was a poet's soul." He gazes pensively down on the houses and docks that stretch along the Liffey: ". . . he looked down the river toward the lower quays and pitied the poor stunted houses. They seemed to him a band of tramps. . . . He wondered whether he could write a poem to express his idea. Perhaps Gallaher might be able to get it into some London paper for him. Could he write something original?" Similarly, in *A Portrait of the Artist* [261] Stephen stands pondering the Dublin waterfront, but his reverie, unlike Little Chandler's, takes him out of himself in his pursuit of an elusive ideal: "A vague dissatisfaction grew up within him as he looked on the quays and on the river and on the lowering skies and yet he continued to wander up and down day after day as if he really sought someone that eluded him."[18]

Little Chandler's reverie on Grattan Bridge concludes with a parody on the epiphany ("A light began to tremble on the horizon of his mind") as he speculates whimsically on how "the English critics" will mark "the melancholy tone" and "Celtic note" of his poems, and on how he will modify his surname to make it more "Irish-looking." His bogus epiphany directs his vision not outward to illuminate reality but inward to compound delusions. Stephen Dedalus's reverie, on the other hand, ends with an angry resolution that seems to burn away the ego. Like Little Chandler, Stephen is also dissatisfied with himself, angry with "the change of future which was reshaping the world about him into a vision of squalor and insincerity," and yet, observes Joyce—again interpolating a significant qualification—"his anger lent nothing to his vision. He chronicled with patience what he saw, detaching himself from it and testing its mortifying flavor in secret."[19] To Stephen Dedalus, and to Joyce the exile, Little Chandler's acrid condemnation of Dublin would have the ring of truth: "There was no doubt about it: if you wanted to succeed you had to go away. You could do nothing in Dublin." In both "A Little Cloud" and *A Portrait of the Artist* the recurring word to describe Dublin is "squalor." "What do you mean," the surly Lynch inquires of Stephen, "by prating about beauty and the imagination in this miserable Godforsaken island?"[20] But Stephen carries within him Ben Jonson's line to give the

---

[18] *Ibid.*, p. 313.
[19] *Ibid.*
[20] *Ibid.*, p. 482.

lie to despair: "I was not wearier where I lay." Dublin is an arid land that withers the creative impulse, and eventually the artist leaves as Joyce and Stephen did—not to escape from life but to experience it freely and fully. During the formative years of incubation, however, the artist transcends rather than flees his environment. He sustains a creative tension between detachment and empathy, an equiponderance of disengagement and commitment, and, in balancing these antitheses, creates a coherent [262] world of purposive order. We see, then, that Little Chandler will never realize his dream of becoming a poet, for he has fled from life into the sterile world of his own identity. Immersed in self-pity and insensitivity, he has become a part of the squalor he loathes.

It is ironic that this indifference to life that Joyce satirizes in Little Chandler is the very quality which critics have attributed to Joyce himself. Confusing what Joyce has firmly implied about the life of the artist with what he has Stephen say in *A Portrait of the Artist* about the artist's technique, critics often assume that Joyce conceived of the ideal artist as being one who, like Little Chandler, turns away from the realities of life and lives in a world of his own creation. Stephen Dedalus's well-known distinction in *A Portrait of the Artist* among the lyric, epic, and dramatic forms on the basis of increasing impersonality in the writer has given rise to this general misconception about Joyce's aesthetics. Stephen's description of the artist as "the God of the creation . . . beyond or above his handiwork invisible, refined out of existence, indifferent, paring his fingernails,"[21] together with Joyce's personal life as an exile and his obscurity as a writer, has encouraged some people to think of Joyce as a *précieux*, an Oscar Wilde or Rimbaud dedicated to art for art's sake with no prevailing interest in the problems of man. To David Daiches, for example, Joyce's work rings alarums to signal a confused evacuation of the world: "It is the aim of the artist who, upset by the confusion and disintegration of values in the world in which he grows up, feels compelled to escape from that world, within which his function as an artist is not clear, and to evoke a view of art which makes that escape into a virtue."[22]

Now no one will question that Joyce's work expresses perplexities regarding religion, politics, family life, and sex,[23] but that there was

---

[21] *Ibid.*, pp. 481–482.

[22] "James Joyce: The Artist as Exile," p. 71.

[23] On the other hand, what modern author's work does not? In every serious literary work there is a discrepancy between the way things are and the way they ought to be, between the world as the author finds it and the world as the author wishes it to be. For an author upset by "a distintegration of values," Joyce managed to retain a rather astonishing stock of not unconventional beliefs. Judging from his work, and what we know of his life, there was certainly nothing confused or ambiguous about his detestation of materialism, puritanism, hedon-

in Joyce himself a parallel confusion about the [263] function of the artist is emphatically contradicted by his work. In *Stephen Hero* and *A Portrait of the Artist,* for example, it is just this concept of the artist which emerges clearly and vividly from the confusion surrounding other problems. And that Joyce ever considered escape from life a virtue is equally doubtful. In *Dubliners* escape from life is condemned not only in "A Little Cloud" but in "A Painful Case," with its dreary portrait of James Duffy, who lives a spiritually exhausted existence cut off from communion with others. There is, too, the case of Richard Rowan in *Exiles,* whose tragedy is implicit in his stolid rejection of normal human needs,[24] and there are *Ulysses* and *Finnegans Wake,* two novels which are, contrary to general opinion, far more deeply concerned with the universal and elemental problems of man than are, say, *An American Tragedy* or *Main Street.* Nor should it be forgotten that *A Portrait of the Artist* has for a conclusion the Whitmanesque apostrophe, "Welcome, O life! I go to encounter for the millionth time the reality of experience and to forge in the smithy of my soul the uncreated conscience of my race."

As the conclusion to *A Portrait of the Artist* suggests, Joyce hoped that his work would sweep a wide arc across the world. For the coterie writer, with his intimate little circle of disciples, Joyce felt a profound contempt.[25] The coterie writer is cauterized in "A Little Cloud" when Little Chandler, standing on Grattan Bridge and dreaming vacantly on Fame, observes: "He would never be popular: he saw that. He could not sway the crowd but he might appeal to a little circle of kindred minds." That Little Chandler foreshadows in this passage the literary reputation of his creator is a coincidence of transcendent irony. The complexity of Joyce's later work took him out of the marketplace and into "a little circle [264] of kindred minds," but he always wished that it could have been otherwise. In fact, Joyce's personal tragedy may well have been that his own literary reputation

ism, war, mass conformity, cruelty, injustice, mediocrity, hypocrisy, bigotry, promiscuity, tyranny; nor about his profound faith in and devotion to art, love, literature, music, laughter, friendship, marriage, freedom, kindness, peace, sincerity, and personal integrity.

[24] For a provocative analysis, see Hugh Kenner, "Joyce's 'Exiles,'" *Hudson Review,* V (1952), 389–403.

[25] Cf. Gorman, p. 283. Gorman's biography gives a very flattering and idealized picture of Joyce as a sublimely independent writer who was haughtily contemptuous of the opinion of the world. That erroneous view has been corrected by Magalaner and Kain, who point out that Joyce worried inordinately about any criticism of his work, and that he desired desperately to be read and appreciated. During his famous correspondence with Grant Richards concerning the publication of *Dubliners,* for example, Joyce went to very great lengths indeed in an effort to get the collection published. In one letter to Richards—which Gorman omits—Joyce offered to drop five stories from *Dubliners* if the publishers would agree to print the rest. (See Marvin Magalaner and Richard M. Kain, *Joyce: The Man, The work, The Reputation* [New York, 1956], p. 20.)

could not be consistent with his idealized concept of the artist's influential place in the world. Stephen Dedalus's surname, it will be recalled, was inspired by that of St. Stephen, the martyr who was torn apart by a mob, and Joyce doubtless fancied himself in that role. He may have come to realize, however, that being torn apart by the mob is not more painful than being sneered at and ignored by it. And yet Joyce hungered for a world of readers: his favorite image of himself was Jolas's cartoon of him as a derby-hatted, bespectacled serpent benignly enfolding the globe in its coils. It is difficult to think of a writer more concerned with the world than was James Joyce.

In regard to Joyce's aesthetics, it should not be forgotten that the serene detachment apotheosized by Stephen in *A Portrait of the Artist* is delivered not as a prescription for the ordering of the artist's life but as an extolment of a literary method analogous to that which Keats referred to as "negative capability" when he paid tribute to Shakespeare. This method requires that the artist omit from his work any vestige of himself. In the creative act the vital imagination refines away the subjectivity of the artist as impure ingredients are burned from a ceramic in the white heat of a flaming kiln: "The personality of the artist, at first a cry or a cadence or a mood and then a fluid and lambent narrative, finally refines itself out of existence, impersonalizes itself. . . ."[26] This is the formula for what Stephen calls "the dramatic form," wherein, he explains, the artist "presents his image in immediate relation to others." Here we take note of an important point: commensurate with the artist's progress toward this ultimate "dramatic form"—from the inchoate "lyrical form," wherein the artist "presents his image in immediate relation to himself," through the penultimate "epical form," wherein he "presents his image in mediate relation to himself and others"[27]—he moves out of himself and into the living world, into "the common tide of other lives."

Here we have treated two different aspects of Joyce's aesthetics. The gathering of the artist's materials has to do with one aspect—his experience in life; the process by which he forges experience into beauty has to do with another—his technique or method, the [265] creative act itself. This bifurcation of life and art is pointed out by Joyce in *Exiles* when the protagonist, Richard Rowan, a writer, confuses the two processes and attempts to approach his personal life with the detachment and objectivity of an artist creating in "the dramatic form." He discovers that neither his wife nor his friend can be manipulated like characters in a novel—at the end of the novel they refuse to resolve the plot Richard has created—nor can Richard as a husband and a father detach himself emotionally from a conflict he has deliberately instigated. The failure of Richard's experiment shows the

[26] *A Portrait of the Artist*, p. 481.
[27] *Ibid.*

inability of the artist to deal with life in the objective spirit with which he organizes and formulates it in a work of art. In Joyce's aesthetics, the experiential and the technical are, then, two different phenomena. To treat them as identical is to imagine Joyce in far off Switzerland or Paris creating his Ireland like the God of creation bringing to life his handiwork from the remote heavens. The simile is absurd. For unlike the artist, and especially unlike the artist Joyce, who once wrote that ". . . he is a very bold man who dares to alter . . . whatever he has seen or heard,"[28] Almighty God does not partake morally and physically in the experience of His creation. He is not pushed into a mudhole at Clongowes, smacked with a pandybat, nor smitten crazily in love by an Irish colleen. In other words, the artist does not share with Divinity any such mystic separation from the life he *recreates* in ordered form from the tumult of life's experiences.

Joyce was Ireland's exile, not life's. Far from being an escapist, "Joyce renews our apprehension of reality," states Harry Levin, "strengthens our sympathy with our fellow creatures, and leaves us in awe before the mystery of created things."[29] Believing with Aquinas that art is "the human disposition of sensible or intelligible matter for an aesthetic end,"[30] Joyce was an empiricist who insisted that the artist was, for better or worse, rooted in an extended, objective reality. To him, life's exiles were the pure conceptualist, the Celtic revivalist living in the past, and the confirmed romanticist "who sees no fit abode here for his ideals." He realized that the romanticist's denial of reality could be a thinly concealed affirmation of his ego. There is a parallel, for example, between [266] the episode in which Little Chandler on Grattan Bridge stands pondering the depths of his poetic soul as he gazes at his own reflection in the water, and the scene in which Stephen Dedalus in *A Portrait of the Artist* sits down to describe in verse an experience with his beloved on a Dublin tram. We have already had occasion to follow the direction of Little Chandler's poetic mood on Grattan Bridge and to remark on the little clerk's ridiculous self-aggrandizement. In a similar situation, Stephen fares scarely better. As Stephen sits down to write, instead of evoking palpable details he introspectively broods until he finds a mélange of clichés about "the night and the balmy breeze and the maiden lustre of the moon." His experiment in verse produces no objective correlatives, no epiphanies:

Now it seemed as if he would fail again but, by dint of brooding on the incident, he thought himself into confidence. During this process all those elements which he deemed common and insignificant fell out of the scene.

[28] Quoted in Gorman, p. 150.
[29] Introduction, *James Joyce*, ed. cit., p. 16.
[30] *A Portrait of the Artist*, p. 472.

There remained no trace of the tram itself nor of the trammen nor of the horses: nor did he or she appear vividly.[31]

"Afterwards," Joyce observes wryly, "he went into his mother's bedroom and gazed at his face for a long time in the mirror of her dressing table." Stephen's romantic afflatus, like Little Chandler's, fans only the ego.

But what is merely an ephemeral stage of immaturity in Stephen is an instance of arrested development in Little Chandler. Little Chandler's fixed puerility is revealed again in the story by his witless devotion to Byron's poetry.[32] Appropriately, the lines Little Chandler quotes from Byron were written when the poet was fourteen. They are also appropriate because they express Little Chandler's lachrymose disposition and represent the kind of turgid doggerel Philistines applaud as "great poetry." Byron's lines have their chief function, however, in defining the limitations of Little Chandler's poetic sensibilities. Nowhere but in Wordsworth's exalted imagination is the child the father of the man. Nor, for that matter, could the poetic mind which conceived of such an [267] astonishing abstraction have been tainted by childishness. When Little Chandler quotes Byron's silly lines we realize, as we have elsewhere in the story, that he will never be a poet because he is, after all, merely a child. In Joyce's mind Byron was associated with adolescence. Stephen Dedalus wrote his first verses in imitation of Byron,[33] and on another occasion defends him to his classmates as the greatest of poets.[34] As a child, Joyce worshipped Byron,[35] although with maturity his literary gods changed from Byron to Ibsen, Zola, and Rimbaud, just as Stephen's idols change from Byron and Newman to Ibsen and Hauptmann. Stephen's Byron, even in adolescence, is obviously not the same as Little Chandler's. To Stephen, Byron is a fellow rebel in the Satanic uprising, a kindred spirit echoing Stephen's cry *Non serviam!* To Little Chandler, he is a reflection of his own childish melancholy and self-absorption.

Little Chandler's pathetic immaturity is again demonstrated in the second episode of the story, after he has left Grattan Bridge to join his friend Gallaher at Corless's restaurant. In this second episode

[31] *Ibid.*, p. 317.
[32] Little Chandler quotes from Byron's "On the Death of a Very Young Lady":

> Hushed are the winds and still the evening gloom,
> Not e'en a Zephyr wanders through the grove,
> Whilst I return to view my Margaret's tomb
> And scatter flowers on the dust I love.

"How melancholy it was!" exclaims Little Chandler. "Could he, too, express the melancholy of his soul in verse?"
[33] *A Portrait of the Artist*, p. 318.
[34] *Ibid.*, p. 329.
[35] Magalaner and Kain, p. 30.

he also reveals that he lacks what every artist has in abundance—the ability to distinguish between appearance and reality. Far from being the towering success Little Chandler thinks he is, Gallaher is a fake and a failure. He has all the conventional symbols of bourgeois triumph—a cosmopolitan vocabulary, expensive clothes, presumably an exciting position in London—but these are fronts to conceal his provinciality and insecurity. Although Little Chandler senses vaguely that there is "something vulgar" about his friend, he quickly attributes it to "the hustle and bustle of the Press." (Like Leopold Bloom in his most relaxed moments, Little Chandler always thinks in clichés and platitudes.) He cannot recognize the real Gallaher for the good reason that Gallaher is his own counterpart, his alter ego, just as the brash boss and his cowed employee in "Counterparts" are doubles in spite of their apparent differences. Consistent with Joyce's technique of "double-writing," Little Chandler and Gallaher appear to be contrasted: Little Chandler is small, Gallaher is large; Little Chandler has remained in Dublin, his friend has gone abroad; Little Chandler is mild and subdued, Gallaher bold and [268] vociferous. Nevertheless these are superficies as deceptive as Gallaher's orange tie and rodomontades.

In the important things, they are similar. Both men are writers (the ironic implication being that Gallaher's newspaper work is no more profitable to himself nor significant to others than Little Chandler's "tiresome writing" at King's Inns). Both are imbued with a melancholy resignation to what they believe is the immitigable stupidity and hopelessness of life: "I'll tell you my opinion," remarks Gallaher, "it's a rum world. . . ." Each is troubled by the prospect of old age, for in "A Little Cloud," as in Mr. Prufrock's plaintive love song, Time is the last refuge of Life's prodigal. On Grattan Bridge Little Chandler had hopefully reassured himself that he was "not so old—thirty-two," and now at Corless's Gallaher inquires pathetically, "Do you see any signs of aging in me—eh, what? A little grey and thin on the top— what?" Both men are afraid of life—Little Chandler remaining in Dublin because he is too timid to leave and Gallaher running away because he is too cowardly to stay. The elemental sameness of the two is emphasized when the obsequious Little Chandler, who has been squirming petulantly before his friend's oppressive hauteur, suddenly seizes an advantage by slyly suggesting that perhaps Gallaher has lost his last chance to make a good marriage. For a revealing moment, Little Chandler slips easily into the role of his bullying counterpart, and we see that the differences between the two are merely symptomatical in that one manifests his neurosis as an introvert, the other as an extrovert.

Whereas the episode at Corless's finds Little Chandler and the big and noisy Gallaher in ironic juxtaposition, the concluding episode at Little Chandler's home shows him and his tiny but equally noisy

child in a similar ironic contrast. Little Chandler exchanges identities
as readily with the child as he did with Gallaher. At the beginning
of the scene, the child bursts into tears and wailing when Little
Chandler roars at him; at the conclusion, the baby is mollified and
it is Little Chandler who weeps. We see that Little Chandler is indeed
capable of change, not to the poet he dreams of becoming, but to an
insensitive bully, as when he reverses roles with Gallaher, or to a
crying baby, as when he exchanges identities with the child. Hence
the last two episodes of "A Little Cloud" are similar to the first two
books of *Gulliver's Travels* in that both view a man from the two
ends of a telescope. [269] Although Little Chandler hungers to "express
the melancholy of his soul in verse," to ascend out of the depths of
his solitary confinement to the lunar heights of the poet, he can do no
more than expand into a garrulous bully or shrink into an infant, always remaining his own inadequate self, like an inflatable ball that
changes in size but never in substance. By the end of the story we
realize the truth of his hollow cry, "It was useless, useless! He was a
prisoner for life."

His life is marked for unfulfillment because, unlike Stephen Dedalus's, its vital forces have been centripetal instead of centrifugal,
have flowed back toward the ego instead of outward into "the common
tide of others"; and now, therefore, his relationship with others becomes
only a grotesque duplication of himself. As he looks at his wife's
photograph, for example, he grows irritated: "Why had he married the
eyes in the photograph?" The answer is that his wife—finicky, neat,
and passionless—is a replica of himself. When he gazes at her photograph, it is as though he were seeing his own reflection in a mirror:
"He looked coldly into the eyes of the photograph and they answered
him coldly."

Ironically, then, Little Chandler's timorous evasion of life has
made any real escape from it impossible, just as Stephen Dedalus's
detachment has, in contrast, enabled him to come to terms with it
and perceive its true pattern. Stephen's detachment represents not a
repudiation of life but a purposive withdrawal to a position from which
it can be viewed more fully. For to Joyce—as to Conrad—life is for
the idealist that destructive element in which he must immerse himself.
It is Stephen's mother who takes the part of a Little Chandler when she
remarks in *Stephen Hero* that she is grateful to art for providing her
with a means of escaping from life, whereupon Stephen retorts: "But
that is wrong: that is the great mistake everyone makes. Art is not
an escape from life! . . . Art's just the opposite. Art, on the contrary,
is the very central expression of life. The artist affirms out of the fulness
of his own life. . . ."[36] Stephen expresses the same idea more elo-
quently in his essay on aesthetics: [270]

[36] *Stephen Hero*, p. 86.

The poet is the intense centre of the life of his age to which he stands in a relation than which none can be more vital. He alone is capable of absorbing in himself the life that surrounds him and flinging it abroad again amid planetary music.[37]

Thus, when "A Little Cloud" is studied in its context with Joyce's other early works, its dimensions quite exceed those of the simple story about married life described by Stanislaus Joyce. By showing how a would-be artist failed to realize his transcendent dream, Joyce has, in a negative way, clearly defined the nature of the true artist and his proper role in life. As we have seen, "A Little Cloud" proclaims the classical virtues of the artist. It teaches us that the genuine artist is not like Little Chandler—a cloud floating above mankind, empty except of rain, and darkening the earth; but like the sun—radiating warmth, sweetness, and light. [271]

[37] *Ibid.*, p. 80. Of Stephen's essay, Joyce states: "Its merit lay in its por-trayal of externals; the realm of its princes was the realm of the manners and customs of societies—a spacious realm" (*ibid.*, p. 78). Compare this statement with Stephen's definition of "the romantic temper," *supra*, p. 259.

Character and Structure in "Counterparts"

JOHN V. HAGOPIAN

"COUNTERPARTS" HAS NOT RECEIVED MUCH CRITICAL ATTENTION FROM Joyce scholars. Even Marvin Magalaner, who deplores the fact that *Dubliners* "has been so throughly ignored by critics,"[1] pays so little attention to this story that he does not even see fit to mention it in his index. Hugh Kenner gives "Counterparts" merely one brief para-graph,[2] and many other examples of indifference could easily be cited. Perhaps the explanation for such neglect is that the story appears to be transparently clear—a simple, realistic narrative written with what

[1] Marvin Magalaner, *Time of Apprenticeship*, p. 7.
[2] Hugh Kenner, *Dublin's Joyce* (London, 1955), p. 57.

From John V. Hagopian, "Counterparts," in John V. Hagopian and Martin Dolch, eds., *Insight II.* Frankfurt: Hirschgraben-Verlag, 1964. Pp. 201–206. Also published as "The Epiphany in Joyce's 'Counterparts,'" *Studies in Short Fiction,* I (Summer 1964), 272–276. Reprinted by permission of the editors and the publisher.

Joyce, himself, called a "certain scrupulous brute force."[3] But it is the brute force rather than the scrupulosity that has been noted, and it is always a mistake to assume that any work of Joyce's will not yield new insights upon close analysis. Although "Counterparts" is by no means one of the richer stories in *Dubliners,* it is (with "The Boarding House") one of two which left Joyce "uncommonly well pleased,"[4] and when he was forced by the publishers to make certain changes he wrote, "I will not conceal from you that I think I have injured these stories by these deletions."[5] In other words, "Counterparts" is a carefully made story which Joyce himself valued rather highly and therefore seems to deserve closer examination than it has heretofore received.

The central character, Farrington, is a scrivener, and the scrivener has almost assumed an archetypal significance in modern literature as the meaningless man, an insignificant victim of the brute forces of society or the universe. In Gogol's "The Overcoat" he was a sentimental, pathetic figure; in Melville's "Bartleby" he was a pale, passive, and futile rebel; in Joyce's "Counterparts" he is a whining, brainless brute. As a Dubliner, Farrington belongs to the "most hopeless, useless, and inconsistent race of charlatans I have ever come across, on the island or on the continent . . . At night when he can hold no more and is swollen up with poison like a toad, he staggers from the side-door, [201] and . . . he goes 'arsing along' as we say in English. There's the Dubliner for you."[6]

Critics have already noted that the images in "Counterparts" suggest that Farrington has been dehumanized by the mechanical nature of his environment. As Hugh Kenner says, he is a "copying-machine geared to a law-machine."[7] As the story opens, "the bell rang furiously . . . Miss Parker went to the tube . . . returned to her machine." Later, Mr. Alleyne's fist "seemed to vibrate like the knob of some electric machine" in Farrington's face. And Kenner's reading would seem to have become definitive; Florence L. Walzl echoes it in one of the most recent studies:

In "Counterparts" the miserliness, dullness, and petty tyranny of a business office destroy initiative and spirit. A very ordinary man, Farrington, trapped by economic need and too weak to rebel, is turned into a brute who visits upon his innocent son at night the ignominy and punishment he has suffered himself all day. The mechanical office routine and clattering, impersonal machines image the sterility of modern business. The unproductive work dehumanizes Farrington as man and father.[8]

[3] Richard Ellmann, *James Joyce* (New York, 1959), p. 217.
[4] *Ibid.,* p. 216.
[5] *Ibid.,* p. 231.
[6] *Ibid.,* pp. 225–226.
[7] Kenner, *op. ct.,* p. 57.
[8] Florence L. Walzl, "Pattern of Paralysis in Joyce's *Dubliners,*" *College English* XXII (January 1961), 226.

This reading is derived from a superficial examination of the story, and if that is all there is to it, "Counterparts" is merely a piece of psycho-social realism with limited value as literary art, regardless of how well made it is. So much of Joyce has a deeper significance than that, has "the true scholastic stink" to it, that it might pay to see if we can sniff it out here.

The story has three parts: two long sequences dealing with events at the office and at the pub, and a brief, whip-lash conclusion at Farrington's home. Each develops a crisis for Farrington, and he responds with gradually increasing intensities of fury. First is the suppressed expression of rage when he reacts to Mr. Alleyne's "Do you take me for a fool?" with the witticism "I don't think, sir, that that's a fair question to put to me"; then a more violent response when the curate at Mulligan's pub comments approvingly on Weathers' victory over Farrington in the trial of strength, "What the hell do you know about it? . . . What do you put in your gab for?" Then, finally, when he strikes his son for letting the fire go out, "Take that, you little whelp!" It is true that in the first part of the story Farrington's humanity has been so reduced by his mechanical environment that Joyce never even refers to him by his name—twenty-one times in the first eight pages he is cited simply as "the man." But in the four pages devoted to the pub scenes he is twenty-two times referred to as "Farrington." It appears to be very important that after he leaves the office and pawns his watch (another mechanical symbol) he walks along "joyfully," feels a "proud satisfaction" at having money, and stares "masterfully" at the office girls. At Davy Byrne's he feels a "great vivacity," finds the drinks "very exhilarating," and for the first time smiles. To be sure, the pubs [202] do not provide a very satisfactory solution to his problems—"he had not even got drunk"—but when he leaves for home he is a man with an identity and a name, not a mere mechanical force. Hence, he is personally responsible for his behaviour to his son.

Many of the stories in *Dubliners* focus on one of the seven deadly sins; the sin in "Counterparts" is wrath. Beginning with "furiously" and "furious" in the very first sentence, specific references to feelings of rage, anger, savagery, violence, passion, and abuse recur frequently throughout the story. It may be said that Farrington and Mr. Alleyne are "counterparts" specifically in their expressions of wrath. (They are also alike in that each is an ineffectual man in a junior position in his rank. Just as Farrington is a copy-clerk subordinate to Mr. Shelley, Alleyne is the junior partner of the firm subordinate to Mr. Crosbie— he twice threatens to report Farrington to Mr. Crosbie.)

However, it is not quite accurate to say that they are exact counterparts. In physical appearance they are diametrically opposed. Farrington is tall and of great bulk, with a dark, wine-coloured face and a moustache; while Mr. Alleyne is a dwarfish little man, pink-headed and clean-shaven. Also, Farrington is a native Dubliner while

Mr. Alleyne is an Orangeman[9] with a North of Ireland accent. But more important is the fact that Mr. Alleyne's wrath stems from a justified indignation over Farrington's incompetence as a copyist, while the latter's wrath derives from his constantly making a fool of himself. Farrington rages against perfectly innocent victims, but he is himself by no means an innocent victim. He does not complete his work on time, he does make mistakes, he does sneak out to the local pub while pretending to go to the toilet, he is not able to produce a complete file on the Delacour case. Thus, it would seem that Farrington is suffering from delusions of persecution and delighting in imaginative or substitute acts of revenge, some of them rather childish. For example, he has been caught mimicking Mr. Alleyne's North of Ireland accent and at the end of the story he mimics his son's flat accent. He enjoys planning a false story of his quip against Alleyne: "So I just looked at him—coolly, you know, and looked at her. Then I looked back at him again—taking my time, you know." But in the original scene he was by no means calm and cool: "almost before he was aware of it, his tongue had found a felicitous moment." He feels that Weathers must have cheated in beating him in the trial of strength: "You're not to put the weight of your body behind it. Play fair." And at his second defeat, he proves to be a bad loser, which is often a symptom of the paranoid personality. Finally, of course, his brutal treatment of his little boy gives him away completely.

The narrative focus is narrowly on Farrington. Even the language sometimes lapses into the central character's idiom: "Blast it! He couldn't finish it in time" and "That was the dart! Why didn't he think of it sooner?" but the [203] narrator's presence is felt in this story (as it is not, for example, in "Eveline") by observations and poetic metaphors that Farrington could not possibly be aware of: "the barometer of his nature was set for a spell of riot." It is also felt in the fact that the story is not merely a smooth flow of realistically rendered experiences. The second and third parts of the story (marked by dotted lines or extra-wide paragraph spacing in most editions) both begin with summaries of the preceding action. In other words, the structure of the story is more obviously signalled than in most of the *Dubliners.*

The ending of "Counterparts" is characterized by a complete shift to the dramatic mode; the narrator withdraws to let the action suddenly speed up toward the powerful close in a sequence of stichomythic dialogue and violent action. Wrath is finally released without any restraints, and the little boy's pathetic and futile plea is completely powerless to stop the fury that has been building up in Farrington all

---

[9] "Orangeman" is now a generic term referring to any Irishman who is loyal to Northern (i.e., Protestant and British, since the days of William of *Orange*) Ireland, in contrast to one who "wears the green" (i.e., the shamrock) on St. Patrick's Day.

day. The conclusion, furthermore, although it has all the surface appearance of Zolaesque realism, is really something quite different. It is one of Joyce's epiphanies, and as is characteristic of the *Dubliners* it comes at the end of the story. Hugh Kenner says of the last line of "The Boarding House," "This is the precarious instant of focus. The story is at that point of balance where the smallest touch will send its extremes into oscillation."[10] The same is true of the last lines of "Counterparts": "I'll say a Hail Mary for you, pa, if you don't beat me . . . I'll say a Hail Mary . . ." In a sudden flash of revelation, we see that the depiction of a seamy side of Dublin life was not an end in itself, that the first two parts of the story actually constitute one long prologue to the final insight—namely, that only a child could be so naive as to believe that the forces of religion and the promise of prayer might stem the tide of the deadly sin of Wrath. Irene Hendry has long ago instructed us that "in *Dubliners, claritas* is achieved most often, although not always, through an apparently trivial incident, action, or single detail which differs from the others making up the story only in that it illuminates them, integrates them, and gives them meaning."[11] In "Counterparts" it is little Tom Farrington's offer to pray that best fits her description. Joyce's technique is such that he could not possibly make the point of the story explicit, but it resounds at the end of "Counterparts" as if he had struck an immense Oriental gong. [204]

[10] Hugh Kenner, *op. cit.*, p. 49.
[11] Irene Hendry, "Joyce's Epiphanies," in John W. Aldridge, ed., *Critiques and Essays on Modern Fiction 1920–51* (New York, 1952), p. 131. Her essay originally appeared in the *Sewanee Review* (Summer 1946).

Virgin and Witch

MARVIN MAGALANER AND RICHARD M. KAIN

THE STORY "CLAY" SHOWS MOST CLEARLY THE OPERATION OF SYMBOLISM on several levels simultaneously.[1] Though a quick reading may deceive the reader into thinking that the sketch concerns nothing more than the frustrated longings of a timid old maid for the joys of life, a husband, children, and romance, careful examination leads to discovery of interesting patterns. All the social relationships in the story, for

[1] Joyce changed the name of this story from "Hallow Eve" to "Clay." See Gorman, *James Joyce*, p. 145.

From Marvin Magalaner and Richard M. Kain, *Joyce: the Man, the Work, the Reputation.* New York: New York University Press, 1956. Pp. 95–101. Reprinted by permission of the authors and the publisher.

instance, are awry. Maria should be married but is not. Alphy and Joe, though brothers, fight continually. Mrs. Donnelly strives to keep peace in the family by calming her drunken husband. The laundresses quarrel often. The saleswoman in the cake shop is impudent to the most inoffensive of customers. The young men on the tram will not rise to give her a seat. And even the innocent children are half accused of stealing the missing cakes. Through this maze of human unpleasantness moves the old maid, Maria, a steadying and moderating influence on all those who have dealings with her.

Her role as peacemaker is stressed. In the Protestant laundry, she "was always sent for when the women quarrelled over their tubs and always succeeded in making peace." Her employer compliments her on her ability as mediator: "Maria, you are a veritable peace-maker." Her calm moderation alone keeps Ginger Mooney from using violence against the "dummy who had charge of the irons." "Everyone," says Joyce, "was so fond of Maria." And rightly so. Her tact prevents a family quarrel over the loss of a nutcracker when she quickly says that "she didn't like nuts and that they [95] weren't to bother about her." Though she does not wish a drink of wine offered by Joe, she "let him have his way." Maria's function as peacemaker, dovetailing as it does with a great many other details of the story, suggests the hypothesis that Joyce intended to build up a rough analogy between the laundry worker Maria and the Virgin Mary. Along certain lines, the relationship is fairly obvious.

Maria, of course, is a variant of the name Mary. Certainly there is nothing subtle about the associations that the name of the main character evokes. The Virgin is well known for her role as peacemaker, for the invocations to her, especially by women, to prevent conflict. Accordingly, she is invoked ("sent for") whenever the laundresses argue and she "always succeeded in making peace." Without her restraining and comforting influence, much more violence would occur. There is surely a suggestion of the church in Maria, for, like Mrs. Kearney and the two sisters, she offers a form of Communion to the women by distributing the barmbracks (raisin bread) and beverage.

Carrying the analogy further, Joyce makes much of the fact that Maria is a virgin. At the same time, and this is significant, she has children, though they are not born from her womb. "She had nursed . . . [Joe] and Alphy too; and Joe used often to say: 'Mamma is mamma but Maria is my proper mother.'" There would seem to be no reason, in a very short story, to quote Joe directly here unless more was intended by the author than the bare statement that Maria had aided his mother in bringing up her sons. There are additional Biblical parallels too. In the Gospel according to Luke, it is Elizabeth who announces to Mary that she is blessed and will have blessed offspring. Interestingly enough, in "Clay" it is Lizzie (Elizabeth) Fleming, Maria's co-worker in the laundry, who "said Maria was sure to get the ring and, though Fleming had said that for so many Hallow Eves, Maria had to laugh and say she didn't want any ring or man either. . . ."

Other similarities crowd in to lend support to the idea. Maria works in a laundry,[2] where things are made clean; Mary is the instrument of cleansing on the spiritual plane. All the children sing for Maria, and two bear gifts to her on a Whitmonday trip. That one gift is a purse has ironic meaning in Joyce's mercenary Dublin. The laundress finds her appearance "nice" and "tidy" "in spite of its years," perhaps a circumspect way of saying that, after centuries, the freshness [96] of Mary as a symbol is still untarnished. On the other hand, Maria finds on the tram that she is ignored by the young men and in the bakeshop treated insolently by the young girl. Only the elderly and the slightly drunk treat her with the respect which she enjoys but which she is too timid to demand. The meaning for Joyce of this situation needs no spelling out. The fact, finally, that Maria gets the prayer book, in the game of the three dishes, and is therefore slated to enter a convent and retire from the world is additional evidence of the author's symbolic intent.

Joyce is not content, however, with working on this single level. He has accomplished one purpose. Just as in *Ulysses* the juxtaposition of the heroic age and the human—of wily Odysseus and sly Leopold Bloom—serves to point up the contrast between the glory that was Greece and the mundane sphere that was Dublin for the artist of 1900, so the superimposition of modern Maria upon the ancient and venerable symbol of Mary is aesthetically effective. Now he goes a step beyond.

The story, originally entitled "Hallow Eve," takes place on the spooky night of the thirty-first of October, "the night set apart for a universal walking abroad of spirits, both of the visible and invisible world; for . . . one of the special characteristics attributed to this mystic evening, is the faculty conferred on the immaterial principle in humanity to detach itself from its corporeal tenement and wander abroad through the realms of space. . . ."[3] Putting this more bluntly than Joyce would have wished, Maria on the spirit level is a witch on this Halloween night, and as a traditional witch Joyce describes her. "Maria was a very, very small person indeed but she had a very long nose and a very long chin." To fix this almost caricature description in the minds of his readers, the author repeats that "when she laughed . . . the tip of her nose nearly met the tip of her chin." And two sentences further on, he reiterates the information for the third time,

[2] For Joyce's comment on the significance of the name, *Dublin by Lamplight Laundry,* see his letters to Stanislaus Joyce in *Letters,* ed. Richard Ellmann (New York: Viking Press, 1966), II, 186 and 192. [Eds.]

[3] Robert Chambers, *The Book of Days: A Miscellany of Popular Antiquities, etc.* (Edinburgh, 1864), II, 519.

and for a fourth before the story is through. The intention is very plain. In addition to these frequent iterations, Joyce's first sentence in "Clay" —and his story openings are almost always frought with special meaning—discloses that this was "her evening out." By right it should be, for witches walk abroad on Allhallow Eve. In itself, however, implying that the old woman is a witch is of minor significance. It derives fuller meaning from the illusion-reality motif.

This motif is central to the story, gives it, in fact, its point. [97] Halloween is famous for its masquerades, its hiding of identities of celebrants, conjuring tricks, illusions of goblins and ghosts—in other words, famed for the illusions that are created in the name of celebrating the holiday. It is a night on which it is hard to tell the material from the spiritual, witch from woman, ghost from sheeted youngster. On this night, things are not what they seem.

In the first paragraph, Joyce touches gently upon the motif more than once. Maria's work in the kitchen is done. Barmbracks have been prepared. It is legitimate to wonder whether the baking was done in accordance with this Irish custom: unmarried girls would knead a cake "with their left thumbs . . . in mute solemnity; a single word would have broken the charm and destroyed their ardent hopes of beholding their future husbands in their dreams after having partaken of the mystic 'dumb-cake.' "[4] The finished barmbracks "seemed uncut; but if you went closer you would see that they had been cut into long thick even slices and were ready. . . . Maria had cut them herself." The contrast between the illusion of wholeness and the reality of the actual slices is given prominent mention only because it belongs within the larger framework of the motif. Also, in the same paragraph, the cook delights in the cleanliness of the big copper boilers in which "you could see yourself," another reference to illusion, possibly connected in Joyce's mind with the Allhallow Eve custom of looking into a mirror to see one's future husband.

In other respects, also, the spirits are at work in this story. Things, as things, lose their materiality and become invisible. At least they are missing and cannot be found. The plum cake disappears. "Nobody could find the nutcrackers." Finally, Joe trying to locate the corkscrew, "could not find what he was looking for." Maria herself is ambiguous, sometimes more a disembodied spirit than a person. Her body, though it exists, is "very, very small," and a hearty burst of laughter grips her "till her minute body nearly shook itself asunder." On this night she is able to get outside her body, almost, and look at it objectively: "she looked with quaint affection at the diminutive body which she had so often adorned . . . she found it a nice tidy little body."

It is in dreams, however, that Maria is able to put the greatest

[4] E. H. Sechrist, *Red Letter Days* (Philadelphia: Macrae-Smith Company, 1940), p. 179. I believe that Mr. Leonard Albert of Hunter College first discussed witchcraft in "Clay" with me.

distance between illusion, namely, the love and adventure which have never entered her life, and reality, the drab, methodical existence of a servant in a laundry. Or if not [98] in dreams, in the reverie induced by a dream song, "I dreamt that I dwelt in marble halls." The whole story builds up to this central split, at which point all the minor examples of the thin line between fantasy and actuality attain meaning and stature. In these rich and sensuous lines, sung in a "tiny quavering voice" by Maria, are packed the antitheses to the frustrating life of the average Dubliner. Mary in contemporary life has decayed in scope to Maria and is no more imposing a spiritual figure than a witch on a broomstick. The marble halls have been converted into laundry kitchens. Most tragic of all, there is no one in the world to whom the old maid can, with truth, sing "that you loved me just the same." In Maria's rendition of the song, she inadvertently omits the second and third stanzas and carelessly sings the first verse twice. Joyce emphasizes that "no one tried to show her her mistake." Little wonder that her audience remains tactfully silent about these missing verses:

> I dreamt that suitors sought my hand
> That knights on bended knee,
> And with vows no maiden heart could withstand,
> They pledged their faith to me.
>
> And I dreamt that one of that noble band
> Came forth my heart to claim,
> But I also dreamt, which charmed me most,
> That you loved me still the same.

Maria's error is probably attributable to an emotional block that prevents her from giving voice to remarks so obviously at variance with the reality of her dull life. Leopold Bloom suffers a similar lapse when of Boylan's affair with Molly he speaks of "the wife's admirers" and then in confusion adds, "The wife's advisers, I mean."[5]

Joyce's decision to change the title of the story from "Hallow Eve" to "Clay" shifts the emphasis from the singing of the song to the ceremony of the three dishes. This familiar Irish fortunetelling game requires blindfolded players to select from a group of traditional objects the one which, so the story goes, will be symbolically revelatory of their future life. Poor Maria puts her fingers into a dish which the thoughtless children have jokingly filled with clay. She is to get neither the prayer book (life in a convent) or the ring (marriage). Death is her fate. There is a subdued shock when even the insensitive [99] people present at the Halloween party realize the symbolic significance

---

[5] Joyce, *Ulysses* (New York: Random House, 1934), p. 307.

of selecting clay as an omen of things to come. Joyce, leaving nothing to chance, has earlier prepared the reader for the symbolic action by showing that Maria is half in love with easeful death: "She had her plants . . . and she liked looking after them. She had lovely ferns and wax-plants. . . ." The emblems of the Virgin Mary, it is interesting to note, are unlike the others, late-flowering plants and late-blossoming trees.

Joyce was a very young writer when he wrote "Clay." He seems uncertain where to place the emphasis, and perhaps he allows too many motifs, even though a tenuous connection among them does exist, to deflect from the central point of his narrative. Perhaps he has not sufficiently reinforced the relationship between the witch and the Virgin,[6] though the history of the church holiday actually establishes all the parallel background he needs: The day set aside in honor of saints (like Mary) by Boniface IV has had its eve perverted by celebrants to the calling forth of witches. The two supernormal female figures, the saint and the witch, share this holiday. The writer who was soon to wrestle with the intricacies of interlocking symbolic levels in *Ulysses* was in "Clay" learning his trade. The result is a much more complicated story than commentators in the past have discovered.

In the B.B.C. magazine, *The Listener* (March 25, 1954), Stanislaus Joyce takes issue with such "scientific" explication of the early works of his brother as has been attempted in this chapter. He attacks particularly an "American critic," undoubtedly Magalaner, who "finds in the short story 'The Clay' [sic] three levels of significance on which Maria is successively herself a witch and the Virgin Mary." He continues:

Though such critics are quite at sea, they can still have the immense satisfaction of knowing that they have dived into deeper depths than the author they are criticising ever sounded. I am in a position to state definitely that my brother had no such subtleties in mind when he wrote the story. In justice, though, I must say that exaggerations like those I have mentioned are not typical of American criticism. . . .[7]

This type of personal-acquaintance criticism is understandably dangerous. What family of a deceased writer has not felt [100] that blood relationship and lifelong closeness afforded deeper insight into the writer's work than detached criticism could? This is a natural and healthy family tendency; yet the results, as evidenced in authorized biographies and critical studies by sons and grandsons and nephews

---

[6] For dissenting views on this point see the following: Richard Carpenter and Daniel Leary, "The Witch Maria," *James Joyce Review*, III (February 1959), 3–7; James R. Baker, "Ibsen, Joyce and the Living-Dead," in *A James Joyce Miscellany*, Series III, ed. Marvin Magalaner (Carbondale: Southern Illinois University Press, 1962), pp. 27–28. [Eds.]

[7] Stanislaus Joyce, "The Background to 'Dubliners,'" *The Listener*, LI (March 25, 1954), 526–527.

of nineteenth-century literary greats, are generally regarded with amusement or dismay by today's scholars. One should respect such prime sources of biographical information, but at the same time, one may suspect critical judgments enunciated by such sources as the last word, on, say, literary symbolism.

Stanislaus Joyce admits that *Ulysses* was "intended by its author" to have "various levels of significance." One wonders whether, if Joyce had not "leaked" his intention to Stuart Gilbert and others, Stanislaus would not be insisting equally on the "pernicious" quality of explications of that novel. It is very difficult to be sure of Joyce's intentions in his poetry and short stories, as it is in *A Portrait*. Eugene Jolas records how "Joyce blanched" when Jolas guessed merely what the title of *Finnegans Wake* was to be. "Ah, Jolas, you've taken something out of me," was the author's sad reply.[8] It is quite possible that the earlier Joyce might have been toying with the idea of multiple symbolic levels in the works before *Ulysses* without discussing his unformulated plans with his younger brother. [101]

[8] Eugene Jolas, "My Friend James Joyce," in *James Joyce, Two Decades of Criticism;* ed. Seon Givens (New York: The Vanguard Press, 1948), p. 16.

Isolation as Motif in "A Painful Case"

JOHN WILLIAM CORRINGTON

HUGH KENNER, WRITING OF "A PAINFUL CASE," HAS CALLED IT "THE heart of the matter," and there would seem to be excellent reason for his choice of words.

"A Painful Case" occupies the mid-point of the book. It gathers up, specifically, the implications of the third group: Chandler's loneliness, Farrington's automatism (Mr. Duffy "lived at a little distance from his body, regarding his own acts with doubtful sideglances"), Maria's living death.[1]

However we choose to measure and evaluate the course taken by Joyce in his development of *Dubliners*, "A Painful Case" serves as penultimate expression of the problems implicit throughout the stories.

[1] Hugh Kenner, *Dublin's Joyce*, Bloomington (1956), 58.

From John William Corrington, "Isolation as Motif in 'A Painful Case,' " *James Joyce Quarterly*, III (Spring 1966), 182–191. Reprinted by permission of the publisher.

In the original manuscript, before Joyce added "The Dead," "A Painful Case" was not only the fullest artistic and dramatic expression in the collection, but also the one upon which Joyce had placed the largest burden of his meaning. In terms of ideas and themes, "A Painful Case" very nearly equals "The Dead" as a kind of synthesizing and focussing medium which, while adding its own dimension to the collection, at the same time serves to sharpen our apprehension of all that Joyce has been patiently moving toward in *Dubliners*.

Mr. Duffy, it must be understood from the onset, is no ordinary man. By comparison with him, the faults and failings of all the characters who have gone before are relatively insignificant. Insofar as Dublin offers scope for great spiritual crime, Mr. Duffy can be said to have exercised himself to the full. If, as has been written, it requires as much energy and dedication to become a great sinner as a great saint, Mr. Duffy manages somehow to defy the rule. For at the root of his character, it seems to me, is a most peculiar blend of spiritual selfishness—and sloth. His predicament seems as much a result of having fallen willing victim to the laziness implicit in compulsive habit as to his terrifying and self-centered withdrawal from every potential contact with life. Duffy is indeed beyond the living death of Maria in "Clay," far beyond the naturalistic automatism of Farrington in "Counterparts." There is little drama in his situation (barring the neat translation of *Michael Kramer* in his desk); drama, by its nature, implies tumult, motion. But it is precisely this kind of thing that Duffy studies to avoid. His is an emptiness, a spiritual torpor fashioned and groomed as assiduously as Corley's crude disregard for the sensibilities of all around him in "Two Gallants." [182]

Yet such a description of Duffy is not without its discrepancies. If his house is "old" and sombre," if his room is "uncarpeted," if he chooses Chapelizod "because he found all the other suburbs of Dublin mean, modern, and pretentious," still there is "a complete Wordsworth" in his bookshelf, and "a black and scarlet rug" covers the foot of the bed. While Mr. Duffy "abhorred anything which betokened physical or mental disorder," still he tells Mrs. Sinico that "for some time he has assisted at the meetings of an Irish Socialist party, where he had felt himself a unique figure. . . . "

Duffy manages to join, apparently, order and punctiliousness with elements of the revolutionary and the chaotic. But behind his fling at socialism, there is that same incredibly vicious self-conciousness which is the hall-mark of his character. He is not concerned so much with socialism as with the vision of himself as "a unique figure."

In the same way, Duffy strikes an attitude with Mrs. Sinico:

. . . he heard the strange impersonal voice which he recognized as his own, insisting on the soul's incurable loneliness. We cannot give ourselves, it said: we are our own.

There are, in this short speech alone, a number of fairly specific hints about Mr. Duffy. The loneliness he speaks of is, at the moment and for him, simply an abstraction, a conversational counter which, like a spotlight, lends a kind of verbally dramatic aura to his obsessively egoistic speech. He is, with the exception of his abortive relationship with Mrs. Sinico, totally alone. But not lonely. He has not yet undergone the sudden and violent vision of mortality and isolation which will lend a measure of terrible reality to his cant phrases. Again, Joyce takes pains to underscore Duffy's character. He gives Duffy's voice a character of its own. ". . . it said:" As Duffy "lived at a little distance from his body," so his voice, "strange and impersonal," seems to have a kind of life and direction of its own—at some distance from him.

Mr. Duffy seems to be the living evidence of his own words, "we are our own." His nearly perfect disregard for everything and everyone around him is flawed only by certain commitments forced upon him by his environment and milieu:

He lived his spiritual life without any communion with others, visiting his relatives at Christmas and escorting them to the cemetery when they died. He performed these two social duties for old dignity's sake, but conceded nothing further to the conventions which regulate the civic life.

But Mr. Duffy does not realize that the very self-possession of which he speaks so glibly is the "beast in the jungle" which threatens [183] all of us. As Eliot has suggested regarding the making of poetry, the great need, the single salvation, of us all is to escape personality, to dilute the corrosive of self-concern by plunging into the being of others.

Duffy is, however, the hermetically sealed man. He is suspended beyond life: there is no friction where there is no contact, and so the need for escape and the gradual impingement of outside corruption are almost irrelevant to Mr. Duffy's situation. This, of course, is temporary. Once the preposterous balance of forces implicit in Duffy's existence is disturbed by the encounter with Mrs. Sinico, the outer world begins to assert its claims and its dominion. And, like a mummy suddenly and violently drawn from its sealed case and exposed to the elements, Duffy begins to crumble. He becomes, for one thing, the dead center of Mrs. Sinico's own dream of escape. Too, his egocentricity which is simply absurd in a single man becomes a towering and destructive vice when he steps into the world beyond his mummy-case. To continue the metaphor, Duffy spreads peculiar germs abroad, and before it is done, Mrs. Sinico dies of the infection.

Duffy's predicament is perilous, perhaps, even before he meets Mrs. Sinico. His tendencies seem to indicate a kind of cleavage between person and ego:

He had an odd autobiographical habit which led him to compose in his mind from time to time a short sentence about himself containing a subject in the third person and a predicate in the past tense.

It would appear that Joyce is leading us to conclude Mr. Duffy is a case even beyond Maria. If Maria is "Death in Life," Duffy is in worse condition. He has systematically deranged his sensibilities, junked the distinctions insisted upon by "church" and "creed," and has made of himself a thing. He lacks the responses and the emotions of a normal man. He has analyzed himself into something other than a human being. He conceives of himself in the third person, in the past tense, and has no associates whatever. His whole spectrum of activities can be divided into two general categories. First, he avoids anything that fails to meet his specifications of order, propriety, and decorum. Thus,

He dined in an eating-house in George's Street where he felt himself safe from the society of Dublin's gilded youth and where there was a certain plain honesty in the bill of fare.

Again, "He never gave alms to beggars." Even his desk and its contents reveal the almost neurotic orderliness of Duffy—except, [184] with typical understated precision, Joyce notes an occasional "overripe apple which might have been left there and forgotten."

The second category of Duffy's doings—and the whole episode dealing with Mrs. Sinico falls into this last—has to do with his "third person" habit of self-dramatization. For, as we see, Mrs. Sinico is no more than an audience, a spectator at the artistic event of *Duffy* being created by Duffy. Mrs. Sinico is sensitive—or at least anxious to make contact with other human beings (the latter often heightening the degree of the former, or even standing counterfeit in its stead), having been "dismissed" by her seafaring husband.

One tends to see the whole relationship between Duffy and Mrs. Sinico as if both of them were sitting in darkened silence watching Mr. Duffy's vision of himself taking shape in cold celluloid on a screen before them:

He went often to her little cottage outside Dublin; often they spent their evenings alone. Little by little, as their thoughts entangled, they spoke of subjects less remote. Her companionship was like warm soil about an exotic. Many times she allowed the dark to fall upon them, refraining from lighting the lamp. The dark discreet room, their isolation, the music that still vibrated in their ears united them. . . . Sometimes he caught himself listening to the sound of his own voice. He thought that in her eyes he would ascend to an angelical stature. . . .

But it is of prime importance to note that, if Duffy manipulates Mrs. Sinico to his own rather unnatural ends, he no less makes use of himself as a kind of raw material in the construction of the surrogate-Duffy he presents to Mrs. Sinico. This, after all, is the significance of his "autobiographical habit," of his listening to the "strange impersonal voice" which is his own, of his living "at a little distance" from his body.

Duffy is the prototype of denatured modern man. As we are told at first he has "neither companions nor friends, church nor creed," we are told at the time of Mrs. Sinico's death that

Some new pieces of music encumbered the music-stand in the lower room, and on his shelves stood two volumes by Nietzsche: *Thus Spake Zarathustra* and *The Gay Science*.

The total effect cannot but put us in mind of the similarities between Duffy and certain minor Nazi functionaries whose whole study was to reduce the animate world to a collection of things, to bring the "order" of death and silence from the "chaos" of brawling undirected humanity. Mr. Duffy's obvious rationalism, his contempt for the ordinary values inherent in life, his total unconcern for human connections, and his rejection of the factitiousness of Irish workmen [185] (recalling Hitler's famous satiric speech on the confusing proliferation of political parties in Germany—which he offered to bring to an end) are all pointers to the conclusion that Duffy is a kind of stand-in for what Joyce considered the end-product of modern urban, industrialized, godless, amoral and fragmented society. Duffy is a man without any inherent identity, as the description of his room and effects suggests. There is nothing behind him that matters: the death of his father is equated, for example, in his mind, with the bank's junior partner retiring. He is, therefore, a sort of pastiche of contemporary bits and pieces without the adhesive of traditional piety or belief to hold things together; he attempts, in the process of creating himself, to substitute habit for purpose. His orderliness and efficiency is that of the crackpot inventor's perpetual-motion machine: it is impressive, but meaningless. Rather than progressive, Duffy's personality is simply, like the avowed purpose of the perpetual-motion machine, an avoidance of attrition.

This is the man, then, who forms a most peculiar relationship with the lonely Mrs. Sinico. Joyce realizes that there is a fairly obvious psychological- and probability-gap between what we know of Duffy and his virtually picking up Mrs. Sinico at a concert and establishing a regular—albeit tame—liaison with her. Joyce says,

Neither he nor she had had any such adventure before and neither was conscious of any incongruity.

But conscious or not, the incongruity is there. Duffy is not the sort for such connections, and indeed, as it turns out, the connection is not to be what at first it seems certain to become.

There is no lust in their affair. There is not even any overt affection until, pressed by her need and her nature beyond the rigid bounds Duffy has intimated, or which his personality indicates, Mrs. Sinico, having "shown every sign of unusual excitement . . . caught up his hand passionately and pressed it to her cheek."

This, of course, is the end of the affair. Mrs. Sinico has destroyed her usefulness, betrayed her function. She has moved from the status of audience and attempted to become an actor in the epic of Duffy's self-revelation. In a single gesture, she has breeched the "third person" fantasy Duffy has erected upon her complacent acceptance, and has demanded of him a new and dynamic relationship grounded in reality, in normal intercourse and exchange on the risk-studded level at which life is commonly lived. Duffy, of course, declines the gambit. He prefers the strait and arid closet of his own escape-mechanism to the raw and emotionally dangerous world in which those unshielded and vulnerable like Mrs. Sinico work out their destinies.

Duffy's rejection ("every bond," he said, "is a bond to sorrow") [186] seems at first to be no more than a return to the introverted order of life he had practiced before meeting Mrs. Sinico. But this is not quite the case. As we have noted, he adds Nietzshe to his bookshelf; he has added to his commonplace book a new sentence:

Love between man and man is impossible because there must not be sexual intercourse, and friendship between man and woman is impossible because there must be sexual intercourse.

But the return to "normality" is illusory. Mrs. Sinico, however much she is victim, has placed a seed in Duffy's psyche. When he reads of her death, he is struck deeply. In his room, he re-reads the newspaper article "by the failing light of the window."

He read it not aloud, but moving his lips as a priest does when he reads the prayers Secreto.

The "failing light" and the implied comparison of Duffy with a priest reading prayers recalls the heavy symbolism of the first few stories. Again, the newspaper article mentions that Mrs. Sinico had been "going out at night to buy spirits," thus injecting alchohol into "A Painful Case," and making its appearance in the stories almost universal.

Duffy is not affected, however, by the pathos of Mrs. Sinico's end. Rather he finds the weakness and squalor of her end "revolting":

The whole narrative of her death revolted him and it revolted him to think that he had ever spoken to her of what he held sacred. The threadbare phrases, the inane expressions of sympathy, the cautious words of a reporter won over to conceal the details of a commonplace vulgar death attacked his stomach. Not merely had she degraded herself; she had degraded him. He saw the squalid tract of her vice, miserable and malodorous. His soul's companion! He thought of the hobbling wretches whom he had seen carrying cans and bottles to be filled by the barman. Just God, what an end!

The depth of Duffy's spiritual corruption is revealed in his total failure to grasp the import of Mrs. Sinico's death. He does not think of her loneliness or desperation. Her long fall into self-destruction or drunken accident does not even occur to him. He is disgusted because his former audience, one privy to the secret construction of his empty monument of ego, has, as he conceives it, cast reflected shame upon him.

He is especially revolted by recalling that he had spoken to her "of what he held sacred." But as we have seen, he holds nothing sacred, and nothing but his own conception of self even in esteem. [187] He refers to Mrs. Sinico ironically as "His soul's companion!" But, after all, it is precisely that he has withheld this status, this sharing of the secret heart, from her that has broken her at last into emotional rubbish.

Evidently she had been unfit to live, without any strength of purpose, an easy prey to habits, one of the wrecks upon which civilization has been reared. But that she could have sunk so low. Was it possible he had deceived himself so utterly about her? He remembered her outburst of that night and interpreted it in a harsher sense than he had ever done. He had no difficulty now in approving of the course he had taken.

Duffy attempts to defend himself. He reaches out desperately to the pseudo-Darwinian-Nietzschian vision of the world in order to justify his acts. Weakness is sin; only that which deserves to survive survives. But in the course of setting down Mrs. Sinico's vices, Duffy, like Prufrock (who condemns himself to be Polonius as he evades the responsibilities of Hamlet), unwittingly indicts himself. What purpose, after all, has Duffy's self-limited life? Is he not more nearly an assemblage of habits than a living man? And, at last, is it not upon the vicious egotism and ruthless self-seeking of numberless Duffys that civilization has been reared—and presently flounders?

Again, it is not possible that Duffy has been guilty of self-deception with regard to Mrs. Sinico. Since he has used her as an object, as a sort of human mirror of the kind that gives answers when applied to as in the fairy-tale; since he has never acknowledged either her humanity or her independent existence—much less evaluated either, how can he have misjudged her?

All this, however, is only Mr. Duffy's initial reaction. The seeds sown by his relationship with Mrs. Sinico have spread deeper roots than that. Mr. Duffy has only the intellect of a Nietzschian: not the profound animal instinct that must accompany it, not the ruthless will to see such matters through.

As he sat there, living over his life with her and evoking alternately the two images in which he now conceived her, he realized that she was dead, that she had ceased to exist, that she had become a memory. He began to feel ill at ease. He asked himself what else could he have done. He could not have carried on a comedy of deception with her; he could not have lived with her openly. He had done what seemed to him best. How was he to blame? Now that she was gone he understood how lonely her life must have been, sitting night after night, alone in that room. His life would be lonely too until he, too, died, ceased to exist, became a memory—if anyone remembered him. [188]

As Kenner points out, "we are entering the regions of "The Dead.""[2] Duffy is caught up in a kind of morbid empathy. The paths of glory, or squalor—or of careful self-serving all lead to the same grave, and the shadow of Mrs. Sinico's loneliness and final end falls across Duffy's consciousness. Not that Duffy undergoes instant conversion. On the contrary, it is the work of only an instant to transfer this concern to himself. That loneliness which he had forced upon her has come back to him. But, unlike Gabriel Conroy in "The Dead," Duffy's realization is of no use to him. He has lived too long within his own fantasy. Now Mrs. Sinico's death has broken a chink in the wall of his self-esteem. But it is a hole only large enough to see through, not large enough for escape.

She seemed to be near him in the darkness. At moments he seemed to feel her voice touch his ear, her hand touch his. He stood still to listen. Why had he withheld life from her? Why had he sentenced her to death? He felt his moral nature falling to pieces.

Duffy is suddenly anxious to feel the very touch which he had rejected so violently when Mrs. Sinico was alive. As he had endlessly talked to her when she was alive ("she listened to all") so now Duffy is silenced at last. He stands still hoping to hear her voice. He begins to understand that beyond the battlements of his own ego other creatures exist. He realizes that he has done irreparable harm. His self-sufficiency, his contempt, his "Übermensch complex," his emotional fascism—all crumble like plaster in the rain. The shabby structure of "his moral nature" is "falling to pieces." He finds that in denying Mrs. Sinico he has betrayed himself. He sees a pair of lovers lying in the darkness. But he is not disgusted by the sight. "Those venal and furtive loves" fill him not with loathing, but despair.

He gnawed the rectitude of his life; he felt that he had been outcast from life's feast. One human being had seemed to love him and he had denied her life and happiness; he had sentenced her to ignominy, a death of shame.

Now Duffy resorts to "threadbare phrases." Now his withdrawal from the agonies and uncertainties of life must be paid for. Having refused to accept the risks, the inescapable vulgarities and compromises of which life in the world is fabricated, he finds that he has lost the precious and meaningful dimension of human love as well. And there is no turning back.

Beyond the river he saw a goods train winding out of Kingsbridge station, like a worm with a fiery head winding through the darkness obstinately and laboriously. It passed slowly out [189] of sight; but still he heard in his ears the laborious drone of the engine reiterating the syllables of her name.

[2] Kenner, p. 58.

The "worm of conscience," soon to appear in Joyce's writing as "agenbite of inwit," adds to Duffy's own self-gnawing. He is enmeshed in, surrounded by Mrs. Sinico's spectre. The sound of the locomotive clatters her name. But there is no release. The gnawing now is only attrition; nothing worthwhile can come of it.

He halted under a tree and allowed the rhythm to die away. He could not feel her near him in the darkness nor her voice touch his ear. He waited for some minutes listening. He could hear nothing: the night was perfectly silent. He listened again: perfectly silent. He felt that he was alone.

In order to grasp the full striking irony of these last lines it is necessary to read forward into "The Dead," where Michael Furey, the prime symbol of selflessness and self-sacrificing love (and closely associated in this and other ways with Mrs. Sinico), is described as "a young man standing under a dripping tree." Joyce goes on to say: "Other forms were near. His [Gabriel Conroy's] soul had approached that region where dwell the vast hosts of the dead."

Duffy's pausing "under the tree" is a pathetic and crippled parody, placing him in devastating contrast to Michael Furey, and in unflattering comparison even with Gabriel Conroy. Duffy has denied love, sexuality, humanity itself, has thwarted Mrs. Sinico's dream of escape, and has opted for a narrow and fruitless life bereft alike of risk and reward. Unlike Furey, he has never committed himself to love of another. And now it is too late. Duffy is trapped at last in the unspeakable corruption of a creature which tries to live on its own waste, on the substance of self-esteem. Unlike Furey, the evocation of his memory will not work its magic in the world after his death. Even Gabriel, who shares a number of Duffy's faults, is more amenable to experience than he. For Gabriel is touched, is changed, is, in a real sense, reborn through his posthumous encounter with his wife's dead lover. But Duffy, straining to hear, desiring nothing more than just a phantom touch in place of the real one he has repudiated, has no such vision. He is beyond that kind—perhaps any kind—of salvation. As he stands beneath his tree (which does not drip with the symbolic water of life) he allows "the rhythm to die away," and the epiphanic moment shared by the boy-narrator of the early stories with Jimmy Doyle, Little Chandler, and Gabriel Conroy fades with the sound of the locomotive "reiterating the syllables of her name." The silence following is perfect and unbroken. It is the same silence that troubled Little Chandler; that of an empty and insentient universe, a universe of inanimate things, a subjective universe designed and [190] perfected by Mr. Duffy, who is, at last, as he has said, "his own." And it is the only universe Mr. Duffy will ever know.

In "Clay," Maria's lack of understanding dehumanizes; in "A Painful Case," total self-interest hallucinates. Duffy thinks he will "ascend to an angelical stature" in Mrs. Sinico's eyes (this is an ironic parody of the position of Michael Furey in "The Dead") and, failing this, gives himself to the study of Nietzsche and the *Übermensch*. Maria is only dead, but Duffy is damned. If there is room for natural salvation in Joyce's scheme, Gabriel Conroy is its beneficiary. [191]

"Ivy Day in the Committee Room": Death Without Resurrection

JOSEPH L. BLOTNER

THE POWER AND IRONY OF JAMES JOYCE'S TREATMENT OF IRISH POLITICS after the death of Parnell in "Ivy Day in the Committee Room" can be seen most clearly by reading this short story from *Dubliners* against the background of the events of Christ's death and resurrection as reported in the Gospel according to St. Luke and St. John and in the Acts of the Apostles. A series of striking parallels appears, reinforced by ironic reversals. These events, separated by time, space, and culture, possess a similarity in which the nature and effect of those which happened in Ireland are emphasized and reinforced by symbolic reference to those which took place in Jerusalem.

An ingenious suggestion of Richard Levin and Charles Shattuck (*Accent*, Winter 1944) posits Joyce's indebtedness to the *Odyssey* in *Dubliners* as well as in *Ulysses*. But it is the Christian tradition to which the critic must turn here rather than the Hellenic. Cranly is perceptive when in *A Portrait of the Artist as a Young Man*, he remarks to Stephen Dedalus, "It is a curious thing . . . how your mind is supersaturated with the religion in which you say you disbelieve."[1] It was this supersaturation, shared by Joyce with Stephen, that served to inform the story of treachery and regret presented in "Ivy Day in the Committee Room" with revealing parallels to the story of that greatest betrayal described in the New Testament.

The nature of Joyce's education, deeply pervaded by the religious atmosphere of Clongowes Wood, Belvedere, and University College, is well known. Equally well established is his awareness, from early childhood, of major issues and events in Irish political history. In his home

---

[1] New York: Compass Books, 1964, p. 240. Subsequent references to the novel are to this edition.

Joseph L. Blotner, " 'Ivy Day in the Committee Room': Death Without Resurrection," *Perspective*, IX (Summer 1957), 210–217. Reprinted in a revised version for this volume by permission of the author and the publisher.

and elsewhere he witnessed the intensity of their effect upon Irishmen of various persuasions. His early emotional involvement in this general subject is demonstrated by his composition, at the age of nine, of a spirited polemic entitled "Et Tu Healy?" This attack, which pleased Joyce's violently partisan father John Stanislaus so well that he had it printed, was directed at Timothy Healy, Parnell's enemy who was later to be Governor General of Ireland. Likening Parnell to Caesar and Healy to Brutus, it was to be followed by a work of Joyce's maturity, *A Portrait of the Artist as a Young Man,* in which he was to raise the quantities in the metaphorical equation several powers: Parnell to be identified with Christ, his enemies with Judas.

In *James Joyce,* Herbert Gorman says that as Joyce prepared to write [210] "The Dead" other titles, "each one conveying to him its peculiar situation, floated through his mind . . ." (176). One of these was "The Last Supper." But he wrote no story under that title. There are several possible reasons why he did not: the protracted difficulties he was experiencing in getting *Dubliners* published may have deterred him from adding to it further; the story may not have finally crystallized in his mind; or, he may have lost interest in it. In any case, his consideration of this title indicates that he was thinking in terms of analogies between events in the lives of his characters and events in the life of Christ at the same time that he was writing some of the stories in *Dubliners.* There is a further possibility, however, which this essay will explore: he had already used a similar analogy in "Ivy Day in the Committee Room." It may be that he was content at this stage of his artistic development to attempt no further extension of these parallels.

The extensive and fundamental correspondences which make Parnell a Christ-figure in Joyce's work and which supply the background for this particular analysis may be seen in the violent quarrel at the Christmas dinner table in the Dedalus home described in *A Portrait of the Artist as a Young Man.* To Stephen's aunt, Dante Riordan, Charles Stewart Parnell was a devil, a fiend who had fortunately been crushed, largely through the efforts of the hierarchy of the Catholic Church in Ireland. To John Casey and Simon Dedalus, he was a saviour betrayed. As Christ was "the Master," so Parnell was "the Chief." At the end of the bitter quarrel, Casey weeps: "—Poor Parnell! he cried loudly. My dead king" (39)! As the disciples wept for the King of the Jews, so this disciple, wounded in the service of his cause, weeps for the King of the Irish. There are other parallels equally apt, as Israel had been subjugated by the military forces of the Roman Empire and its people governed by puppets of Britain. The function of Caiaphas, the chief priests, and the elders is fulfilled by the Irish clergy. "—Didn't the bishops of Ireland betray us in the time of the union when Bishop Lanigan presented an address of loyalty to the Marquess Cornwallis?" John Casey demands. "Didn't the bishops and priests sell the aspirations of their country in 1829 in return for Catholic emancipation? Didn't they denounce the fenian movement from the pulpit and in the confession box" (38)? And Dante has already exclaimed, "The priests were right to abandon him" (38). One parallel between the two sets of circumstances results in a reversal. As Mary Magdalene followed Christ, so Kitty O'Shea followed Parnell, but whereas Christ was Mary's salvation, Kitty O'Shea was the means of Parnell's destruction. Despite this divergence, the parallels implicit in this portion of Joyce's novel are both extensive and consistent. This symbolic [211] equation of Parnell with Christ carried over into Joyce's journalistic work of the Trieste period. In Ellsworth Mason's translation (*Twentieth Century Literature*, for October 1956) of "Home Rule Comes of Age," published in *Il Piccolo della* on May 19, 1907, Joyce concludes his indictment of the Irish parliamentary party thus: "They have given proof of their altruism only in 1891, when they sold their leader, Parnell, to the pharasaical conscience of the English Non-conformists without exacting the thirty pieces of silver."[2]

Read only on the narrative level, "Ivy Day in the Committee Room" is deceptively simple. A group of canvassers gather in their campaign headquarters to await the arrival of their candidate who is to pay them for their services. They come and go, joined briefly by a priest and a canvasser for the rival candidate. They converse more or less desultorily. Their leader does not appear and neither does their reward. Finally, to the drinking of bottles of stout, one of the men reads an amateurish poem commemorating the death of Parnell. As the brief applause dies away, the story quickly comes to an end. This apparent simplicity led Padraic Colum to write in his introduction to *Dubliners*[3] that this story "has been completely rendered for us" (x), that Joyce seemingly "had decided to illustrate the life of Dublin through a series of reports, taking this and that incident and being as clear and as unconcerned in the reporting of it as a scientific historian might be" (11). But it is only on the narrative level that the story is completely rendered for us and reported as clearly and unconcernedly as a scientific historian might do it. Read on the symbolic level, this short story is both rich and complex in meanings.

The parallels between the New Testament and "Ivy Day in the Committee Room" are, unlike those in *A Portrait of the Artist as a Young Man*, ironic rather than direct. And this suits Joyce's purpose exactly. In those well-known words to Grant Richards before he published *Dubliners*, Joyce wrote: "My intention was to write a chapter of the moral history of my country and I chose Dublin for the scene be-

---

[2] In "Joyce and the Three Ages of Charles Stewart Parnell," *A James Joyce Miscellany*, Second Series, Southern Illinois University Press, 1959, Adaline Glasheen admirably traces Joyce's changing use of Parnell in *A Portrait, Dubliners*, and *Ulysses*. She explains the historical bases of the references to Parnell's career and the extent to which Joyce alters or deviates from them. Pp. 151–178. The subsection "Parnell as God in 'Ivy Day in the Committee Room'" explores Parnell's kingship, his role as "slain god," and the lines drawn between Parnellites, Fenians, and Clericals.

[3] New York: Modern Library, n.d.

cause that city seemed to me the centre of paralysis" (Gorman, p. 149). In another letter to the same correspondent, he had written, "I think people might be willing to pay for the special odour of corruption which, I hope, floats over my stories" (146). The gathering place of Christ's apostles was a center of vitality, not paralysis; their odor, if any, was one of health rather than corruption. Thus Joyce could oppose and cause to illuminate each other the static and dynamic, the impure and the pure. The parallels, then, had to be ironic and thus doubly effective in emphasizing the essence of the phenomena he was treating.

The locale of "Ivy Day in the Committee Room" is an upper room in a building in Dublin. The room's elevation is emphasized when Mr. Henchy [212] grasps a candlestick at Father Keon's departure "to light him downstairs" because " 'the stairs is so dark.' " This suggests the upper room which was the meeting place of the apostles in Jerusalem in which the Last Supper was held (Luke, 22:12) and in which the election of Matthias to fill the place of Judas took place (Acts, 1:13). It seems logical to assume that it was this same upper room in which the spirit of the Holy Ghost descended upon the apostles at Pentecost (Acts, 2:12). More important for purposes of this analysis, it can be assumed that it was probably this same upper room in which the risen Christ appeared to the apostles (John, 20:19,26).

Even the story's title is rich in allusion. Ivy Day is a commemoration of the death of Parnell, the lost leader. "Committee Room" here denotes the place in which the canvassers meet; but for these men and nearly all of Joyce's Irish readers, it would connote a vastly different place: Committee Room No. 15 in the House of Commons in London, where, after days of fierce recriminations, Parnell had been deposed from the leadership of the Irish parliamentary party following Gladstone's letter declaring that the Irish cause would be injured and his own position made untenable if Parnell retained his post. The starkness of the contrast is clear: on the one hand, a tense and crowded chamber in the seat of the oldest legislative body of the English-speaking peoples, where national issues and the fate of national figures hung upon the action; on the other hand, a cold and shabby room in an undistinguished section of Dublin, where nothing is accomplished politically, which is a genuine "centre of paralysis." The ivy, which is green and perennial, a symbol of life and rebirth, is worn here with a fundamentally ironic effect for a man who is dead, and with whose death had departed the fire and spirit which he had infused into the movement he led.[4]

[4] In their textbook, The Worlds of Fiction (Houghton Mifflin, 1964), T. Y. Greet, Charles E. Edge, and John M. Munro draw upon Sir James Frazer, Robert Graves, and others for pagan lore about ivy and also primitive leader-worship. They further provide background material on Irish history and politics. Pp. 249–253.

Interpreted still another way, the wearing of the ivy leads deeper into the symbolism of the story. Both O'Connor and Hynes wear the ivy leaf in their lapels. This marks them, just as the symbol of the fish marked the early Christians, signalling their commitment to a leader, an ideal, and a cause. For the Christians there was the hope of a resurrection that would make their symbol more than a memento. For a time, some of the Parnellites had cherished the same hope. "—Some say he is not in that grave at all," says John Power in awed tones in *Ulysses*, "That the coffin was filled with stones. That one day he will come again" (111). But the same Hynes shakes his head, "—Parnell will never come again, he said. He's there, all that was mortal of him. Peace to his ashes" (111).

Against this background one can proceed to further parallels and contrasts. In John, 20:18, Mary Magdalene has told the disciples that she has seen the risen Christ. In the next verse John relates how they gathered together, [213] probably in the upper room, a group of men consecrated to their work, awaiting the appearance of their leader who would bring to them the reward of everlasting life. It was this same upper room, one can assume, that was later illuminated by the heavenly light of the "cloven tongues like as of fire" (Acts, 2:3) in which the Holy Ghost descended upon these same apostles on the day of Pentecost. The upper room in Joyce's story is in a building located on Wicklow Street. Joyce's propensity for punning makes this choice of a place-name meaningful. When a wick is low the light cast is, of course, diminished. As Hynes enters he asks, jocosely yet significantly (in Catholic Dublin): "Is this a Freemason's meeting?" The meagre fire gives little illumination, and Hynes asks another question: "What are you doing in the dark?" This query is meaningful for both O'Connor and Hynes, each at loose ends, politically in the dark, and essentially directionless since the light had gone out of the movement to which they had devoted themselves. Very shortly, Old Jack, the caretaker, places two lighted candles on the table, an action suggestive of the preparations for the celebration of the Mass, the rite in which, to the faithful, Christ is present. Thus the scene is set. These two are joined by other canvassers. Rather than being consecrated to their work, they are halfhearted. O'Connor, who lights cigarettes with his employer's cards, has shirked his job, spending most of the wet day in the committee room. Crofton has come to work for O'Connor's candidate with reluctance and only because his former employer has withdrawn from the contest. And it is this new employer whom Henchy, another canvasser, calls a "Mean little schoolboy of hell." Later they drink warm stout, in obvious contrast to the group in the Biblical upper room which at the celebration of the Last Supper had drunk the consecrated sacramental wine. And thus they wait for their reward: money.

The Christian names which Joyce supplies are also meaningful. Those of Crofton and Lyons (called "Bantam" in *Ulysses*), we do not know, but the names of Henchy, O'Connor, and Hynes are given: John, Matthew, and Joseph. The first two, of course, are identical with names of apostles. But the circumstances suggest a more subtle correspondence. The Acts of the Apostles, 1:13, describes the gathering in the upper room called by Peter to name a disciple to replace Judas. Two candidates are selected: Joseph, "called Barsabas, who was surnamed Justus, and Matthias" (Acts, 2:23). The similarity between "Matthew" and "Matthias" is interesting here. In the Biblical account, "the lot fell upon Matthias; and he was numbered with the eleven apostles" (Acts, 2:26). Ironically, Joe Hynes, the one character in the story who remains undeviating in his loyalty to Parnell, is the outsider, the one regarded with suspicion. Old Jack, in view of his age and his hearkening back to earlier days ("'Musha, God be with them [214] times!' said the old man. 'There was some life in it then'") may perhaps suggest a forerunner of the apostles, John the Baptist.[5]

The immediate political background of the situation in Joyce's story buttresses this interpretation. In the light of Joyce's fondness for word-play, the name of the ward in which the candidate, Richard J. Tierney, is standing for election is revealing. It is the Royal Exchange Ward. Joyce knew slang, and the slang connotation of the word "royal" is consistent with the political exchange so many Irishmen had made: Parnell for the likes of Timothy Healy and "Tricky Dicky" Tierney; the greatest figure in modern Irish politics as opposed to one who, to the young Joyce, was scarcely better than an outright renegade, and another, a "tricky" man with "little pigs' eyes" who is supported by the clergy and who is the son of the keeper of a second-hand clothing store. And the characters in the story have either ignored or failed to perceive the fact that Colgan, the Labor candidate, is closer to the spirit of Parnell than Tierney, even though Tierney is standing for election as a Nationalist candidate. This exchange, and the values which underlie it, is hypocritical in the extreme. Mr. Henchy, defending a proposed address of welcome to Edward VII (which Hynes thinks Tierney will sign) should Edward visit Ireland, declares that they should overlook his notorious private life: "He's fond of his glass of grog and he's a bit of a rake, perhaps, and he's a good sportsman." When Lyons protests that he is unfit for this distinction, just as Parnell was unfit to lead the Irish after his breach of their moral code, O'Connor quickly intervenes: "'This is Parnell's anniversary . . . and don't let us stir up any bad blood. We all respect him now that he's dead and gone. . . .'" But the choice has been made, before this, and too many of the Irish, like Henchy, are ready to render what is Christ's unto Caesar.

The climax of the story comes as Hynes is asked by O'Connor to

[5] In "'Two Gallants' and 'Ivy Day in the Committee Room,'" *James Joyce Quarterly*, Fall 1963, Robert Boyle, S.J., notes revealing details about the canvassers and their functions, then goes on to comment on the uses of Hynes's poem. Pp. 3–9.

recite a poem written in memory of Parnell. By this time Hynes has emerged as the dominating living character in Joyce's story. He is distinguished by his appearance as well as his steadfastness, whereas all the others are unattractive in some way. Old Jack is marked by the decrepitude of age, and O'Connor is "a grey-haired young man, whose face was disfigured by many blotches and pimples . . ." (and who speaks in "a husky falsetto"). Mr. Henchy is "a bustling little man with a snuffling nose. . . ." Crofton is "a very fat man . . . [with a] sloping figure . . . [and] a big face which resembled a young ox's face in expression . . ." whereas Lyons is frail and thin. The shabbily-dressed Father Keon's rain-wet face has "the appearance of damp yellow cheese save where two rosy spots indicated the cheek bones." Resembling a poor clergyman or a poor actor, the priest has a very long mouth and speaks in "a discreet, indulgent, velvety voice." This clergyman, who is close to Mr. Fanning, one of Tierney's financial backers, is called by Henchy "a black sheep . . . an unfortunate man of some kind. . . ." Both he and Father Burke (who does not appear), interesting themselves in Tierney's candidacy, are representative of those among the clergy who had helped to bring about Parnell's downfall. Symbolically they are analogous to Caiaphas, the scribes, and the priests of the temple who had conspired against Christ. Contrasted with Keon and the canvassers is Hynes, "a tall, slender young man with a light brown mustache," and the only character in the story this favorably described. It is he alone who makes his loyalty to Parnell unequivocally clear: " 'If this man was alive,' he said, pointing to the leaf, 'we'd have no talk of an address of welcome!' "

Finally, near the end of the story, Hynes, at the urging of O'Connor and Henchy, recites his poem, "The Death of Parnell." A few of the eleven quatrains will serve to further emphasize Parnell's role as a Christ-figure:

> He is dead. Our uncrowned King is dead.
>   O, Erin, mourn with grief and woe
> For he lies dead whom the fell gang
>   Of *modern* [italics mine] hypocrites laid low.
>
>   ❁   ❁   ❁
>
> Shame on the coward, caitiff hands
>   That smote their Lord or with a kiss
> Betrayed him to the rabble rout
>   Of fawning priests—no friends of his
>
>   ❁   ❁   ❁
>
> He fell as fall the mighty ones,
>
>   ❁   ❁   ❁
>
> They had their way: they laid him low.
>   But Erin, list, his spirit may
> Rise, like the Phoenix from the flames,
>   When breaks the dawning of the day.

There is a burst of applause and then silence as the auditors ranged about the mute and motionless Hynes drink from their bottles of stout. One of Joyce's epiphanies has occurred for Hynes, and perhaps for some of those around him.

By this time another irony has become increasingly clear. When Christ had reappeared, only one of the eleven apostles, Thomas, had separated himself from the rest by his lack of faith and devotion (John, 20:24–29). In this story only one of five (Crofton, a Conservative, is excluded here) has retained his faith and loyalty, becoming, as shown by Henchy's speculation that he is a spy of Colgan, an object of suspicion to the others.

So, in "Ivy Day in the Committee Room" a group of followers wait in a candle-lit room for the leader, who has said "I won't forget you," [216] to reappear and bring to them the reward which they anxiously await. One says: " 'I hope to God he'll not leave us in the lurch tonight.' " But the leader does not appear. Joyce has delineated the characteristic of which he said Dublin was the center, and he has strengthened this delineation through an implicit ironic comparison with the towering events of the New Testament. The contrasts are illuminated; on the one hand: betrayal, death, faith, resurrection, and dedication; on the other: betrayal, death, faithlessness, disappearance, and paralysis. [217]

A Portrait of a Lady

WILLIAM YORK TINDALL

THIS STORY ["A MOTHER"] OCCUPIES THE MIDDLE PLACE IN A TRILOGY about Dublin's more or less adult social interests, a trilogy which balances the opening trilogy about youth.[1] "Ivy Day," the first of the second trilogy, concerns political life, and "Grace," the third, concerns religious life. "A Mother" displays Dublin's cultural interests and pretensions. The third-rate concert of "artistes" in the Antient Concert Rooms is as desolating as the meeting of third-rate politicians in Wick-

---

[1] Tindall is referring to the division of the stories that Joyce outlined in a letter to Grant Richards on May 5, 1906. See the second letter in "Three Letters to Grant Richards." [Eds.]

---

low Street. Plainly Dublin suffers from cultural as well as political paralysis.[2] [36]

The characters, somewhat more elegant than those in the committee room, belong not only to Dublin's middle class but to its nationalistic faction. Kathleen, who bears the name Ireland takes for herself when assuming body for allegorical purposes, has studied Gaelic, and knows a few words of it. Her friends, also participants in the "language movement" (which Joyce, good European, thought provincial), sing local songs and recite patriotic pieces.

Not about Kathleen, however, but about her terrible mother, this story is essentially a portrait of this lady. Our problem is whether to take her literally or figuratively or both. If, in consideration of her name, Kathleen can be taken for Ireland in one of its aspects, can we or should we take her mother and manager as something equally important—Ireland's Church maybe? We seem invited to dare this hypothesis. Like the Church, Mrs. Kearney slips "the doubtful items in between the old favourites." Like the Church, she offers wine and biscuits to the visitors whom she dominates. Like the Church, she insists on being paid; and like the Church, she futilely excommunicates those who displease her.

These possibilities—and they are no more than that since Joyce was not writing allegory—expand the meaning of one who, however surrounded with implications of something almost general and abstract, remains a particular woman nevertheless. But that this particular, solidly-presented woman carries suggestions beyond her apparent capacity seems an obvious improvement. If we take her not only as an obnoxious Dubliner but as an unassigned symbol—that is as a meaningful thing of uncertain meaning—we must admit that she is more narrowly assigned by the context than Mr. O'Madden Burke's mysterious umbrella, which occupies the middle and end of this story, as Stein's butterfly occupies the middle and end of *Lord Jim*. Guessing the significance of butterfly or umbrella, trying our ingenuity on the scrutinized text, we remain blameless until dogmatic about our guesses and our scrutiny.

Aside from this shady object and Mrs. Kearney herself, Joyce's story of the concert offers a simple and agreeable surface for our [37] enjoyment. People, we conclude, are odd and this story funny. Far from bare and scrupulously mean, the manner is one of polished irony, as urbane as the matter is provincial. The deadly sins encountered here

---

[2] Tindall sees "paralysis" as central to *Dubliners*. Earlier in his study he writes: "Paralysis is moral and central. The moral center of *Dubliners*, however, is not paralysis alone but the revelation of paralysis to its victims. Coming to awareness or self-revelation marks the climax of these stories or of most at least; for knowing oneself, as the Greeks knew, is a basis of morality if not the thing itself" (p. 4). Tindall develops this argument in his interpretation of each of the stories in *Dubliners*. [Eds.]

are pride, wrath, and covetousness. (Mrs. Kearney's demand for payment is even louder than that of the politicians in "Ivy Day.") The
virtues, save for a kind of ignominious fortitude, are hardly there at
all. [38]

"Grace" and Joyce's Method of Parody

CARL NIEMEYER

"GRACE" IS NOT ONE OF THE MORE FREQUENTLY DISCUSSED OR ANTHOLO-
gized stories in James Joyce's *Dubliners*. No one has tried to justify
V. S. Pritchett's judgment of it as, along with "The Dead," the best in
the book, and no one has looked deeply into Stanislaus Joyce's observation that the story is based on Dante's *Commedia*. Yet before he wrote
"The Dead" Joyce intended to make "Grace" the last story, and hence
an important one, in the *Dubliners* collection, and the title itself, the
name of one of the most difficult and profound of theological concepts,
should warn us not to overlook it. Furthermore, it is the first example
of Joyce's method of parody. Here as in *Ulysses* he takes a great book
and by deliberately echoing it, by applying it to squalid situations, of
which we get no suggestion in the book itself, makes fun not of the
original but of an age or civilization so debased that, measured by the
great classics, it is ridiculous. In "Grace" and in *Ulysses* Joyce's very
method suggests the theme of *Finnegans Wake*—the world is deteriorat-
ing from the greatness of its past, and ours is the age of the commonplace. It is the argument of *The Battle of the Books,* and like Swift,
Joyce awards the palm to the ancients.

Except for the three obviously marked off parts into which the
story is divided, "Grace" at first seems remote enough from Dante. It is
about Tom Kernan, who has fallen down a flight of steps leading to a
barroom lavatory. His clothes are "smeared with the filth and ooze of
the floor on which he had lain, face downwards." Two men, also present in the lavatory, try to help him up. If he is not unconscious, he is at
least helpless, and to get him upstairs on to the bar floor the two men
need the aid of the bar assistant. No one knows Kernan's name, and
the manager sends for a constable. Nor does anyone try to help him, in-

Carl Niemeyer, "'Grace' and Joyce's Method of Parody," *College English,*
XXVII (December 1965), 196–201. Reprinted by permission of the National
Council of Teachers of English and Carl Niemeyer.

cluding the stupid constable, until out of nowhere "a young man in a cycling-suit" kneels beside him, washes the blood off his mouth, and administers brandy. Revived, Kernan avoids answering the constable's questions about his identity and is luckily recognized by a certain Mr. Power, who vouches for him and with the help of the young man leads him out of the bar. Mr. Power calls for an "outsider," on to which Kernan is hoisted. The young man in the cycling-suit leaves, never to reappear. Kernan now reveals that in the fall he has bitten off a small piece of his tongue. We learn he is a tea-taster, grown a little seedy. Mr. Power takes him home, where Mrs. Kernan tells him her husband has been drinking since Friday. Mr. Power, while Mrs. Kernan is taking care of Tom, talks to the three children, whose bad manners and accents surprise him. He leaves assuring Mrs. Kernan that he and another friend, Martin, will make a new man of her husband. The first part ends.

Two days later Mr. Power returns in the company of Martin Cunningham and Mr. M'Coy. They reveal to Mrs. Kernan that they have contrived a plot to reclaim Tom. Though disillusioned about the efficacy of religion, she is willing that the attempt be made. Mr. Kernan is a Catholic since his marriage, but has not been in church for twenty years. [196] The three men join Tom, who is still in bed. His tongue appears to be healing; at least his speech is no longer impeded as in the first episode. An amiable and brainless discussion ensues. Tom cannot at first remember whom he was with when he fell; one was a "little chap with sandy hair," he finally recalls; the other is one Harford, who is partnered with a Jew in the business of money lending. The young man in the cycling-suit is remembered and described as "a decent young chap, that medical fellow," but for whom Mr. Power believes Kernan would have been jailed for seven days. The constable too is recalled and his ignorance jeered at. Mrs. Kernan brings refreshments and treats the men with courtesy, although she and Tom exchange a couple of sharp sentences. The plot is now introduced, which is to inveigle Tom to go with the three men to make a retreat. Cunningham with a cunning appropriate to his name wisely does not press Tom at once. Instead, there is general and approving discussion of the Jesuits, one of whom, Father Purdon, will conduct the retreat. Tom is promised he will not be hard on them. Another famous preacher is recalled, and the essential likeness of Catholics and Protestants is proclaimed, with Mr. Cunningham asserting that the Catholic is "*the* religion, the old, original faith." To this, Mr. Kernan, despite some of his earlier remarks, assents. Mr. Fogarty, the grocer, arrives with a gift of whiskey. Mr. Cunningham continues the conversation by commending Leo XIII, and contributes a good deal of erroneous and opinionated information. The conversation is full of non sequiturs.

"I remember reading," said Mr. Cunningham, "that one of Pope Leo's poems was on the invention of the photograph—in Latin, of course."

"On the photograph!" exclaimed Mr. Kernan.

"Yes," said Mr. Cunningham.

He also drank from his glass.

"Well, you know," said Mr. M'Coy, "isn't the photograph wonderful when you come to think of it?"

"O, of course," said Mr. Power, "great minds can see things."

"As the poet says: *Great minds are very near to madness*," said Mr. Fogarty.

Martin admits Tom's somewhat hesitant objection about the morality of the popes, but affirms that none of them ever uttered false doctrine. Papal infallibility is discussed. Mr. Kernan is told that at the retreat he has only to stand with a lighted candle and renew his baptismal vows. He agrees to the retreat and confession but demurs at the candles. The second part ends.

The brief third section takes place in the Jesuit Church in Gardiner Street. It is full of "well dressed and orderly" gentlemen. The five men from the preceding section are there, seated in the form of a quincunx. The presence of Mr. Harford and the others comforts Mr. Kernan. Father Purdon after prayer delivers his sermon, using as his text Luke xvi 8–9: "For the children of this world are wiser in their generation than the children of light. Wherefore make unto yourself friends out of the mammon of iniquity so that when you die they may receive you into everlasting dwellings." Father Purdon calls this a particularly good text for business men and fulfills Cunningham's prediction by promising to speak to them in a business-like way. He asks them to open the books of their spiritual lives and tally them with their consciences. If they find anything wrong they are to say, "But, with God's grace, I will rectify this and this. I will set right my accounts." Here the story abruptly ends.

One may well ask how in this commonplace narrative Joyce expects his reader to be reminded of the *Commedia*. The answer is the number of small details, trivial in themselves, which taken together point strongly to the equation. For instance, the climax of the *Commedia*, [197] in the last canto, is a revelation to Dante of God, the source of grace, attained after an arduous spiritual and intellectual pilgrimage. In the Joyce story the characters are in search of grace, but their pursuit is so ignorant and vulgar that they find no revelation and are not even aware of their own failure. One of Dante's important concerns is the medieval church, which he is not afraid to criticize if necessary. The church is also the concern of the Dubliners in Tom's bedroom, but their praise of it is fulsome and their ignorance of it as great as their complacency. So, too, the Dubliners' jokes about the ignorant policeman suggest Dante's interest in civil life and the working of the Empire. Hugh Kenner has suggested that Tom Kernan at the foot of the lavatory stairs is in a *selva oscura* (*Dublin's Joyce*, p. 61), out of which he is led "through a Dublin *Commedia*." As we shall see, the foot of the stairs indicates something other than Dante's

dark wood, for strictly there is no parallel to Dante himself in "Grace."
Kernan, however, is the central figure with Power as a kind of Virgilian
guide, who is prominent in Part One as a savior, "outgeneralled" in
Part Two, and merely mentioned in Part Three. (In Dante Virgil disappears from Dante's side in Purgatorio, and is only mentioned in
Paradiso, xvii, 19; and xxvi, 118.) If the Dubliners are prideful in their
smug self-satisfaction, we are perhaps expected to be reminded of
Mars by Martin Cunningham's first name, since Dante locates Mars in
the first circle of Purgatorio (xii, 31) among the prideful, and Martin
appears first in the story in Part Two.

Actually, however, "Grace" is less a story parodying a spiritual
pilgrimage than it is the account of a particular kind of sin, of which
all the Dubliners are guilty. Here the link with Dante is unmistakable.
The clue is Tom Kernan's fall. His position at the foot of the stairs in
a privy, "smeared with the filth and ooze of the floor on which he had
lain, face downwards," refers to the Malebolge of the Eighth Circle of
the Inferno.

> There we came and down in the ditch
> I saw people plunged in excrement
> such as seemed to come from human
>   privies
> And while my eye was seeking there
>   below
> I saw one with his head so weighted
>   with dung
> that it did not appear whether he was
>   clerk or layman.
>   (Inferno, xviii, 112–17)

In other words, Kernan is one of the fraudulent. More specifically, like
Alessio Interminei, he is a flatterer. To underscore this point, Joyce has
made him a tea-taster, a man who makes his living by his tongue. (It
is surely significant that biting off a "minute piece" of his tongue is
enough to put him to bed for three days.) Later, to demonstrate his
character, he speaks flatteringly to his wife when she insults him, and
he always acquiesces in Cunningham's judgments.

"These yahoos coming up here," he said, "think they can boss the
people. I needn't tell you Martin, what kind of men they are."
    Mr. Cunningham gave a qualified assent.
    "It's like everything else in this world," he said. "You get some bad
ones and you get some good ones."
    "O yes, you get some good ones, I admit," said Mr. Kernan, satisfied.

During the second part of the story, when the men are assembled in
Kernan's sickroom, however, it becomes evident that, like Tom, they
are all guilty of the sin of flattery. They resemble the harlot whom
Dante introduces to end his canto, whose thanks to her lover were not

merely *"grandi"* but *"maravigliose,"* or in Joyce himself they resemble Richie Goulding in *Ulysses* with his automatic superlatives. They are blarneyers. Their [198] flattery is not necessarily of those in their presence, but of persons and things with whom they identify themselves, for instance the Jesuits. Tom expresses himself mildly about them—they are an educated order and mean well, but Cunningham calls them the grandest order in the Church; and Mr. M'Coy praises them for their influence. Again, Kernan, who has not always been a Catholic, finds some of the secular priests ignorant and bumptious. Cunningham, echoed by Mr. Power and Mr. M'Coy, says the Irish priesthood "is honoured all the world over," and Mr. Kernan, easily convinced, says, "Perhaps you're right," flattering Cunningham by agreeing with him. Mr. Fogarty, who joins the group later, is a grocer who "flattered himself, his manners would ingratiate him with the housewives of the district. He bore himself with a certain grace, complimented little children and spoke with a neat enunciation." His flattery of the group takes tangible form. He brings with him half a pint of whiskey.

All these flatterers are in search of grace, as shown by their attendance at the retreat, and hence resemble Dante. Their Paradiso is the church in Gardiner Street, where they sit with other "well dressed and orderly" gentlemen gazing "at the distant speck of red light which was suspended before the high altar," possibly mentioned to suggest Paradiso xiv, the heaven of Mars, with its red glow.

> I noted well that there I was more
> exalted
> by the flaming smile of the star,
> which seemed to me redder than
> usual. (85–87)

In the story this is the heaven of Martin rather than Mars, for he has taken the lead in getting the group together. The five friends, seated in the form of a quincunx are in ironic contrast with the souls of those who fought for Christ, whom Dante arranges in the form of a cross. That all the souls in canto xiv are in the form of lights may explain why in the preceding section of "Grace" a point has been made of each man's carrying a candle. Kernan's firm refusal to be a candle bearer (we never learn whether he makes it stick) might then humorously suggest his unwillingness to become a spirit, or it might be a sudden refusal to acquiesce, a hint that he at least is on the road to redemption. Joyce does not use such details with the expectation that the reader make a precise application of them. They are suggestive rather than explicit. Primarily, Joyce wants to show how far these neatly dressed and unexciting gentlemen are removed from the blazing glory of Dante's vision of Christ's warriors. Mediocrity, indeed, is one of their characteristics; although it may be only a striking coincidence that Dante's flatterers are in the middle of the Inferno, that Mars is the fifth of the nine heavens, and that in Purgatorio the sin of sloth, the deliberately chosen paralysis of which the Dubliners are guilty, is the fourth of the seven deadly sins.

There is still another flatterer in Joyce's story. At the Jesuit church Father Purdon preaches on the text from Luke, "one of the most difficult . . . in all the Scriptures . . . to interpret properly." It comes from the parable of the steward who wastes his master's goods and then, in danger of losing his position, renounces his commission from two of the debtors in order to gain their friendship in the uncertain future. His master commends him for doing "wisely," his explanation being the text quoted. The passage has troubled commentators because in it Jesus seems to be commending the ways of the world which elsewhere He rejects. Without discussing the exegesis the passage has aroused, one may conclude that Jesus is obviously not praising sharp practice but rather suggesting the difference between the life of calculation and the life of the spirit. The word "wise" used both in the Douay and the King [199] James versions is a misleading translation of the Greek word *"phronimos,"* whose meaning is rather "prudent" or even "businesslike." In other words, the master of the "steward of unrighteousness" thinks it is good business to make influential friends and commends his steward for doing so. This text fits Joyce's purposes beautifully. Not only does Father Purdon reveal his own shallowness by ignoring the subtleties of the passage; he is as much a flatterer as his hearers. He tells them he is a man of the world like themselves, a business man who will speak to them in a businesslike fashion. He tells them Christ understands "our little failings" and "the temptations of this life." Ironically, the text gives him away. Father Purdon himself is a type of the unjust steward. By reducing their indebtedness, the steward made friends of his master's debtors. So Father Purdon by reducing the obligation of the Dubliners to God, as he does when he instructs them that salvation is simply a matter of keeping a good set of books, ingratiates himself with his hearers. Harford, the usurer, must have been particularly well pleased to hear his own technical vocabulary on the priest's lips. Subconsciously, Cunningham must feel that he is now repaid for his own early flattery of the Jesuits. Joyce is emphasizing the difference between spiritual grace and the ingratiation of men trying to gain others' good will. Father Purdon, using his holy office in order that he may be a good fellow and enjoy his hearers' favorable opinion, is literally making unto himself friends out of the mammon of iniquity, friends of the complacent, successful business men sitting before him. No doubt they will receive him into their everlasting dwellings, but Joyce does not mean his reader to confuse these dwellings with the paradise described in the last canto of the *Commedia.*

Dante's poem closes in a dazzling vision, which we may take as a verbal representation of the grace of God. Then because we can probe no deeper and ascend no higher, the poem stops. We have reached man's ordained limits. In parody of Dante, "Grace" too simply stops. Father Purdon is well embarked upon his sermon, having said enough to demonstrate to the reader his incompetence, when the story breaks off. Grace has not been attained or even perceived, but the characters can go no farther, for none of them, including the priest, has or ever will have any idea what grace is. There is no equivalent here of the human reason of Virgil or of the divine knowledge of Beatrice. In the moral world, power and cunning cannot lead us to grace. These men, significantly named Power and Cunningham, are as poor examples of man's reason as Father Purdon is of theology, and the Dubliners have none of the despair of one who finds himself in a *selva oscura*. The nearest we get to grace in the story is through the man in cycling clothes, who administers aid and then disappears. Maybe the cycling clothes, otherwise unexplained, are intended to suggest the circles of the last canto. The interpretation may be far-fetched, but there is something mystical about the young man. He is the Macintosh of "Grace," but unlike the figure in *Ulysses* he represents salvation, not death. His sudden appearance, his equally sudden vanishing, Kernan's vagueness about him ("a decent young chap, that medical fellow") all suggest that Joyce wishes us to see in him some deeper significance.

Though a parody, "Grace" is a moral story. Subtly invoking the greatest of Christian allegories, with its suggestion of the depths to which man's grossness may fall and the heights to which his spiritual nature may rise, Joyce asks the reader to see in Dante's light the paralysis of the Dubliners. Here, as in parts of *Ulysses* and in *Finnegans Wake*, talk, for Joyce the most human of man's activities, is the subject; but it is debased [200] talk, blarney and flattery, ignorant and futile. Dante's words are of grace; these are of ingratiation. Etymologically identical, the two terms are as far apart as revelation and damnation. The title of the story is ironic, for "grace" remains a word and does not become a reality. With no better men than the Dubliners to illustrate it, Dante's "Comedy" turns into pointless farce. [201]

Characterization in "The Dead"

LIONEL TRILLING

" 'HE DIED WHEN HE WAS ONLY SEVENTEEN!' " SAYS GRETTA CONROY when she tells her husband about Michael Furey. " 'Isn't it a terrible thing to die so young as that?' " But no reader will give the answer that Gretta seems to expect from her husband. No reader upon whom the story has had its intended effect can fail to know that it is better to have died as Michael Furey died than to have lived after the fashion of Gabriel Conroy and all the other guests at the Christmas party. And this is the answer that Gabriel Conroy does indeed give when he lies down beside his sleeping wife. "Better pass boldly into that other world," he thinks, "in the full glory of some passion, than fade and wither dismally with age." The title of the story, we eventually understand, refers less to Michael Furey than to Gabriel Conroy, to the guests at the Christmas party, to all the people of Ireland as Conroy now perceives them. They, although still breathing, are the truly dead, and young Michael Furey, if only because he exists as he does in the minds of Gretta and Gabriel Conroy, is alive, a clearly defined personal entity, a strong energy.

"The Dead" is the last, the longest, and the most complex of the stories of James Joyce's first volume of fiction, *Dubliners*. Of this book Joyce said, "My intention was to write a chapter of the moral history of my country and I chose Dublin for the scene because the city seemed to me the centre of paralysis."[1] What Joyce had in mind when he spoke of "paralysis" is suggested by an incident in "The Dead," Aunt Julia's singing. For a fleeting moment there is a remission of the "paralysis," for the old lady sings surprisingly well, and we are told that "to follow the voice was to feel and share the excitement of swift and secure flight." *The excitement of swift and secure flight:* here is life as the poets wish it to be, as we all at some time imagine it possibly can be. But in quoting the sentence, I have omitted a qualifying clause. The whole sentence reads: "To follow the voice, without looking at the singer's face, was to feel and share the excitement of swift and secure flight." If one did look at her face, Joyce is telling us, one saw the ap-

[1] See "Three Letters to Grant Richards" in Part One. [Eds.]

Lionel Trilling, Commentary by Lionel Trilling from *The Experience of Literature* edited by Lionel Trilling. Copyright © 1967 by Lionel Trilling. Pp. 652–655. Reprinted by permission of Holt, Rinehart and Winston, Inc.

proach of death and the limitation of mind and spirit that marks not Aunt Julia alone but all the relatives and friends who are gathered around her. One saw the poverty of experience and passion, of gaiety, wit, intelligence—the death-in-life of a narrow, provincial existence.

Joyce writes of his own nation and city with passionate particularity. But when we consider the very high place that "The Dead" has been given in the canon of modern literature, and the admiration it has won from readers of the most diverse backgrounds, we must say that Joyce has written a chapter in the moral history not only of his own country but of the whole modern western world. Gabriel Conroy's plight, his sense that he has been overtaken by death-in-life, is shared by many in our time: it is one of the characteristics of modern society that an ever-growing number of people are not content to live by habit and routine and by the unquestioning acceptance of the circumstances into which they have been born. They believe they have the right to claim for themselves pleasure, or power, or dignity, or fullness of experience; a prerogative which in former times was exercised by relatively few people, usually members of the privileged classes, and which now seems available to many people regardless of class. Yet almost in the degree that modern man feels free to assert the personal claims which are the expression of a heightened sense of individuality, [652] he seems to fall prey to that peculiarly modern disorder so often remarked by novelists, psychologists, and sociologists—an uncertainty about who the person is who makes the claims, a diminished sense of his personal identity.

Identity is the word that Gabriel Conroy uses when he thinks about death: he sees "his own identity . . . fading out into a grey impalpable world." And his imagination of death provides the image of his life. All through the evening his identity had been fading out into the grey impalpable world of his aunts' party. All through his youth and his early middle-age his identity had been fading out into the grey impalpable world of Dublin society.

It is sometimes said that Gabriel Conroy is what James Joyce would have been, or what he supposed he would have been, if he had not fled Dublin at the age of twenty, with no resources but his talent and his youth, risking privation for the sake of achievement and fame. And certainly the juxtaposition of the author and his character helps us understand Gabriel Conroy. Joyce was one of an old and rare species of man: he was a genius, with all the stubborn resistance and courage, all the strong sense of identity, by which, in addition to great gifts, genius is defined. Gabriel Conroy is one of a new, and very numerous, kind of man whose large demand upon life is supported neither by native gift nor moral energy. He has the knowledge of excellence but cannot achieve it for himself; he admires distinction and cannot attain it.

Poor Conroy's deficiency manifests itself most saliently and sadly in his relation to his wife. Gretta is a person of rather considerable distinction; among the guests at the party she is the only woman who possesses beauty, charm, and temperament. She is vivacious and spirited, and, as her evocation of the dead Michael Furey suggests, she has a capacity for intense feeling. To this endowment her husband responds with admiration and love, but he has the dim, implicit knowledge that he cannot match it with qualities of his own. When his wife tells him the story of her girlhood romance, his inarticulate self-knowledge is suddenly made explicit and devastating. The sharp clarity with which Michael Furey has remained in Gretta's consciousness, his embodiment of will and passion, make plain to Gabriel Conroy how fully he himself has succumbed to his aunts' impalpable grey world of habit, respectability, and mediocrity.

The literary means by which Joyce represents the world of Conroy's friends and relatives are striking in their subtlety and diversity. If Joyce has an opinion about the people who gather at the old aunts'—and we know he has—he does not express it overtly. At times he seems to subordinate his own judgment to theirs, as when he gravely tells us about the serving maid Lily that she "seldom made a mistake in the orders, so that she got on well with her three mistresses. They were fussy, that was all. But the only thing they would not stand was back answers." Now and then he seems to yield to the spirit of the party and uses a prose which, in a fatigued way, takes on something of the consciously fanciful humor of Dickens in his scenes of jollification: "On the closed square piano a pudding in a huge yellow dish lay in waiting and behind it were three squads of bottles of stout and ale and minerals, drawn up according to the colours of their uniforms, the first two black, with brown and red labels, the third and smallest squad white, with transverse green sashes." For the most part, however, the tone of the prose is neutral and a little naive, as if Joyce has no point of view of his own, or as if he were saying that he has no wish to judge, let alone to blame—for how can one blame the dead for being dead? [653]

Nothing could be more brilliant and subtle, or humane, than Joyce's management of his own—and our—relation to Gabriel Conroy. All the details of Conroy's behavior at the party contribute to our perception of his second-rateness. But we are never invited to despise him, we are never permitted to triumph over him. Joyce spares him nothing in making us aware of his mediocrity: we know all about his nervous desire to be liked and approved, his wish to be thought superior, his fear of asserting whatever superiority he may actually have, his lack of intellectual and emotional courage, his sulky resentment when he feels slighted, his easy sentimentality. But at the same time Joyce does not obscure Conroy's genuine intention of kindness, his actual considerateness, his demand upon himself that he be large-minded and generous. And he protects Conroy from our ultimate contempt by making plain the extent of his fairly accurate self-knowledge; there is little we discern to Conroy's discredit that the unhappy man does not himself know and deplore.

But self-knowledge cannot save Conroy from being the kind of man he is, and when we try to say what that kind is, we are bound to think of his commitment to galoshes. In the British Isles, much more than in America, the wearing of galoshes and rubbers is regarded as an excessive and rather foolish caution about one's health. The fact that Conroy makes such a great thing of wearing them himself and urges them on his wife—but on the night of the party she defies him— puts him in almost too obvious contrast with Michael Furey, who had died from standing in the rain to bid his love farewell. It is Conroy's sense of his vulnerability, his uneasy feeling that almost every situation is a threat, that makes him what he is. He has no valid reason to think that the servant girl is really angry with him; when she responds to his remark about her getting married, her "great bitterness" is directed not at him but at the conditions of her life, yet Conroy feels that "he had made a mistake," that he had "failed" with her, and he is extravagantly distressed. He is equally self-conscious and timorous in his half-flirta-tious dispute with Miss Ivors, feeling that the nature of their relation makes it impossible for him to "risk a grandiose phrase with her." He does indeed achieve a moment of dignity when he is moved by desire for his wife, but even here he protects himself, resolving to postpone his wooing until he is certain of being fully responded to. And when he does at last speak, it is to make an irrelevant and banal remark that quite belies his emotion.

Conroy's own last adverse judgment on himself is extreme—he sees himself as "a ludicrous figure, acting as a pennyboy for his aunts, a nervous, well-meaning sentimentalist, orating to vulgarians and idealis-ing his own clownish lusts, the pitiable fatuous fellow he had caught a glimpse of in the mirror." This extravagance of self-contempt is not only the outcome of self-knowledge; it is also the expression of Con-roy's self-pity, an emotion which we are taught to despise. But Joyce does not despise it and he does not permit us to despise it. As Conroy lies in defeat and meditation beside his sleeping wife, his evocation of the sadness of life under the dominion of death is the climax of his self-pity, yet when his commiseration with himself reaches this point of intensity, the author's own emotion is seen to be in active accord with it. This sudden identification of the author with his character is one of the most striking and effective elements of the story. Joyce feels exactly what Conroy feels about the sadness of human life, its terrible nearness to death, and the *waste* that every life is; he directs no irony upon Conroy's grief but makes Conroy's suffering his own, [654] with no reservations whatever. At several points in the story he has clearly regarded Conroy's language, or the tone of his thoughts, as banal, or vulgar, or sentimental. But as the story approaches its conclusion, it becomes impossible for us to know whose language we are hearing,

Conroy's or the author's, or to whose tone of desperate sorrow we are responding. It is as if Joyce, secure in his genius and identity, were saying that under the aspect of the imagination of death and of death-in-life there is no difference between him and the mediocre, sentimental man of whom he has been writing. [655]

The Snow

JACK BARRY LUDWIG

GABRIEL CONROY, IN "THE DEAD," THE APTLY NAMED CODA TO *Dubliners,* [387] is a later, totally defeated version of the young boy of "The Sisters." Like his prototypes, Chandler and Duffy, he has *not* flown the nets[1] of Ireland. If Stephen Dedalus had remained in Ireland till he was Gabriel Conroy's age, he might have been Gabriel Conroy; for Gabriel is Stephen . . . less hope, less courage, less heroic Dedalean stature. Where Stephen's discovery of the nets leads to an affirmation of life, a determination to journey eastward to the continent the nationalists despise, Gabriel's discovery leads to a readying for "the journey westward," for his "final end."

The snow that Gabriel watches at the end of the book is the snow that is introduced into Dublin town with him. At first it seems to be no more than a symbol of escape, a symbol of the world outside the pettiness and the ugliness of the "Misses Morkan's annual dance." The things Gabriel wishes to escape from form the microcosm of the Ireland Stephen Dedalus *did* fly from, the nets from which his soul escaped. Stephen had no illusions about the world in which he found himself. Opposition he met head on, whether it was from friend, foe, family, or female. Only in this way are the nets evaded. Gabriel, on the other hand, keeps insisting to himself, in his vapid illusions and romantic imaginings, that the nets are but gossamer webs. Unlike Stephen, he attempts to temporize, to assume the attitudes of the different members of the different cultural levels meeting in the home of his aunts. But nothing works: he has an unpleasant encounter with the

---

[1] In *A Portrait of the Artist as a Young Man* (New York, 1964) Stephen says to Davin, the Irish nationalist: "When the soul of a man is born in this country there are nets flung at it to hold it back from flight. You talk to me of nationality, language, religion. I shall try to fly by those nets" (203). [Eds.]

From "James Joyce's *Dubliners,*" in Jack Barry Ludwig and W. Richard Poirier, eds., *Stories: British and American.* Boston: Houghton Mifflin Company, 1953. Pp. 384–391. Copyright by Jack Ludwig. Reprinted by permission of Jack Ludwig and the publisher.

rude maid, Lily, when he—unseeing—attempts casual conversation in order to communicate with somebody—anybody—at the party. Loud, corny, self-styled humorists like the Protestant Browne ("'I hope, Miss Morkan . . . that I am brown enough for you because, you know, I'm all brown'"), ignorant, quarreling drunks like the "aesthetically-involved" Freddy Malins ("'And why couldn't he have a voice too?' asked Freddy Malins sharply. 'Is it because he's only a black?'"), tremendous architectural bores like Mrs. Malins ("Her son-in-law was a splendid fisher. One day he caught a beautiful big fish and the man in the hotel cooked it for their dinner"), prudish fanatics like Miss Ivors ("She did not wear a low-cut bodice and the large brooch which was fixed in the front of her collar bore on it an Irish device and motto"), are much more successful at the party than the sensitive intellectual, Gabriel. They all have levels on which they can communicate with someone—he none. The unpleasantness which follows his encounter with each of the members of the different levels induces in Gabriel a desire to escape; the symbols of snow and cold, which are introduced into the story with Gabriel's entrance into the house of the Misses Morkan, become more [388] and more meaningful till they are fully understood at the very end of the story.

The first description of Gabriel contains other details which later assume larger meaning. "A light fringe of snow lay like a cape on the shoulders of his overcoat and like toe-caps on the toes of his goloshes; and, as the buttons of his overcoat slipped with a squeaking noise through the snow-stiffened frieze, a cold, fragrant air from out-of-doors escaped from crevices and folds." The reappearance of snow and cold mark the successive stages of Gabriel's failure of communication. After the rude answer from Lily, after he has assumed the failure with Lily to portend the inevitable failure of his speech, after the slight unpleasantness with his aunt over the "continent" (the incident of the goloshes), after being revealed as a nervous, ill-at-ease man who frets over his children and his wife, after his tiff with Miss Ivors and gruffness with Gretta, Gabriel returns to thoughts of the cold, snow-covered outside. Inside is isolation, outside solitude:

Gabriel's warm trembling fingers tapped the cold pane of the window. How cool it must be outside! How pleasant it would be to walk out alone, first along by the river and then through the park! The snow would be lying on the branches of the trees and forming a bright cap on the top of the Wellington Monument. How much more pleasant it would be there than at the supper-table!

The symbols begin to take on added meaning. After the faked heartiness of the carving rites, just before beginning the much worried-over speech, Gabriel once more returns to thoughts of escape, again symbolized by the world of snow and cold: "People, perhaps, were standing in the snow on the quay outside, gazing up at the lighted windows and listening to the waltz music. The air was pure there. In the distance lay the park where the trees were weighted with snow. The Wellington Monument wore a gleaming cap of snow that flashed westward over the white field of Fifteen Acres."

Away from the party, his speech over, Gabriel reacts to the cold and the snow; even though the surroundings are anything but what his illusions are fixed on, he feels liberated, happy, ready for anything. The movement away from the party is treated with a sudden change of pace and the diction is foreboding, dwelling on all the unpleasantness of the winter scene:

> The morning was still dark. A dull, yellow light brooded over the houses and the river; and the sky seemed to be descending. It was slushy underfoot; and the only streaks and patches of snow lay on the [389] roofs, on the parapets of the quay and on the area railings. The lamps were still burning redly in the murky air and, across the river, the palace of the Four Courts stood out menacingly against the heavy sky.

However, Gabriel is unconscious of these surroundings; only Gretta means anything to him now: "Gabriel's eyes were still bright with happiness. The blood went bounding along his veins; and the thoughts went rioting through his brain, proud, joyful, tender, valorous." His gaiety is a new mood and the tone of the section that follows is new to the story. But Joyce does not forget the meaning of the symbols of snow and cold: even in his gaiety, when he waves at the statue of Daniel O'Connell—another dead hero like Wellington, and another symbol of snow-covered greatness—"on which lay patches of snow," and when he tips the cabman handsomely, Gabriel is moving toward the epiphany in which the full meaning of all the symbols becomes clear.

Gabriel believes he has escaped, that he and Gretta have flown the world of ugliness, that they will "run away together with wild and radiant hearts to a new adventure"; in sentimental language he recalls their days of happiness together, when "Birds were twittering in the ivy." But once alone with Gretta, once in the hotel room where, like Lochinvar finding an unattended Guinevere, he locks the door in readiness for his great moment of love, all his diffidence returns. "He longed to cry to her from his soul, to crush her body against his, to overmaster her," but what he says is dull, prosaic, inspiring neither lust nor love in Gretta.

His patient wait for her to come to him as he wishes her to is destroyed by the tale she tells of Michael Furey. Gabriel finds that Gretta—and Michael—were capable of a kind of love he can conceive of only dimly. His defeat is completed. In the epiphany which follows, all his temporizing, all his illusions, all his sentimental nostalgia, appear to him for what they are. He sees himself whole, giving up in the act the possibility of a future with meaning:

A shameful consciousness of his own person assailed him. He saw himself a ludicrous figure, acting as a pennyboy for his aunts, a nervous, well-meaning sentimentalist, orating to vulgarians and idealising his own clownish lusts, the pitiable fatuous fellow he had caught a glimpse of in the mirror.

The tableau of the sobbing Gretta and the inadequate Gabriel dramatizes his complete isolation: "Gabriel held her hand for a moment longer, irresolutely, and then, shy of intruding on her grief, [390] let it fall gently and walked quietly to the window." The act of dropping Gretta's hand is the act of recognition: Gabriel now knows that his last hope of achieving identification—for all his other attempts have been failures just as his acts at the party ended in failure—is gone: "His own identity was fading out into the grey impalpable world: the solid world itself, which these dead had one time reared and lived in, was dissolving and dwindling."

It is here that the careful reader must recall other details which previously appeared in the story. Recalling the description of Gabriel on his entrance into the house, he will see that the details are substantially the same as those which describe the snow-covered statues of the departed great, Wellington and O'Connell. He will see that by connecting Gabriel with the statues, Joyce is saying that Gabriel is without life, inanimate, made of stone, a paralytic after his final stroke, like Father Flynn of "The Sisters." Now he will recall that the description of Gabriel was that of a harbinger of death ("a cold, fragrant air from out-of-doors escaped from crevices and folds"); now he will recall Gabriel's fixation with the dead past (and past dead) and the story of Johnny the horse: "Poor Aunt Julia! She, too, would soon be a shade with the shade of Patrick Morkan and his horse." Now the reader will recall that Gabriel's mother was very conscious of the dignity of names, naming the son who became a "senior curate in Balbriggan," Constantine, after the famous emperor and Christian, and the son who tells of the "final end," the one with the task of singing a requiem, Gabriel.

Now it is seen that there is nothing of romantic escape about the symbols of snow and cold: Gabriel's escape is the escape into death. The snow that formed a cape on his overcoat, the snow that formed a bright cap on the Wellington Monument, the snow that covered Daniel O'Connell's statue in patches, snow like this is beginning to blanket all, "falling faintly through the universe and faintly falling, like the descent of their last end, upon all the living and the dead." Snow, as Mary Jane reported and Gabriel now recalls in the coda to the volume, is "general all over Ireland." Paralysis is general all over Ireland. Death is general all over Ireland. For his own death Gabriel not waits. He merges with the dead of the past and the dead of the present, watching the snow—the death of all—"falling faintly . . . upon all the living and the dead."[391]

APPENDICES

Chronology

A. WALTON LITZ

1882   James Joyce born in Dublin on February 2, the eldest son of John Stanislaus Joyce, an improvident tax collector, and Mary Jane Joyce.

1884   Birth of Stanislaus Joyce. Of the ten Joyce children who survived infancy, Stanislaus was closest to James.

1888   In September Joyce entered Clongowes Wood College, a Jesuit boarding school; there he remained (except for holidays) until June, 1891.

1891   A crucial year in Joyce's life. Financial difficulties forced John Joyce to withdraw James from Clongowes Wood in June. The death of Parnell on October 6 deeply affected the nine-year-old boy, who wrote a poem, "Et Tu, Healy," denouncing Parnell's "betrayer," Tim Healey; John Joyce was so pleased that he had the poem printed, but no copy has survived. Christmas dinner in the Joyce household was marred by a violent scene later described in *Portrait of the Artist.*

1893   In April Joyce entered another Jesuit school, Belvedere College, where he remained until 1898, making a brilliant academic record.

1898   Joyce began to attend University College, Dublin, a Jesuit institution founded by Cardinal Newman. While there, his revolt against Catholicism and provincial patriotism took form.

1899   In May Joyce opposed his fellow students and refused to sign a letter attacking the "heresy" of Yeats's *Countess Cathleen.*

1900   A year of literary activity. In January Joyce read a paper on "Drama and Life" before the college literary society (see *Stephen Hero*); in April his essay on "Ibsen's New Drama" appeared in the distinguished *Fortnightly Review.*

1901   Late in the year Joyce published "The Day of the Rabblement," an essay attacking the provincialism of the Irish theater (originally designed for a college magazine, it was rejected by the Jesuit adviser).

A. Walton Litz, "Chronology," in his *James Joyce.* New York: Twayne Publishers, Inc., 1966. Reprinted by permission of the publisher.

1902   In February Joyce read a paper on the Irish poet James Clarence Mangan, claiming that Mangan had been the victim of narrow nationalism.

Joyce, who received his degree in October, finally decided to study medicine in Paris. He left Dublin in the late autumn, pausing briefly in London to visit Yeats and to investigate possible outlets for his writing.

1903   Once in Paris, Joyce soon lost interest in medicine and began to write reviews for a Dublin newspaper. On April 10 he received a telegram, "MOTHER DYING COME HOME FATHER," and immediately returned to Dublin. His mother died on August 13.

1904   Early in 1904 Joyce began work on his autobiographical novel with a short piece called "A Portrait of the Artist": this was later expanded into *Stephen Hero* and then recast to make *A Portrait of the Artist as a Young Man*.

The situation of the Joyce family had worsened after Mary Joyce's death, and James gradually withdrew from the family. In March he took a job as teacher in a Dalkey school, remaining there until the end of June. On June 10 Joyce met Nora Barnacle and soon fell in love with her. Since he was opposed to marriage as an institution, and could not live with Nora in Dublin, Joyce decided to make his way in Europe. He and Nora left Dublin on October 8, traveling through London and Zurich to Pola, where Joyce began teaching English at the Berlitz School.

1905   Joyce moved to Trieste in March, and a son, Giorgio, was born on July 27. Three months later Joyce's younger brother, Stanislaus, joined him in Trieste. Late in the year Joyce submitted the manuscript of *Dubliners* to a publisher, but it was not until 1914—after years of controversy—that the book appeared.

1906– In July 1906 Joyce moved to Rome, where he worked in a bank
1907   until March of the next year; he then returned to Trieste and resumed his language teaching. In May a London publisher issued *Chamber Music*. A daughter, Lucia Anna, was born on July 26.

1908   In September Joyce began revising *Stephen Hero* and continued this work into the next year, but after finishing three chapters he temporarily abandoned the manuscript.

1909   On August 1 Joyce traveled to Ireland for a visit. The next month he came back to Trieste, gained financial support, and returned to Dublin where he opened a cinema.

1910   Joyce returned to Trieste in January, and the cinema venture soon collapsed. During his first visit to Dublin, Joyce underwent an emotional crisis later transformed into the substance of his play, *Exiles*.

1911– During these years the controversy over *Dubliners* became an obses-
1912   sion with Joyce. Finally, in July, 1912, he made his last trip to Dublin, but was unable to arrange for publication. Joyce left Dublin

in great bitterness, and on the return journey to Trieste wrote a savage broadside, *Gas from a Burner.*

1913   Late in the year Joyce began to correspond with Ezra Pound; his luck was changing.

1914   Joyce's *annus mirabilis.* Serial publication of *A Portrait of the Artist as a Young Man* began in the *Egoist* (installments ran from February, 1914, to September, 1915). *Dubliners* was finally published in June. In March Joyce began drafting *Ulysses;* but he soon suspended work on the novel to write *Exiles.*

1915   *Exiles* was completed in the spring. In spite of the war Joyce was allowed to depart in June for neutral Switzerland.

1916   *Portrait* was published in book form on December 29.

1917   During this year Joyce underwent his first eye operation. By the end of 1917 Joyce had finished drafting the first three episodes of *Ulysses;* the structure of the novel was already taking shape.

1918   In March the *Little Review* (New York) began to serialize *Ulysses.* *Exiles* was published on May 25.

1919   In October Joyce returned to Trieste, where he taught English and drove *Ulysses* toward completion.

1920   At the insistence of Ezra Pound, Joyce moved to Paris in early July. In October a complaint from the Society for the Suppression of Vice stopped publication of *Ulysses* in the *Little Review* (the opening pages of "Oxen of the Sun" were the last to appear).

1921   This year was devoted to completing the last episodes of *Ulysses* and to revising the entire work.

1922   *Ulysses* was published on February 2, Joyce's fortieth birthday.

1923   On March 10 Joyce wrote the first pages of *Finnegans Wake* (known before publication in 1939 as *Work in Progress*). He had been actively planning for this new work through several years.

1924   The first published fragment of *Finnegans Wake* appeared in April. During the next fourteen years Joyce was to publish most of *Finnegans Wake* in preliminary versions.

1927–   Between April, 1927, and November, 1929, Joyce published early
1929   versions of *Finnegans Wake,* Parts I and III, in the experimental magazine *transition. Anna Livia Plurabelle* (FW I. viii) was published in book form on October 20, 1928. During the next ten years several sections of *Work in Progress* were published as books (see Bibliography).

1931–   In May the Joyces traveled to London, and on July 4 James and
1932   Nora Joyce were married at a registry office ("for testamentary reasons"). Joyce's father died on December 29; and a grandson, Stephen Joyce, was born on February 15 of the next year. Both

events affected Joyce profoundly: see his poem written at the time, "Ecce Puer." In March Joyce's daughter, Lucia, suffered a nervous breakdown; she never recovered, and the remainder of Joyce's life was darkened by this event.

1933   Late in the year an American court ruled that *Ulysses* was not pornographic; this famous decision led to the first authorized American publication of the work in February of the next year (the first English edition was issued in 1936).

1934   Most of this year was spent in Switzerland, so that Joyce could be near Lucia (who was confined to an institution near Zurich) and could consult a Zurich doctor who had cared for his failing eyesight since 1930.

1935–   During these years Joyce labored slowly to complete *Finnegans*
1938   *Wake;* residence in Paris was broken by frequent trips through France, Switzerland, and Denmark.

1939   *Finnegans Wake* was published on May 4, but Joyce received a copy in time for his fifty-seventh birthday.

1940–   After the fall of France, the Joyces managed to reach Zurich; James
1941   Joyce died there on January 13, 1941, after an abdominal operation.

Suggestions for Study

"Drama and Life"

1. In "Drama and Life" Joyce writes: "Human society is the embodiment of changeless laws which the whimsicalities and circumstances of men and women involve and overwrap. The realm of literature is the realm of these accidental manners and humors—a spacious realm; and the true literary artist concerns himself mainly with them." In what way does this statement reflect Joyce's rationale for the title *Dubliners* and for the collection and division of the stories?

2. How does Joyce's disagreement with Mr. Tree explain to some degree his method in *Dubliners?*

3. Joyce maintains in this essay that man longs to become "a maker and a moulder" and that in this longing is the necessity of art. He goes on to say that life itself provides the stuff out of which drama is made and that "drama arises spontaneously out of life and is coeval with it." What evidence

do you find in *Dubliners* to indicate that Joyce is engaged in writing "drama"?

"The Dramatic Form"

1. Joyce writes: "The artist, like the God of the creation, remains within or behind or beyond or above his handiwork, invisible, refined out of existence, indifferent, paring his fingernails." Is Joyce this impersonal in *Dubliners* or does he fail to achieve this detachment? If he fails, do you think that it is to the detriment or benefit of his art?

2. "The dramatic form is reached when the vitality which has flowed and eddied round each person fills every person with such vital force that he or she assumes a proper and intangible esthetic life." Consider one story from *Dubliners* and show in it how Joyce has or has not reached "dramatic form" according to his definition.

3. Stephen mentions here the old English ballad "Turpin Hero" as one which "begins in the first person and ends in the third person." Is it worth remarking, in connection with Joyce's theory excerpted above, that *Dubliners* does the same? Develop your remarks fully.

"Epiphany"

1. Discuss the function of the "epiphany" in one of the first three stories in *Dubliners*. Does the epiphany in the story seem to coincide with Stephen's theoretical explanation?

2. Speaking here of "epiphany," Joyce says that "the apprehensive faculty must be scrutinised in action." By examining the series of apprehensions which lead up to the epiphany in "Araby," show to what extent Joyce makes it possible for this faculty to be scrutinized in action.

3. Is there an inherently *positive* quality in epiphany? Is this true even when the knowledge or understanding brought out is tragically late for the person involved?

4. Reread carefully Stephen's explanation of *claritas* and *quidditas* in this selection. Stephen is, of course, deliberately investigating this concept for the tremendous forces of emotion and understanding which it releases from everyday objects and situations. Choose one story from *Dubliners* and show how its protagonist experiences *claritas*, "radiance," revealed in the world around him.

5. In the portion of *Stephen Hero* reprinted here, we see how Stephen's sensitiveness is "afflicted" by a keen impression gathered "as he passed on his quest." That word *quest* seems to assume great importance in the light of what follows in Stephen's conversation with Cranly. What would you say that quest is, in light of that conversation? What is its unstated importance for Stephen's idea of epiphany?

"A Succession of Epiphanies"

1. Spencer writes that *Dubliners* "is a series of epiphanies." Do you agree with his contention? Is the epiphany an essential element in each story?

2. You may or may not agree that any of his works are, as Spencer says of *A Portrait of the Artist as a Young Man,* a "showing forth—of Joyce himself." Be that as it may, do you see in the first three stories of *Dubliners* any sort of unified (fictional character) "showing forth"? Describe this "character."

"Three Letters to Grant Richards"

1. Among many other things, these letters reveal the great difficulty Joyce had in getting *Dubliners* published. To what extent do you feel this difficulty influenced the collection? In what specific ways? See Ellmann's biography of Joyce for further background and also the pertinent letters to Grant Richards and others in the *Letters* (see bibliography).

2. The three letters reprinted here reflect a growth in Joyce's ambitions and a broader purpose for *Dubliners.* Why do you think that Joyce was so persistent in his refusal to make changes and what does the fact that he was willing to give in to Richards on some points but remained rigid on others reveal?

3. Once an author has struggled successfully and fixed his works as permanently as Joyce has fixed them as objects of our attention, we can afford the luxury of reviewing his forewarnings. Compare, for instance, Joyce's three letters reprinted here with his essay "Drama and Life." Formulate as best you can the principles implicit in these letters; discover to what extent they appear five years previously in the essay.

"*Dubliners* and the Short Story"

1. In this essay the authors point out that critics of *Dubliners* most frequently cite Chekhov and Maupassant as Joyce's models. But Joyce is really quite different in his approach from both of these writers. In what ways does he differ from them? In what ways are these three writers similar in their approach to the short story?

2. In what manner do the stories in *Dubliners* reflect many of the criteria of naturalistic fiction found in Zola's movement? Is Joyce's adherence to these tenets more than superficial and accidental? In what ways does he go beyond scientific objectivity in these stories?

3. Another strong movement in the literature of English-speaking countries which made itself felt at the time Joyce came to maturity was "organized symbolism." In what way does Joyce use suggestive detail and symbol in *Dubliners*? Does his use of symbol become part of his theory of "epiphany"? In what way? See Baker's essay and Joyce's "Epiphany."

"Virtues and Limitations"

1. Goldberg instances four stories—"Eveline," "After the Race," "The Boarding House," and "Counterparts"—which he says are "too intent upon their analytical purposes" so that in them "the art comes to seem almost programmatic." Choose one of the four stories and demonstrate how Goldberg's criticism is or is not justified.

2. If it is true that, as Goldberg says, the young Joyce had "an uncertain grasp of the values by which others are criticised," we see how Joyce might very well have oversimplified the conditions which illustrate the judgment implicit in each story. Do you find this to be the case in *Dubliners*? Illustrate your answer fully.

3. Goldberg says that in *Dubliners* Joyce chose "to work through the limited consciousness of his characters" and moreover that "he could not see more in his characters than their limitations." Refer back to the selection from *Stephen Hero* reprinted in this volume; explain how this impression of the technique in *Dubliners* as "limited" does or does not fit into Stephen's claims for the artist.

"The Unity of *Dubliners*"

1. Ghiselin says that in the fifth through eleventh stories in *Dubliners* the "seven deadly sins" are portrayed "successively in action, usually in association with other sins adjacent in the list." Examine those stories in order to show how each of the "seven deadly sins" is presented, how each contributes to a "unified" paralysis. (Consult a standard reference such as the *Catholic Encyclopedia* for traditional definitions and analyses of the so-called "seven deadly sins.")

2. Assume for a moment that *Dubliners* ends with "Grace" as Joyce originally planned. On this basis, trace, as a theme participating in a structure with such an ending, the notion of the Catholic Church in Ireland as a "false east." Then show how the addition of "The Dead" affects such a theme and structure.

3. Ghiselin says that *Dubliners* is a novel as well as a group of short stories, that in this "novel" the separate histories of various protagonists compose "one essential history, that of the soul of a people." Make an abstract of this *Dubliners* novel, a précis showing the progress of this people-protagonist from beginning to denouement.

"Ibsen, Joyce, and the Living-Dead"

1. The author of this essay speaks of "epiphany" as having "the saving quality of a revelation containing the seeds not only of suffering but resurrection." Is this aspect manifest in all the epiphanies in the *Dubliners,* or only in certain of them? Demonstrate how your findings affect the work as a whole.

2. Read Ibsen's *When We Dead Awaken.* Formulate from it, as best you can, the "neatly condensed version of the symbolic parable" which Baker claims to be of such importance to Joyce in all his works. What is the "epiphany" in the play? Does your investigation add anything to Baker's discussion of this "parable" in *Dubliners?*

3. Compare Baker's sketch of the progress in "tragic" capacity of Joyce's characters with Friedrich's idea of "perspective."

"The Perspective of Joyce's *Dubliners*"

1. Friedrich mentions the importance of the first and last stories for the perspective of *Dubliners* as a whole. Show how the first paragraph of "The Sisters" and the last paragraph of "The Dead" taken together suggest a perspective for the whole work.

2. Joyce is quoted here as saying: "I call the series *Dubliners* to betray the soul of that hemiplegia or paralysis which many consider a city." How completely did Joyce present the city itself? Is the total picture provided by the collection one of general, or only local, paralysis?

3. Compare Friedrich, Baker, and Ghiselin on the structure and development of *Dubliners.*

"Joyce's 'The Sisters' "

1. Connolly says: "It seems to me to stretch the story beyond its limits to make the cream crackers and sherry the bread and wine of the Mass as one critic has done." You may be puzzled by this objection to a complexity of symbol which some critics in this volume and elsewhere seem to accept as part and parcel of Joyce's technique. Is there something special about this instance or its context? Or would you be inclined to accept the bread-and-wine identification?

2. The purpose of this article is to restore "The Sisters" to a "simple reading," one free from critical distortions. Consider very carefully the "reading" so restored and evaluate it on the strength of your experience thus far with both Joyce and his critics.

3. Connolly makes much of the boy's first reaction to death in "The Sisters." In what way would Gabriel Conroy be experiencing a similar first reaction to death in "The Dead"?

"The Wings of Daedalus"

1. What evidence do you find throughout *Dubliners* for the importance of the father-quest emphasized in this article? (It may help you to clarify for yourself the meaning of the "wings of Daedalus.")

2. Look at "An Encounter" in two ways: first, as a simple descriptive narrative (the literal level only); second, as the complex symbolic structure revealed by Kaye. Evaluate the difference in terms of the literary experience provided by the two readings. What details of Kaye's reading seem dubious or forced?

3. Where would you say the climax occurs in "An Encounter"? What does Kaye's treatment of the story contribute to your understanding of it as more than a narrative of incident?

"The Chalice Bearer"

1. The authors of this essay explain only those "apparently irrelevant items" which illustrate their concern with one area of symbolism in "Araby." Discover another area of symbolism in the story and show how it accounts for similarly apparently irrelevant items.

2. Compare the use of the "journey" or "quest" motif in "An Encounter" and "Araby." If you find the significance of the protagonist's experience to be greatly similar in these stories, find some justification for there being *two* stories.

3. Develop as fully as you can the analogies between the boy and the priest. Show how these similarities serve to illuminate the theme of quest and disappointment here and in "The Sisters."

"Eveline"

1. Dolch mentions that "Eveline" was written in 1903, not long after Joyce eloped with Nora Barnacle. As an exercise in comparing "the raw material of life" with literary expression, read that portion of Richard Ellmann's biography which deals with Joyce's elopement. Do you find that such a comparison increases your understanding of literature, of the literary experience?

2. Joyce critics have paid comparatively little attention to "Eveline." Give reasons—from the story itself, or from its relationship to the collection —why you think this is so. Should it be so?

3. Consult some standard reference (such as Butler's *Lives of the Saints*) for the "promises" made to Blessed Margaret Mary Alacoque. Do the promises themselves add anything to "Eveline," or is Dolch's mention of Blessed Margaret Mary's miraculous cure enough to clarify his account of her presence in the story?

"A Study in Weakness and Humiliation"

1. What evidence do you find in "After the Race" to support Adams's statement that "there are some reasons why the figure of Jimmy Doyle is not simply contemptible, contemptible though he doubtless is"?

2. Mrs. Mooney of "The Boarding House" is described as one who "deals with moral problems as a cleaver deals with meat." Is the moral problem in "After the Race" dealt with in a similar manner?

"Two Gallants"

1. What is the moment of "epiphany" in "Two Gallants" and how does it reflect Joyce's ability to further the reader's insight into his characters through the epiphanic strategy?

2. Father Noon states that a calculated arrangement of words and images is necessary to achieve the right adjustment of symbolic insight in a story. How does Joyce manage to prepare the reader for the moment of "epiphany" in "Two Gallants"?

3. What are some of the images in "Two Gallants" that carry Joyce's theme through the "symbolic dimensions of language" and in what way do they function?

"The Boarding House"

1. Develop the idea that "Polly is Corley's female counterpart."

2. Mrs. Mooney has been called, by her admirers, one of the most horrible women in literature. What is so horrible about her?

3. This story has not been frequently analyzed by the critics. Why? Is it transparent and simple compared with "The Sisters"? Are the details less significant, less "symbolic," than those in the earlier story? Or have they simply been neglected by ingenious critics?

" 'A Little Cloud': Joyce's Portrait of the Would-Be Artist"

1. Given Stanislaus Joyce's description of it, do you think that you would find in "A Little Cloud" more or less of what Joyce defined as art, "the very central expression of life"? Does Joyce mean that the artist, or would-be artist, is somehow representative of people in general?

2. Ruoff quotes widely from both primary and secondary materials on Joyce. Using his article as the base for your "research," develop the idea that Joyce pictured the failure of the ordinary man to become an artist as a *typical* failure symptomatic of the paralysis analyzed in *Dubliners*.

3. Taking a hint from Joyce's critics' examinations of the significance of names, discover for yourself the possible significance of Little Chandler's name.

"Character and Structure in 'Counterparts' "

1. The central character in "Counterparts," Farrington, is a scrivener. For what reasons does Hagopian suggest that the scrivener has assumed an archetypal significance in modern literature?

2. The author states that many of the stories in *Dubliners* focus on one of the seven deadly sins. With what sin is "Counterparts" concerned? Support your answer with specific references in the text of the story.

3. How does the end of "Counterparts" reflect Irene Hendry's statement that "in *Dubliners, claritas* is achieved most often, although not always, through an apparently trivial incident, action, or single detail which differs from the others making up the story only in that it illuminates them, integrates them, and gives them meaning"?

"Virgin and Witch"

1. The authors of this article say that "the superimposition of modern Maria upon the ancient and venerable symbol of Mary is aesthetically effective." Explain how such a "superimposition" is effective in "Clay." (You will, of course, want to specify what "aesthetically effective" means.)

2. If it were true (as Stanislaus Joyce is quoted as maintaining) that James Joyce had "no such subtleties in mind" as those suggested in this article by Magalaner and Kain—what then does "Clay" offer the reader? Do your findings lead you to accept or reject Stanislaus Joyce's testimony?

3. Martin Dolch, in his essay printed above, speaks of celibacy as "implicitly condemned by Joyce." Do you find in "Clay" a similar condemna-

tion? Keep in mind that virgins as well as some witches may be said to be "celibate."

"Isolation as Motif in 'A Painful Case' "

1. Develop fully the reasons why Maria in "Clay" is "only dead," whereas Mr. Duffy in "A Painful Case" is "damned," according to Corrington.

2. Study "A Painful Case" carefully and explain more fully than Corrington does how Mr. Duffy comes to change from his attitude of self-righteousness ("He had no difficulty now in approving of the course he had taken") to one of self-incrimination ("Why had he withheld life from her? Why had he sentenced her to death?"). Compare here Baker's idea that epiphany is potentially redemptive or "saving."

3. Review the selection of Joyce's own critical writing reprinted in this volume. What evidence do you find in them to support the notion that "A Painful Case" is the portrait of a man who lacks the *essential* quality of an artist? Does Duffy's excruciating final remorse take him any closer to their vital "quality" of mind?

" 'Ivy Day in the Committee Room': Death Without Resurrection"

1. Analyze the strength of Hynes's position as central character in "Ivy Day." How strongly is his position challenged by the figure of Parnell? Compare the function of Parnell here with that of the dead boy Michael in "The Dead."

2. Read the Christmas scene in Joyce's *A Portrait of the Artist as a Young Man* (Part I, section 3). How does it serve to clarify for you the nature of the emotions aroused by the memory of Parnell in "Ivy Day in the Committee Room"?

3. Refer to footnote 2 of the Blotner essay. Read the subsection on "Ivy Day in the Committee Room" and the references concerning Parnell. Show how that information illuminates the story.

"Portrait of a Lady"

1. Tindall sees the theme of "paralysis" as central to *Dubliners*. In what specific ways is this theme reinforced in "A Mother"? Do any of the characters reach a state of awareness or self-revelation?

2. In what ways do Kathleen and her mother reflect Joyce's views on the "language movement" going on in Ireland at this time? How does Mrs. Kearney reflect his views on the Church?

3. What manner does Joyce assume in this story? Is he "scrupulously mean" as in some of the other stories?

" 'Grace' and Joyce's Method of Parody"

1. Joyce sent this version of the outcome of the 1870 Vatican Council to his brother in 1906: "Before the final proclamation many of the clerics left Rome as a protest. At the proclamation when the dogma of papal infallibility was read out the Pope said 'Is that all right, gents?' All the gents said 'Placet' but two said 'Non placet.' But the Pope 'You be damned! Kissmearse! I'm infallible!' " (Ellmann, *James Joyce*, 1959, p. 238.) Of course the Council receives more subtle treatment in "Grace." Nevertheless, compare the two "parodies" of the Council and show how Joyce, in "Grace," is master of subsurface irony. (Would you suspect, moreover, that as blatant a parody is hidden under the surface of Father Purdon's sermon?)

2. Given a definition of grace as "divine assistance given man for his regeneration," show how the theme of the necessity for grace is important throughout *Dubliners*. Show too how this necessity sharpens the indictment of the Irish Church throughout.

3. Compare Niemeyer's interpretation of this story as parody with the theory of Levin and Shattuck (see bibliography) that *everything* in *Dubliners* is parody of Homer's Odyssey. Does the use of parody indicate a negative moral judgment by the author? Try to define Joyce's moral position or judgment on Mr. Kernan.

"Characterization in 'The Dead' "

1. Trilling says: "But as the story approaches its conclusion, it becomes impossible for us to know whose language we are hearing, Conroy's or the author's, or to whose tone of desperate sorrow we are responding." This statement points to a very important problem of point of view in the whole of *Dubliners*. Do you find any justification, from the stories themselves, for Trilling's suggestion that creator and character merge in "The Dead"?

2. In what respects does this story contain the elements of tragic drama? See Baker's essay for analysis of Gabriel's growth.

3. Gabriel Conroy is protected from our contempt, Trilling says, by the "extent of his fairly accurate self-knowledge." Cite examples of other Dubliners who do *not* possess self-knowledge. How is this fact indicated in each case? Does it invariably arouse our contempt for them?

"The Snow"

1. Show how Joyce uses the snow not only to illuminate Gabriel's inner condition but also to state in symbolic terms the condition of the Irish

people, whose representative Gabriel is. (You may want to pay particular attention to the meaning behind references to Irish history.)

2. Compare the analysis of snow in the Ghiselin and the Ludwig essays. What do these treatments illustrate with respect to focus and perspective in dealing with the symbolic treatment of the snow?

3. Show how the power and variety of the snow symbol in "The Dead" gives to *Dubliners* a higher level of mastery than that indicated by the stories through "Grace."

Bibliography of Criticism on *Dubliners*

The following bibliography does not aim to be all-inclusive, but it does attempt to list all the works of criticism on *Dubliners* that are generally available to students in the United States. The editors have included several foreign items of significance, but we have avoided listing articles that appear in foreign journals unless they are especially vital. The articles reprinted in this volume are also listed here.

The divisions are self-explanatory: general studies of *Dubliners* are listed first, and studies of specific stories are divided under separate sections. If an article deals with more than one story, it is cross listed under the specific story which it covers.

The editors are grateful to Maralee Frampton for her preliminary compilation and research. To update this bibliography the reader should check the annual bibliography published in the May issue of *PMLA* and the annual bibliographical supplements compiled by Alan Cohn and published in the *James Joyce Quarterly*.

General Studies of *Dubliners*

1. Adams, Robert M. *James Joyce: Common Sense and Beyond.* New York: Random House, 1966. Pp. 63–90.

2. Atherton, James S. "The Joyce of *Dubliners*." In Thomas F. Staley, ed., *James Joyce Today: Essays on the Major Works.* Bloomington: Indiana University Press, 1966. Pp. 28–53.

3. Baker, James R. "Ibsen, Joyce and the Living-Dead." In Marvin Magalaner, ed., *A James Joyce Miscellany,* Third Series. Carbondale: Southern Illinois University Press, 1962. Pp. 19–32.

4. Burgess, Anthony. *ReJoyce.* New York: Norton and Co., 1965. Pp. 35–48.

5. Carrier, Warren. *"Dubliners:* Joyce's Dantean Vision." *Renascence,* XVII (Summer 1965), 211–215.

6. Church, Margaret. *Time and Reality.* Chapel Hill: University of North Carolina Press, 1963. Pp. 27–30.

7. Colum, Padraic. "Dublin in Literature." *Bookman,* LXIII (July 1926), 555–561.

8. _____. Introduction to *Dubliners.* New York: The Modern Library, 1926. Pp. v–xiii.

9. Coveney, Peter. "Joyce, Virginia Woolf, D. H. Lawrence." In *Poor Monkey: The Child in Literature.* London: Rockliff, 1957. *Passim.*

10. Daiches, David. *The Novel and the Modern World.* Chicago: University of Chicago Press, 1939. Pp. 80–100.

11. Eliot, T. S., ed. *Introducing James Joyce.* London: Faber and Faber, 1962. Pp. 5–7.

12. Ellmann, Richard. *James Joyce.* New York: Oxford University Press, 1959.

13. Freidrich, Gerhard. "The Gnomonic Clue to James Joyce's *Dubliners." Modern Language Notes,* LXII (June 1957), 421–424.

14. _____. "Joyce's Pattern of Paralysis in *Dubliners." College English,* XXII (April 1961), 519–520.

15. _____. "The Perspective of Joyce's *Dubliners." College English,* XXVI (March 1965), 421–426.

16. Ghiselin, Brewster. "The Unity of Joyce's *Dubliners." Accent,* XVI (Spring 1956), 75–88; XVI (Summer 1956), 196–213.

17. Gilbert, Stuart. Introduction to *The Letters of James Joyce.* New York: Viking Press, 1957. Pp. 60–64.

18. Goldberg, S. L. *James Joyce.* New York: Grove Press, 1962. Pp. 29–46.

19. _____. "Joyce and the Artist's Fingernails." *A Review of English Literature,* II (April 1961), 61.

20. Golding, Lewis. *James Joyce.* London: Thornton Butterworth, 1933. Pp. 22–33.

21. Goldman, Arnold. "The Early Stories in *Dubliners."* In *The Joyce Paradox.* Evanston: Northwestern University Press, 1966. Pp. 1–21 *et passim.*

22. Gorman, Herbert. *James Joyce.* New York: Rinehart, 1940. Pp. 28–64.

23. Guidi, Augusto. "Il Primo Joyce." *Storia e Letteratura.* Rome: Edizioni, 1954. Pp. 7–40.

24. Hodgart, Matthew J. C., and Mabel P. Worthington. *Song in the Works of James Joyce.* New York: Columbia University Press, 1959. P. 60.

25. Hone, Joseph. "A Recollection of JJ." *Envoy,* V (April 1951), 44–45.

26. Howarth, Herbert. *The Irish Writers 1880–1940.* New York: Hill and Wang, 1958. Pp. 245–287.

27. Jacquot, Jean. "Exégètes et Interprètes de James Joyce." *Études Anglaises*, XII (January–March 1959), 30–46.

28. Jaloux, Edmond. *Au Pays du Roman*. Paris: A. Carrea, 1931. Pp. 97–109.

29. Jones, W. Powell. *James Joyce and the Common Reader*. Norman: University of Oklahoma Press, 1955. Pp. 9–23.

30. Joyce, Stanislaus. "The Backgrounds to *Dubliners*." *Listener*, LI (March 1954), 226–227.

31. _____. "James Joyce: A Memoir." *Hudson Review*, II (1949–1950), 502.

32. _____. *My Brother's Keeper*, ed. Richard Ellmann. New York: Viking Press, 1958. *Passim*.

33. Kenner, Hugh. *Dublin's Joyce*. Bloomington: Indiana University Press, 1956. Pp. 48–68.

34. Kiely, Benedict. *Modern Irish Fiction: A Critique*. Dublin: Golden Eagle Books, 1950. *Passim*.

35. Levin, Harry. *James Joyce: A Critical Introduction*. Norfolk, Conn.: New Directions, 1941. Pp. 27–37.

36. Levin, Richard, and Charles Shattuck. "First Flight to Ithaca: A New Reading of Joyce's *Dubliners*." In Seon Givens, ed., *James Joyce: Two Decades of Criticism*. New York: Vanguard Press, 1947. Pp. 47–94.

37. Litz, Walton. *James Joyce*. New York: Twayne, 1966. Pp. 47–59.

38. Ludwig, Jack B., and W. Richard Poirier, eds. "James Joyce's *Dubliners*." In *Stories British and American*. Boston: Houghton Mifflin, 1953. Pp. 384–391.

39. Magalaner, Marvin. "James Joyce and the Uncommon Reader." *South Atlantic Quarterly*, LII (April 1953), 267–276.

40. _____. *Time of Apprenticeship: The Fiction of Young James Joyce*. New York: Abelard-Schuman, 1959. Pp. 72–96.

41. _____, and Richard M. Kain. *Joyce: The Man, the Work, the Reputation*. New York: New York University Press, 1956. Pp. 53–101.

42. Mercanton, Jacques. "James Joyce." In *Poetes de l'Univers*. Paris: Editions Albert Skira, 1947. Pp. 70–76.

43. Morse, J. Mitchell. *The Sympathetic Alien*. New York: New York University Press, 1959. Pp. 59, 62, 73, 103–110.

44. O'Connor, Frank. "Joyce and the Dislocated Metaphor." In *The Mirror in the Roadway: A Study of the Modern Novel*. New York: Knopf, 1956. Pp. 295–312.

45. Ostroff, Anthony. "The Moral Vision in *Dubliners*." *Western Speech*, XXI (Fall 1956), 196–209.

46. Pound, Ezra. "*Dubliners* and Mr. James Joyce." *Egoist*, I (July 1914), 267. Reprinted in *Pavannes and Divisions*. New York: Knopf, 1918. Pp. 156–160.

47. Pritchett, V. S. "The Short Story and J. J." *New Statesman and Nation,* XXI (February 15, 1941), 162.

48. Rubinstein, Joseph, and Earl Farley. *He who destroys a good Booke, kills reason it selfe: An exhibition of books which have survived Fire, the Sword, and the Censors.* Lawrence: University of Kansas Press, 1955. P. 10.

49. Ryan, Marjorie. "*Dubliners* and the Stories of Katherine Anne Porter." *American Literature,* XXXI (January 1960), 464–473.

50. Ryf, Robert S. *A New Approach to Joyce.* Los Angeles: University of California Press, 1962. Pp. 59–76.

51. Sanchez, Luis Alberto. *Panorama de la Literatura Actual,* 3rd ed. Santiago de Chile: Biblioteca America, 1936. Pp. 109–112.

52. Scholes, Robert. "Further Observations on the Text of *Dubliners.*" *Studies in Bibliography,* XVII (1964), 107–122.

53. _____. "Grant Richards to James Joyce." *Studies in Bibliography,* XVI (1963), 139–160.

54. Stewart, J. I. M. *James Joyce.* London: Longman, Green, 1957. Pp. 11–16.

55. Steif, Carl, ed. *Modern Litteratur Efter 1914.* Copenhagen: Gyldendal, 1950. Pp. 132–135.

56. Strong, L. A. G. *The Sacred River: An Approach to James Joyce.* New York: Pellegrini and Cudahy, 1951. Pp. 17–23.

57. Tindall, William York. *A Reader's Guide to James Joyce.* New York: Noonday Press, 1959. Pp. 3–49.

58. _____. *James Joyce: His Way of Interpreting the Modern World.* New York: Scribner's, 1950. *Passim.*

59. Verhaeghen, Victor. "Capriolen om Joyce." *De Periscoop,* VIII (September 1, 1958), 7.

60. Walzl, Florence. "The Liturgy of the Epiphany Season and the Epiphanies of Joyce." *PMLA,* LXXX (September 1965), 436–450.

61. _____. "Patterns of Paralysis in Joyce's *Dubliners.*" *College English,* XXII (January 1961), 221–228.

62. Weathers, Winston. "A Portrait of the Broken Word." *James Joyce Quarterly,* I (Summer 1964), 27–40.

Individual Studies of "The Sisters"

Benstock, Bernard. "Joyce's 'The Sisters.'" *The Explicator,* XXIV (September 1965), Item 1.

Connolly, Thomas. "Joyce's 'The Sisters': A Pennyworth of Snuff." *College English,* XXVII (December 1965), 189–195.

Fahey, William A. "Joyce's 'The Sisters.'" *The Explicator,* XVII (January 1959), Item 26.

Gleeson, W. F., Jr. "Joyce's 'The Sisters.' " *The Explicator,* XXII (December 1963), Item 30.

Kaye, Julian B. "Simony, the Three Simons, and Joycean Myth." In Marvin Magalaner, ed., *A James Joyce Miscellany.* New York: The James Joyce Society, 1947. Pp. 20–36.

Kuehl, John. "À la Joyce: The Sisters Fitzgerald's Absolution." *James Joyce Quarterly,* II (Fall 1964), 2–6.

Magalaner, Marvin. " 'The Sisters' of James Joyce." *University of Kansas City Review,* XVIII (Summer 1952), 255–261.

Senn, Fritz. "He Was Too Scrupulous Always: Joyce's 'The Sisters.' " *James Joyce Quarterly,* II (Winter 1965), 66–72.

Speilberg, Peter. " 'The Sisters': No Christ at Bethany." *James Joyce Quarterly,* III (Spring 1966), 192–195.

Stein, William Bysshe. "Joyce's 'The Sisters.' " *The Explicator,* XX (March 1962), Item 61.

—————. "Joyce's 'The Sisters.' " *The Explicator,* XXI (September 1962), Item 2.

Walzl, Florence. "A Date in Joyce's 'The Sisters.' " *Texas Studies in Literature and Language,* IV (Summer 1962), 183–187.

See also "General Studies" items 3, 5, 10, 12, 13, 14, 15, 16, 18, 20, 22, 29, 32, 33, 35, 36, 40, 41, 43, 45, 50, 56, 57, 60, 61, 62.

Individual Studies of "An Encounter"

Beja, Morris. "The Wooden Sword: Threatener and Threatened in the Fiction of James Joyce." *James Joyce Quarterly,* II (Fall 1964), 33–34.

Feshbach, Sidney. "Death in 'An Encounter.' " *James Joyce Quarterly,* II (Winter 1965), 83–89.

Kaye, Julian B. "The Wings of Daedalus: Two Stories in *Dubliners.*" *Modern Fiction Studies,* IV (Spring 1958), 31–41.

See also "General Studies" items 3, 4, 10, 12, 16, 18, 22, 29, 32, 33, 35, 36, 40, 41, 43, 45, 50, 56, 57, 60, 61, 62.

Individual Studies of "Araby"

Ap Roberts, Robert Pigott. " 'Araby' and the Palimpsest of Criticism; or, Through a Glass Eye Darkly." *Antioch Review,* XXVI (Winter 1966–67), 469–489.

Bonazza, Blaze O., and Emil Roy. *Instructor's Manual to Accompany "Studies in Fiction."* New York: Harper & Row, 1965. Pp. 1–2.

Brooks, Cleanth, and Robert Penn Warren. *Understanding Fiction.* New York: Crofts, 1944. Pp. 420–423.

—————, John T. Purser, and Robert Penn Warren. *An Approach to*

Literature, 3rd ed. New York: Appleton-Century-Crofts, 1960. Pp. 108–111.

Burto, William. "Joyce's 'Araby.'" *The Explicator,* XXV (April 1967), Item 67.

Collins, Ben L. "Joyce's 'Araby' and the Extended Simile." *James Joyce Quarterly,* IV (Winter 1967), 84–90.

Dadufalza, Concepcion D. "The Quest of the Chalice Bearer in James Joyce's 'Araby.'" *Diliman Review,* VII (July 1959), 317–325.

Davis, Robert Gorham. *Ten Modern Masters.* New York: Harcourt, Brace, 1959. Pp. 40–42.

Friedman, Stanley. "Joyce's 'Araby.'" *The Explicator,* XXIV (January 1966), Item 5.

Fuller, James A. "A Note on Joyce's 'Araby.'" *CEA Critic,* XX (February 1958), 8.

Going, William T. "Joyce's 'Araby.'" *The Explicator,* XXVI (January 1968), Item 39.

Magalaner, Marvin. "James Mangan and Joyce's Dedalus Family." *Philological Quarterly,* XXXI (October 1952), 363–371.

Male, Roy R., ed. *Types of Short Fiction.* Belmont, California: Wadsworth Publishing Co., 1962. Pp. 31–34.

Stein, William Bysshe. "Joyce's 'Araby': Paradise Lost." *Perspective,* XII (Spring 1963), 215–222.

Stone, Harry. "'Araby' and the Writings of James Joyce." *Antioch Review,* XXV (Fall 1965), 375–410.

See also "General Studies" items 3, 4, 10, 12, 15, 16, 18, 22, 29, 32, 33, 35, 36, 40, 41, 43, 45, 50, 57, 60, 61, 62.

Individual Studies of "Eveline"

Connolly, Thomas. "Marriage Divination in Joyce's 'Clay.'" *Studies in Short Fiction,* III (Spring 1966), 293–299.

Dolch, Martin. "Eveline." In John V. Hagopian and Martin Dolch, eds., *Insight II.* Frankfurt: Hirschgraben Verlag, 1964. Pp. 193–200.

Stein, William Bysshe. "The Effects of Eden in Joyce's 'Eveline.'" *Renascence,* XV (Winter 1962), 124–126.

Taube, Myron. "Joyce and Shakespeare: 'Eveline' and *Othello.*" *James Joyce Quarterly,* IV (Winter 1967), 152–153.

See also "General Studies" items 4, 12, 14, 16, 18, 20, 22, 24, 29, 32, 35, 36, 40, 41, 43, 50, 57, 60, 61, 62.

Individual Studies of "After the Race"

Joyce, James. *The Critical Writings,* ed. Elsworth Mason and Richard Ellmann. New York: Compass Books, 1959. Pp. 106–108.

Ward, David. "The Race Before the Story," *Eire-Ireland*, II (Samhradh 1967), 27–35.

See also "General Studies" items 4, 12, 15, 16, 18, 20, 22, 29, 32, 33, 35, 36, 40, 43, 50, 56, 57, 60, 61, 62.

Individual Studies of "Two Gallants"

Boyle, Robert, S.J. " 'Two Gallants' and 'Ivy Day in the Committee Room.' " *James Joyce Quarterly*, I (Fall 1963), 3–9.

Walzl, Florence. "Symbolism in Joyce's 'Two Gallants.' " *James Joyce Quarterly*, II (Winter 1965), 73–81.

See also "General Studies" items 3, 4, 5, 12, 16, 18, 20, 22, 24, 29, 32, 33, 35, 36, 40, 41, 43, 45, 50, 56, 57, 60, 61, 62.

Individual Studies of "The Boarding House"

Kenner, Hugh. *Studies in Change: A Book of the Short Story*. Englewood Cliffs, N.J.: Prentice-Hall, 1965. Pp. vii–x.

Rosenberg, Bruce A. "The Crucifixion in 'The Boarding House.' " *Studies in Short Fiction*, V (Fall 1967), 44–53.

See also "General Studies" items 4, 12, 16, 18, 22, 29, 33, 35, 36, 40, 41, 43, 50, 57, 60, 61, 62.

Individual Studies of "A Little Cloud"

Brodbar, Harold. "A Religious Allegory: Joyce's 'A Little Cloud.' " *Midwest Quarterly*, II (Spring 1961), 221–227.

Harmon, Maurice. "Little Chandler and Byron's First Poem." *Threshold*, XVII (1962), 59–61.

Heilman, Robert B., ed. *Modern Short Stories: A Critical Anthology*. New York: Harcourt, Brace, 1950. Pp. 133–147.

Perrine, Laurence, ed. *Story and Structure*, 2nd ed. New York: Harcourt, Brace, 1966. Pp. 88–99.

Ruoff, James. " 'A Little Cloud': Joyce's Portrait of the Would-Be Artist." *Research Studies of the State College of Washington*, XXV (September 1957), 256–271.

Schorer, Mark, ed. *The Story: A Critical Anthology*. Englewood Cliffs, N.J.: Prentice-Hall, 1950. Pp. 288–305.

Short, Clarice. "Joyce's 'A Little Cloud.' " *Modern Language Notes*, LXXII (April 1957), 255–258.

See also "General Studies" items 4, 12, 16, 18, 20, 22, 29, 32, 33, 35, 36, 40, 41, 43, 45, 50, 57, 60, 61, 62.

Individual Studies of "Counterparts"

Chatterjee, Sisir. *James Joyce: A Study in Technique*. Calcutta: Dos Gupta and Co., Private Ltd., 1957. Pp. 22–23.

Davis, Robert Gorham. *Ten Modern Masters* (Instructor's Manual). New York: Harcourt, Brace, 1959. Pp. 42–43.

Foff, Arthur, and Daniel Knapp, eds. *Story: An Introduction to Prose Fiction.* Belmont, California: Wadsworth Publishing Co., 1964. Pp. 142–145.

Hagopian, John V. "The Epiphany in Joyce's 'Counterparts.'" *Studies in Short Fiction*, I (Summer 1964), 272–277.

—————. "Counterparts." In John V. Hagopian and Martin Dolch, eds., *Insight II*. Frankfurt: Hirschgraben Verlag, 1964. Pp. 201–206.

Hendry, Irene. "Joyce's Epiphanies." In Seon Givens, ed., *James Joyce: Two Decades of Criticism*. New York: Vanguard Press, 1948. P. 30.

Stein, William Bysshe. "'Counterparts'" A Swine Song." *James Joyce Quarterly*, I (Winter 1964), 30–32.

See also "General Studies" items 4, 5, 6, 12, 16, 18, 20, 22, 29, 33, 36, 40, 41, 43, 45, 50, 57, 60, 61, 62.

Individual Studies of "Clay"

Brooks, Cleanth, John T. Purser, and Robert Penn Warren. *An Approach to Literature*, 3rd ed. New York: Appleton-Century-Crofts, 1952. Pp. 137–140.

Carpenter, Richard, and Daniel Leary. "The Witch Maria." *James Joyce Review*, III (February 1959), 3–7.

Connolly, Francis. *The Types of Literature*. New York: Harcourt, Brace, 1955. Pp. 127–130.

Connolly, Thomas. "Marriage Divination in Joyce's 'Clay.'" *Studies in Short Fiction*, III (Spring 1966), 293–299.

Cowan, S. A. "Joyce's 'Clay.'" *The Explicator*, XXIII (March 1965), Item 50.

Davies, Phillips G. "Maria's Song in Joyce's 'Clay.'" *Studies in Short Fiction*, I (Winter 1964), 153–154.

Hudson, Richard B. "Joyce's 'Clay.'" *The Explicator*, VI (March 1948), Item 30.

Lynskey, Winifred, ed. *Reading Modern Fiction*, 3rd ed. New York: Scribner's, 1962. Pp. 311–317.

Madden, David. "James Joyce's 'Clay.'" *The University Review*, XXXIII (March 1967), 229–233.

Magalaner, Marvin. "The Other Side of James Joyce." *Arizona Quarterly*, IX (Spring 1953), 5–16.

Mathews, F. X. "Punchtime: A New Look at 'Clay.'" *James Joyce Quarterly*, IV (Winter 1967), 102–106.

Noon, William T., S.J. "Joyce's 'Clay': An Interpretation." *College English*, XVII (November 1955), 93–95.

Pearson, Norman H. "Joyce's 'Clay.'" *The Explicator*, VII (October 1948), Item 9.

Short, Raymond W., and Richard B. Sewall. *A Manual of Suggestions for Teachers Using "Short Stories for Study,"* 3rd ed. New York: Holt, 1956. Pp. 4–5.

Smith, G. Ralph, II. "A Superstition in Joyce's 'Clay.'" *James Joyce Quarterly*, II (Winter 1965), 133–134.

Staley, Thomas F. "Moral Responsibility in Joyce's 'Clay.'" *Renascence*, XVIII (Spring 1966), 124–128.

Walzl, Florence L. "Joyce's 'Clay.'" *The Explicator*, XX (February 1962), Item 46.

Weber, Robert. "Clay." In John V. Hagopian and Martin Dolch, eds., *Insight II*. Frankfurt: Hirschgraben Verlag, 1962. Pp. 206–212.

See also "General Studies" items 3, 4, 5, 12, 16, 18, 20, 22, 24, 29, 32, 33, 35, 40, 41, 43, 45, 50, 56, 57, 60, 61.

Individual Studies of "A Painful Case"

Barrows, Herbert. *Suggestions for Teaching "Fifteen Stories."* Boston: Heath, 1950. Pp. 19–22.

Corrington, John W. "Isolation as Motif in 'A Painful Case.'" *James Joyce Quarterly*, III (Spring 1966), 182–191.

Duffy, John J. "The Painful Case of M'Intosh." *Studies in Short Fiction*, II (November 1964), 183–185.

Gettmann, Royal A., and Bruce Harkness. *Teacher's Manual for "A Book of Stories."* New York: Rinehart, 1955. Pp. 7–9.

Kranidas, Thomas. "Mr. Duffy and the Song of Songs." *James Joyce Quarterly*, III (Spring 1966), 220.

Lyons, John O. "The Man in the Macintosh." In Marvin Magalaner, ed., *A James Joyce Miscellany*, Second Series. Carbondale: Southern Illinois University Press, 1959. Pp. 133–138.

Magalaner, Marvin. "Joyce, Nietzsche, and Hauptmann in James Joyce's 'A Painful Case.'" *PMLA*, LXVIII (March 1953), 95–102.

Miller, James E., Jr., and Bernice Slote. *Notes for Teaching "The Dimensions of the Short Story."* New York: Dodd, Mead, 1964. Pp. 22–23.

Reid, Stephen. "'The Beast in the Jungle' and 'A Painful Case': Two Different Sufferings." *American Imago*, XX, 221–239.

Wright, Charles D. "Melancholy Duffy and Sanguine Sinico: Humors in 'A Painful Case.'" *James Joyce Quarterly,* III (Spring 1966), 171–181.

See also "General Studies" items 3, 4, 5, 12, 16, 18, 20, 22, 29, 32, 33, 35, 36, 40, 41, 43, 50, 51, 57, 60, 61.

Individual Studies of "Ivy Day in the Committee Room"

Benstock, Bernard. "A Covey of Clerics in Joyce and O'Casey." *James Joyce Quarterly,* II (Winter 1965), 20–21.

Blotner, Joseph L. "'Ivy Day in the Committee Room.'" *Perspective,* IX (Summer 1957), 210–217.

Boyle, Robert, S.J. "'Two Gallants' and 'Ivy Day in the Committee Room.'" *James Joyce Quarterly,* I (Fall 1963), 3–9.

——————. "A Note on Mr. Hynes's 'The Death of Parnell.'" *James Joyce Quarterly,* II (Spring 1965), 133.

Glasheen, Adaline. "Joyce and the Three Ages of Charles Stewart Parnell." In Marvin Magalaner, ed., *A James Joyce Miscellany.* Second Series. Carbondale: Southern Illinois University Press, 1959. Pp. 151–178.

Stegner, Wallace, Richard Scowcroft, and Boris Ilyin, eds. *The Writer's Art.* Boston: Heath, 1950. Pp. 92–95.

See also "General Studies" items 3, 4, 5, 10, 12, 16, 18, 20, 22, 26, 29, 32, 33, 35, 36, 40, 41, 43, 45, 50, 56, 57, 60, 61, 62.

Individual Studies of "A Mother"

O'Neill, Michael. "Joyce's Use of Memory in 'A Mother.'" *Modern Language Notes,* LXXXIV (March 1959), 226–230.

See also "General Studies" items 3, 4, 12, 16, 22, 29, 33, 35, 36, 40, 41, 43, 50, 57, 60, 61.

Individual Studies of "Grace"

Baker, Joseph E. "The Trinity in Joyce's 'Grace.'" *James Joyce Quarterly,* II (Summer 1965), 299–303.

Benstock, Bernard. "A Covey of Clerics in Joyce and O'Casey." *James Joyce Quarterly,* II (Winter 1965), 20–21.

Gould, George. "A Review of *Dubliners.*" *The New Statesman,* III (June 27, 1914), 374–375.

Jackson, Robert S. "A Parabolic Reading of James Joyce's 'Grace.'" *Modern Language Notes,* LXXXVI (December 1961), 719–724.

Kaye, Julian B. "Simony, the Three Simons, and Joycean Myth." In Marvin

Magalaner, ed., *A James Joyce Miscellany.* New York: The James Joyce Society, 1947. Pp. 20–36.

Magalaner, Marvin. "Leopold Bloom Before *Ulysses." Modern Language Notes,* LXXVI (December 1965), 110–112.

Newman, F. X. "The Land of Ooze: Joyce's 'Grace' and the *Book of Job." Studies in Short Fiction,* IV (Fall 1966), 70–79.

Niemeyer, Carl. " 'Grace' and Joyce's Method of Parody." *College English,* XXVII (December 1965), 196–201.

Scholes, Robert, and Richard M. Kain. *The Workshop of Daedalus.* Evanston: Northwestern University Press, 1965. P. 68.

See also "General Studies" items 3, 4, 5, 12, 13, 15, 18, 20, 22, 29, 32, 33, 35, 36, 40, 41, 43, 44, 45, 50, 56, 57, 60, 61, 62.

Individual Studies of "The Dead"

Barr, Isabelle H. "Footnote to 'The Dead.' " *A. D.,* II (Autumn 1951), 112.

Bates, H. E. "Is This the Greatest Short Story?" *Irish Digest,* LV (January 1956), 103.

_____. *The Modern Short Story: A Critical Survey.* London: Thomas Nelson, 1943. Pp. 154–156.

Benstock, Bernard. "A Covey of Clerics in Joyce and O'Casey." *James Joyce Quarterly,* II (Winter 1965), 20–21.

Bierman, Robert. "Structural Elements in 'The Dead.' " *James Joyce Quarterly,* IV (Fall 1966), 42–45.

Blum, Morgan. "The Shifting Point of View: Joyce's 'The Dead' and Gordon's 'Old Red.' " *Critique,* I (Winter 1956), 45–66.

Brandabur, Edward. "Arrayed for the Bridal: The Embodied Vision of 'The Dead.' " In William T. Moynihan, ed., *Joyce's "The Dead."* Boston: Allyn and Bacon, 1965. Pp. 108–119.

Burke, Kenneth. "Three Definitions." *Kenyon Review,* XIII (Spring 1951), 186–192.

Cox, Roger. "Johnny the Horse in Joyce's 'The Dead.' " *James Joyce Quarterly,* IV (Fall 1966), 36–41.

Damon, Phillip. "A Symphasis of Antipathies in 'The Dead.' " *Modern Language Notes,* LXIV (February 1959), 111–114.

Davis, Robert Gorham. *Ten Modern Masters.* New York: Harcourt, Brace, 1959. Pp. 43–45.

Detoni, Gianantonio. "Su una Pagina di Joyce." *Aut Aut,* II (1952), 138–147.

Ellmann, Richard. "Backgrounds of 'The Dead.' " *Kenyon Review,* XX (Autumn 1958), 507–528.

Felheim, Marvin, Franklin Newman, and William Steinhoff. *Study Aids for Teachers of "Modern Short Stories."* New York: Oxford University Press, 1951. Pp. 55–57.

Friedrich, Gerhard. "Bret Harte as a Source for James Joyce's 'The Dead.'" *Philological Quarterly,* XXXIII (October 1954), 442–444.

Gordon, Caroline, and Allen Tate. "Commentary on 'The Dead.'" In *The House of Fiction.* New York: Scribner's, 1950. Pp. 279–282.

Gould, Gerald. "A Review of *Dubliners.*" *The New Statesman,* III (June 27, 1914), 374–375.

Hutton, Virgil. "James Joyce's 'The Dead.'" *East-West Review,* II (1963), 124–139.

Kaye, Julian B. "The Wings of Daedalus: Two Stories in *Dubliners.*" *Modern Fiction Studies,* IV (Spring 1958), 31–41.

Kelleher, John V. "Irish History and Mythology in James Joyce's 'The Dead.'" *Review of Politics,* XXVII (July 1965), 414–433.

Knox, George. "Michael Furey: Symbol-Name in Joyce's 'The Dead.'" *Western Humanities Review,* XIII (1959), 221–222.

Loomis, C. C., Jr. "Structure and Sympathy in Joyce's 'The Dead.'" *PMLA,* LXXV (March 1960), 149–151.

Mannin, Ethel. "Contemporary Irish Fiction." In Denys V. Baker, ed., *Modern British Writing.* New York: Vanguard Press, 1947. Pp. 165–167.

Miller, Milton. "Definition by Comparison: Chaucer, Lawrence, and Joyce." *Essays in Criticism,* III (October 1953), 369–381.

Mosley, Virginia. " 'Two Sights for Ever a Picture' in Joyce's 'The Dead.'" *College English,* XXVI (March 1965), 426–433.

Moynihan, William T., ed. *Joyce's 'The Dead.'* Boston: Allyn and Bacon, 1965.

Neider, Charles. "James Joyce." In *Short Novels of the Masters.* New York: Rinehart, 1948. Pp. 37–40.

Noon, William T., S.J. *Joyce and Aquinas.* New Haven: Yale University Press, 1957. Pp. 84–86.

O'Connor, Frank. "At the Microphone." *The Bell,* III (March 1942), 415–419.

O Hehir, Brendan P. "Structural Symbol in Joyce's 'The Dead.'" *Twentieth Century Literature,* III (April 1957), 3–13.

Sale, William, Jr., James Hall, and Martin Steinmann, Jr. *Short Stories: Tradition and Direction.* Norfolk, Conn.: New Directions, 1949. Pp. 178–224.

Scheuerle, William H. " 'Gabriel Hounds' and Joyce's 'The Dead.'" *Studies in Short Fiction,* II (July 1965), 369–371.

Schmidt, Hugo. "Hauptmann's *Michael Kramer* and Joyce's 'The Dead.'" *PMLA,* LXXX (March 1965), 141–142.

Scholes, Robert. "Some Observations on the Text of *Dubliners:* 'The Dead.' " *Studies in Bibliography,* XV (1962), 191–205.

Smith, Thomas F. "Color and Light in 'The Dead.' " *James Joyce Quarterly,* II (Summer 1965), 304–309.

Tate, Allen. "Three Commentaries: Poe, James and Joyce." *Sewanee Review,* LVIII (Winter 1950), 10–15.

Tindall, William York. *The Literary Symbol.* Bloomington: University of Indiana Press, 1955. Pp. 224–226.

Trilling, Lionel. *The Experience of Literature.* New York: Holt, 1967. Pp. 652–655.

Walzl, Florence L. "Gabriel and Michael: The Conclusion of 'The Dead.' " *James Joyce Quarterly,* IV (Fall 1966), 17–30.

See also "General Studies" items 3, 4, 5, 10, 12, 13, 15, 16, 18, 20, 22, 24, 26, 29, 32, 33, 35, 36, 38, 40, 41, 43, 44, 45, 49, 50, 54, 56, 57, 60, 61, 62.